MARTIN PIPE

The Champion Trainer's Story

MARTIN PIPE
The Champion Trainer's Story

Martin Pipe
with Richard Pitman

HEADLINE

First published in 1992
by HEADLINE BOOK PUBLISHING PLC

10 9 8 7 6 5 4 3 2 1

British Library Cataloguing in Publication Data

Pipe, Martin
    Martin Pipe: Champion Trainer's Story
    I. Title   II. Pitman, Richard
    798.40092

    ISBN 0–7472–0602–3

Typeset by Keyboard Services, Luton
Printed and bound in Great Britain by
Clays Ltd, St Ives plc

HEADLINE BOOK PUBLISHING PLC
Headline House
79 Great Titchfield Street
London W1P 7FN

Contents

MARTIN PIPE'S RECORD OF SUCCESS

Season	Number of Winners	Winning Prize Money (£)	Major Triumphs
1974/75	1	272	
1975/76	5	2,059	
1976/77	5	2,460	
1977/78	2	768	
1978/79	6	3,233	
1979/80	12	6,908	
1980/81	14	25,765	Baron Blakeney, Triumph Hurdle
1981/82	20	16,318	
1982/83	23	25,538	
1983 (Flat)			Right Regent, Ascot Stakes
1983/84	32	35,382	Corporal Clinger, Swinton Insurance Hurdle
1984/85	51	95,732	Corporal Clinger, Bula Hurdle
1985 (Flat)			Atall Atall, Windsor Castle Stakes
1985/86	79	121,536	
1986/87	106	166,058	High Knowl, Welsh Champion Hurdle
1987/88	129	249,792	Beau Ranger, Mackeson Gold Cup Sabin Du Loir, Racecall Ascot Hurdle
1988/89	208	630,647	Bonanza Boy, Welsh National Strands Of Gold, Hennessy Gold Cup Travel Mystery, William Hill Imperial Cup Sondrio, Waterford Crystal Novice Hurdle Sayfars Lad, Sun Alliance Novice Hurdle Sabin Du Loir, Racecall Ascot Hurdle Liadett, Victor Ludorum Hurdle
1989/90	224	668,606	Sayparee, Scottish Champion Hurdle Liadett, William Hill Handicap Hurdle Bonanza Boy, Welsh National Regal Ambition, Sun Alliance Novice Hurdle
1990/91	230	956,894	Omerta, Kim Muir Irish National Tyrone Bridge, Challow Hurdle Sabin Du Loir, Newton Chase, Grade I Rolling Ball, Sun Alliance Novice Chase Chatam, Cathcart Chase Aquilifer, Martell Cup Chase
1991/92	224	724,442	Chatam, Hennessy Gold Cup Miinnehoma, Sun Alliance Novice Chase Carvill's Hill, Irish Gold Cup Granville Again, Scottish Champion Hurdle Carvill's Hill, Welsh National

Prologue

Carrie Ann

Milestones, barriers and records have been reached, passed and cast aside with accelerating frequency over the past few years by Martin Pipe – without his ever specifically aiming at them. Fastest fifty, quickest ton, topping £1 million in prize money in a season, eclipsing Michael Dickinson's seemingly unbeatable total of winners in a campaign, then breaking into uncharted territory by sending out over 200 winners a season for the past four years: all this is now racing history. Yet among the historic moments that Pipe himself treasures, one that still gives him as much pleasure as any is that of a day in 1980, when a small-time West Country trainer with a gaggle of moderate horses took a home-bred filly called Carrie Ann to Haydock Park for an undistinguished selling hurdle.

To all but the handful in the know, the Makerfield Hurdle on 5 January looked to be nothing more than just another seller. No one witnessing the horse's boisterous reception in the winner's enclosure on that cold day had the faintest idea of the success's worth or indeed just how far the trainer would have gone in the subsequent auction to retain his home-bred mare Carrie Ann. But the gamble landed that day proved conclusively to Martin that he really knew what he was doing. The diminutive Carrie Ann, winning first time out and despite persistent leg trouble, set a pattern that has been the Pipe hallmark ever since.

Pipe
I had opened up to those nearest to me, convincing them this was

1

the bet of a lifetime. Everything was right: the course, the soft ground, the two-mile trip, the opposition; the mare was sound and, most of all, she was fit to run for her life.

Fitness is often taken for granted by casual punters, but there are numerous reasons why horses run when not fully tuned up. Fitness should not be taken as a matter of course. When you consider that the previous nine meetings in Britain before that day at Haydock had been abandoned through frost, the lay-off could easily have jeopardized our most carefully laid plans. What's more, this came at a time when the all-weather gallop had not even been planned.

Carrie Ann was out of Clever Caroline, a mare Father had raced from other yards before deciding I would become a trainer. It really did appear to be as simple as that: there was no room for argument, I would learn the trade and that was final. By the time I put my training theories to the real test, I had five years of practice behind me. During that time I had pulled off lesser gambles and of the nineteen victories we had tucked away prior to the make-or-break Haydock coup, little Carrie Ann had already provided two. One of them was a dress rehearsal in selling class at Chepstow, when we backed her from 6–1 down to 7–4 and she won under Graham Thorner. No one bid for the filly after the race, giving us double cause for celebration.

Carrie Ann then bolted up ten days later under Ron Atkins in a non-selling novice hurdle at Devon and Exeter. By now I had a clear indication of her ability, although it was another three years before I put her to the ultimate test at Haydock Park. By running her below her class when the time came, we once again proved sound the old racing adage: keep yourself in the best company and your horse in the worst.

The lengthy period between victories was not entirely planned; it was forced on me by the mare's leg problems. However, it had its advantages in giving the bookies time to forget about her. Carrie Ann was off the racecourse for the whole of 1978, eventually reappearing twice within a fortnight the next March.

A quiet run over three miles at Plumpton, a trip she could not win over, saw Ron Atkins pull the mare up before the last hurdle, having done enough to prove her soundness. I again used the racecourse to confirm her ability to stand up to the rigours of competition in a long-distance hurdle at Devon and Exeter. As the race was fully a mile further than her optimum distance there was little chance she would show the world at large any obvious signs of a return to form. In the event, Carrie Ann led two hurdles from home before fading. What was of most interest to me was that she finished sound under a good ride from Rod Millman, and she impressed him enough for him to tell me she would win in better than selling company over a shorter trip.

Having seen enough to convince myself Carrie Ann could still win, all I had to do was find the right race. I had not stopped the filly from winning her two comeback races, just run her in contests she could not win. This tactic has been and will continue to be used by trainers to ready horses for their objectives without contravening the rules. Anyone studying the form daily can, of course, spot the pattern, yet the volume of racing in Britain makes it likely to be overlooked until after the coup has been landed.

There was no suitable race left that season to guarantee me a successful gamble, so I put Carrie Ann out to grass for the summer. After a search through the programme book, I earmarked the race that would be our target, even though it was fully nine months away. This particular selling hurdle at Haydock Park in January had attracted moderate performers, even by selling standards, in the past. Being the final race of a day with three decent sponsored contests on the card, the seller would not arouse much interest and with luck the bookies would have already enjoyed a good day. What's more, the ground ought to be soft enough at that time of the year not to put any strain on the mare's suspect legs.

The gallops at home were less than adequate at that time, prompting me to carry out full-scale trials at Taunton and Devon and Exeter racecourses after the spectators had departed. Millman, with five wins on the Flat and just two successes in selling hurdles, got the ride for the gamble at Haydock. I was far more nervous than normal, mainly because I had staked so much on this race in my own mind. If the result went wrong – unless through some stroke of bad luck – it would sink everything I believed about getting a horse ready to run. As you can imagine, I left the jockey in no doubt about the importance of the occasion.

3

Rod and head man Dennis Dummett drove Carrie Ann up to the course while my friend Chester Barnes and I motored up, planning how and by whom the money would be placed. Dad had given me a very hard time before we left that morning, goading me with all sorts of accusations that almost had me doubting my own judgement. He said I was mad going all that way. He pointed out the cost of taking a bad-legged screw that far from home, the folly of three of us being away – Chester didn't count then – and that with twenty-three runners in the race there was sure to be something good enough to beat us. Naturally I defended myself, insisting that Carrie Ann was a certainty. There was nothing better than selling class in the race – except our mare, who certainly was. All the conditions were right for her, it really was no contest. I could not have been more adamant: the race was ours. Dad pretended not to be convinced and let me leave still fuming that he had challenged my judgement to such an extent. I set off with my hackles still well and truly up.

In time it came out that Dad had got me all fired up to gauge the strength of the information; he'd decided to go for a massive bet himself and reckoned the best way to confirm the worth of the operation was to rile me. My vehement defence convinced him to go ahead. Dad later admitted that whenever he wants proof of someone's intentions he questions that person's ability to produce the goods; and the more fierce the defence, the better.

This was only the second day's racing Chester had gone to with me. The prospect of a touch at long odds appealed to him, yet it took most of the journey to convince him it was feasible. On the strength of the animal's apparently moderate form, the only way he could bring himself to get involved was if either he saw me back her or I placed the commission with him.

The bookies offered Carrie Ann at odds varying from 14–1 to 20–1, although Pat Whelan went as high as 33–1, a price Chester snapped up to the tune of £100. Pat never even flinched and had the cheek to leave her price the same, almost daring Chester to have some more, so he had another hundred on. At the same time I worked my way around the ring, placing tens, twenties and tons on the filly without any of the layers taking a blind bit of notice. Chester continued to put money on until the off, by which time he'd parted with over £800. Still, it was a certainty, wasn't it? In those days he was so naïve he thought if the trainer said a horse would win, there was no question about the outcome.

Our former jockey Len Lungo wandered up to me in the parade ring, casually inquiring what chance the mare held. I could not put Lenny away but nevertheless it seemed prudent to stem the potential leak by promising him a drink to keep his mouth shut. Chester (dressed in a wolfskin coat) and I (looking every bit as if I'd been let out for the day) would not cause the bookies to take much notice. If faces known to be friendly with a jockey were noted backing her, it would soon become obvious it was not mugs' money.

During the race itself, Rod never had a single doubt as to the outcome. Keeping out of trouble after Priddy Friendly, one of the joint favourites, fell at the third hurdle, he moved through the big field to join the issue approaching the final flight. Mindful of the long run-in, Rod resisted the temptation to go for a medal, kept a tight hold of the mare's head and popped the jump, needing only to let out half an inch of rein to win unextended by two and a half lengths.

We were the only people shouting Carrie Ann home among the huge Haydock crowd. People must have thought we were mad. When we posed either side of the mare's head for the sole remaining photographer to record the momentous occasion neither of us kept hold of her head as we were too busy giving the victory salute – and the mare started to wander off.

As the race was a seller, Carrie Ann had to be offered for auction after the weighed-in signal. Unbelievably, no one made even a half-hearted bid for her. Collecting the winnings gave us a great sense of achievement; trotting down the line picking up from most bookies was like a dream. We kept stuffing notes of every denomination into our pockets and eventually also into my hat.

It takes wins like that, or perhaps, these days, victories in Cup races, to lift you off the ground. We didn't want to leave the course in case it all dissolved once we broke the spell. Eventually we headed south – only to realize that neither of us had thought to collect our Tote winnings. The ten miles back to the course saw us chattering away like a pair of monkeys and we were still riding on a wave of euphoria when we collected the remaining £7,000 from the sole Tote lady waiting to pay us out. The dividend returned odds of 240–1 on the machine, which is surprising when you consider Dad had placed most of his bet with the Tote, spread around quite a few shops and credit firms. Nowadays, with outlets linked to a central office, the money would dilute the payout no end.

I never did learn the extent of my father's take-out and although my wife Carol was still the office accountant she never discussed his business with me. She did express surprise, though, that Dad never mentioned his involvement; after all, she logged all the incoming cheques from the win as well as handling the string of correspondence that followed closing his accounts.

A day like that one is, of course, a one-off. To arrive home able to litter the kitchen with money is a dream and as we are not in the game of putting huge amounts on shorter-priced horses, it will probably never happen again. We filled two buckets with notes totalling over £53,000, all from a little bad-legged mare no one wanted. Chester thought this was far better than working.

The irony of human nature came home the next day when I met Simon Crook's father in Taunton. Simon looked after Carrie Ann at home, often schooling her or riding the mare in gallops. He'd told his father she was expected to win, yet when seeing Carrie Ann actually drift in the betting instead of hardening, he assumed the plan had changed. Imagine the dreadful sinking feeling as Mr Crook watched his inside information come good without a penny of his money riding on her back.

Carrie Ann ran six times the following season, finishing third once, back at Haydock, then reappeared only twice the next term when her legs flared up. At the age of eleven she obliged twice more, including another selling hurdle at the Lancashire course. This time the bookies took far more notice of the West Country visitors, offering no more than 7–4 about her chances.

The story had an unfortunate sequel for Chester, who unwisely put his share of the loot away in a building society under an assumed name. The Inland Revenue inspector who unearthed it six years later refused to believe Chester had won the money, despite a letter of support from Pat Whelan who vividly remembered the bloke in the outrageous wolfskin fur coat relieving him of £6,600 for a £200 stake. His field book corroborated the story; but as the racecourse has been used to launder ill-gotten cash in the past, the inspector would not accept the evidence, and Chester had no chance of convincing him that the rest of his £26,000 winnings were above board. The Inland Revenue ordered Chester to find £47,000 in back tax, penalties and interest, and his luxury Brixham home had to be sold to clear the debt. Chester has always attracted controversy one way or another, yet despite the backlash of the gamble that started off his racing involvement, he's well and truly hooked now.

Rod Millman, the winning jockey on that memorable day, is now in his third year training at Cullompton in Devon. He looks back with admiration and a tinge of regret that he cut loose too soon.

Millman
Prior to joining the Pipes I'd been with Reg Akehurst and David Barons. Martin was always pumping me for information regarding their training methods – not that he wanted to copy them, more to see if he was doing something wrong.

I moved on to Gerald Cottrell when Paul Leach seemed too well entrenched as jockey at Martin's to allow me much scope. Gerald is the opposite to Martin; he brings them on very slowly and would rarely win first or even second time out. Having studied them both I'm convinced some horses from each establishment would have benefited from being trained by the other.

I saw one winner get away in the days when gambling ruled the roost at Pond House. Starting at the mouthwatering price of 20–1, Chicita Beetle went in at Worcester in a National Hunt flat race in September 1980, leaving Martin and Chester open-mouthed in disbelief. The reason she was left unbacked probably had something to do with the fact she had planted herself flat-footed on her intended debut. She simply had a seizure on the way to the start and after trying all the usual ploys from talking to her to turning in small circles, I gave her a slap down the shoulder. The result was both immediate and explosive: she simply threw herself on to the ground and refused to get up until we took the saddle off. Naturally she was withdrawn from the race, the vets diagnosing an extreme case of stage fright. So next time, at Worcester, they were all taking the mickey out of me, only to watch with astonishment as she strode in, beating sixteen others. It was a one-off performance, though; she never won again.

Another horse to get the laugh on Martin while I was there was Pauw. He was totally wild, we couldn't even catch him in his stable. He would either kick you or bite you or do both at once. We kept a headcollar on him all the time and caught him by using a pole with a hook in the end. When he won for us at Devon, Martin forgot all about his wayward tendencies in the euphoria of the victory. He walked in behind us to the winner's enclosure and patted the horse on the hindquarters, only to be rewarded by a kick on the knee. It must have caught an artery as blood spurted everywhere, confining the boss to bed for two weeks.

We also caught a cold after a little filly called Cherchez La Femme fooled us. Strangely enough, she ran above previous form when I rode her for the first time behind Baron Blakeney on his pre-Cheltenham Festival run at Worcester in March. Baron was the fancied one while I was told to enjoy my ride and not get in his way. I finished sixth of sixteen, beaten only eight lengths without being hard on her. She ran just three days later to get the wages at Market Rasen, which in retrospect was far too quick for a small filly.

As it is almost 300 miles from the Devon border to Market Rasen we set off in the Range Rover and trailer at 3.10 a.m. Martin treated me with kid gloves then as I had a crucial part to play in the afternoon. He and Chester took it in turns to drive while I slept in the back to conserve my strength – just as the equine part of the equation was, we hoped, doing in the trailer behind us.

The race turned out badly. The filly dropped out tamely, finishing in the ruck having felt lifeless after halfway. When she had recovered from her exertions we set off home; and it was a very different story from setting off fourteen hours before. I was voted driver as Martin and Chester settled down to sleep on the homeward journey.

Martin goes quiet when things go wrong, especially if the horse has been backed. Provided the rider has done nothing wrong there are no recriminations, just atmospheric silences. Even Chester's jokes peter out. He can usually perk Martin up

when pressure mounts, yet seems to know when not to attempt it
– which is probably why the two of them hit it off.

Imagine me, though, only five feet high and barely able to
reach the controls in a Range Rover and not a clue how to get
from Market Rasen to Devon. It was dark, I'd never driven
anything towing a trailer, let alone with a horse in the back.
Common sense directed me from Lincoln to Leicester then
southwest towards the M6. Somehow after such a promising
start to the journey I ended up in the middle of Birmingham and
could not get out. A sixth sense must have alerted my passengers
as they both woke up together, stretched, looked out of the
windows and shouted '—kin' 'ell Rod, where are we?'

None of us had ever been to Birmingham's Bull Ring in our
lives and I certainly didn't let on it was the third time I'd been
around it in the past half hour.

Chapter 1

A Budding Little Einstein

On 29 May 1945 Martin Charles Pipe weighed into this world in the Wellington Maternity Hospital. His parents, Dave and Betty, lived in a flat in Cheddon Road, Taunton and Martin is their only child.

In the formative years, the budding genius looked distinctly ordinary: small, pale, quiet, he was just another child, showing few signs of devilment and not encouraged to develop any. In those days Dave Pipe was still more of a punter, although his bookmaking business had stuttered into life. The future looked hopeful rather than promising, and life set off at a gentle pace for the son and heir. In fact little, if anything, took root in Martin's memory in those early years. It is obvious, though, that even at a tender age he had strong feelings for animals.

Pipe
Dad kept a few greyhounds and when one got loose, chased a neighbour's cat and killed it, I was extremely upset. I also spent hours digging for worms to feed my grandparents' chickens. Somehow I doubt if the worms involved in this act of kindness to the fowls appreciated the thought.

My first school was Northtown in Taunton. It was only a hundred yards from Dad's first credit betting office and it was there, under the direction of the ferocious headmistress, Miss Marshall, that I found my love of figures.

Maths was the only thing I was any good at. We worked from cards with ten questions on each. I used to devour them like

11

sweets, I couldn't get enough. Other than that, the only memories to stick are the embarrassment of being forced to act in school plays and dance around the maypole. I passed the school recently and saw they had restrung it, so other action men must still be dancing around it as uncomfortably as I did.

My maternal grandmother, Granny Nation, encouraged my early penchant for maths by leaving sixpence on the mantelpiece for her budding little Einstein every time I did well in tests. Invariably the reward went on sweets or ice cream, still my biggest weakness today. Immediately behind the school the aroma of Brunts' sweet factory continually filled the air, luring me on like the Pied Piper of Hamelin. Potatoes, peas or meat came, and still come, a very long way down the list. I was a chubby baby until recovering from a particularly nasty bout of chicken-pox. I went right off my food then, and in order to get me to eat, Mum would put potatoes, peas and meat all on separate plates. I have remained completely spoiled ever since!

At eight I went to Queens College in Taunton, and it was here that being good at maths, coupled with a growing interest in racing, started a friendship which is just as strong now.

Richard Lewis and I teamed up together along with another lad called Johnie Van Trump. We both always had plenty of folding money in our pockets, which tends to bind people together. Johnie has disappeared since we've grown up, but Richard and I are still kids at heart. Now, almost forty years later, I go to the Lewis household every Monday evening to escape from the incessant telephone calls at Pond House. While Carol holds the fort at home I pencil in the entries for the following week helped by Richard's wife Rosie. We have developed a rating system when entering horses, placing a star beside the races we think they have won even before the horses have been entered. When favourable conditions are married to the right horses it adds up to winners, unless luck goes against you – and as long as you can eliminate most of the risks, more luck will go for you than against.

Rosie and Richard provide a haven for me on these Monday evenings – somewhere I can live a normal life for a few hours away from the incessant demands of controlling so many horses and the people that go with them. Carol makes sure no one gets to me at the Lewises' – and similarly, when she and I nip down to the sea-view flat in Brixham to keep the lid on life, there is no phone in the place. The phone is one of the vital pieces of equipment in our business but every now and then the lifeline can choke you.

After we've done the entries there's a light supper, snooker with Richard, a few drinks, and then it's home to the conveyor-belt existence such a large stable of horses demands. I thrive on it, of course, but I do need that Monday night escape to stay sane.

There is one other regular break I find imperative in order to maintain the pace. Every day I sneak up to the house to have a cup of tea with Carol at eleven o'clock. While I'm in the yard there is a constant bombardment from the secretaries, Dennis, the staff, the phone, or Dad. After five minutes away from it all I'm refreshed again and itching to get back into the fray – but I do need that break.

At Queens I continued to develop my maths under the guidance of tutor Nobby Hyland, to the extent of joining the Maths Society in the evenings. I loved solving problems and as there were no calculators in those days, everything had to be worked out mentally. It was a good grounding for my job later when settling bets. I was absolutely thick otherwise, eventually scraping together three O levels.

As for games, cricket came easily to me, especially as Dad gave me a shilling for every run I made. Annoyingly, though I got to forty-eight on many occasions, I never quite made two pounds ten shillings in a match. I was coached by Bill Alley, the Australian player who joined Somerset and I became the youngest boy in the school First Eleven. It looked as if I was popular when all the other lads scrambled to sit next to me after matches, but in fact it was simply because I'd never touch my food and anyone sitting near enough got my share! Rugby absolutely petrified me. Although I could run a bit then, the players were so big . . . Swimming was another dodgy area for me. To get out of it I regularly altered Mum's original sick note to whatever day was needed and I'm still terrified of the water today. I only learned to swim when we put a pool in here. Carol kept throwing me in and happily I kept coming back up.

Dad did not believe in such extravagances as holidays, and I was fourteen years old before Richard Lewis's father took me along with their family to Newquay. I was really skinny then and all the clothes Mum bought me were miles too big. One particular check shirt with large orange and white squares came down to my knees. It was like a tent and I was always the only one on the whole beach still clothed. But that wasn't the only reason I was still lily-white when we got back, because even then Rich and I spent more time in Jack Tully's betting shop than on the beach.

I can remember that first holiday clearly. We stayed in the Hotel Bristol in Newquay during Glorious Goodwood week and had a real touch on Tudor Monarch in the Stewards' Cup. By then I was well into gambling, unknown to my parents, who had made a conscious decision to steer me away from the family business. If only they knew to what extent their only child had already emulated his father! Richard and I always had money and if it didn't go on the horses it went on snooker, pontoon or darts. Whatever we did we bet on the result.

We also regularly made a book at school which I typed up daily. It was amazing how easily a carefully floated rumour about a good thing spread around. Our mates often bet with us on moderate horses, not thinking for a moment it was only our duff information they were following. Thanks to my upbringing I have quite high moral standards, but when it comes to gambling, it's everyone for themselves! Still, in order to keep our school-boy clients happy we did let them in on some genuine punts but when we did we were careful to lay the bets off along with our own.

One horse we will never forget from our days as under-aged punters is Sweet Solera, trained by Reg Day, who took the One Thousand Guineas under Bill Rickaby in 1961 at 4–1. Rich and I had £40 on for ourselves and a further £25 from our schoolchum clients. Everyone was geed up as the off time approached. Richard and I were in different classrooms so had decided we'd both pretend to be feeling ill twenty seconds before the official start time of the race. Once we were reunited in the loo I whipped out an old transistor radio and we proceeded to shout Sweet Solera home to beat Ambergris by one and a half lengths, never in danger of defeat! We dashed back to our respective classes far healthier than we'd purported to be on leaving them. The classroom doors were half glazed and as I reached for the handle all eyes were on me instead of the history teacher who was writing on the blackboard. A jubilant thumbs up prompted a whispered reaction which rapidly spread among the other winning punters in the class. The master never did know why the class was quite so pleased to see me back and healthy.

Obviously the Grand National figured top in our book as even the schoolboys who were not regular punters dabbled then. We never had a losing year during all our time at Queens. Even the Latin master Mr Geary had a bet in the annual Aintree lottery. He'd always look for something with a Latin connection and put half a crown on it. Hardly surprising he never looked like collecting any winnings from us.

I suppose my aspiration to win that elusive prize now, as a trainer, probably stems from those far off illegal bookmaking days.

Just as Rich and I hit it off, so our parents did too. The family relationship started when Richard's younger brother Danny ran away from Queens. I told him to seek refuge with Mum and, several ice creams and sweets later, life seemed a little better. Danny's father came to collect him in a huge great Rolls-Royce which really impressed us. After that he came down every Sunday with chocolates and presents for everyone in order to stop Danny's antics.

The Lewises' father Charlie liked a daily bet too, preferring to go in for accumulators on outsiders, and he came within a Lester Piggott short head of cleaning Dad out. It was a question of likes attracting: Dad loved taking the bets and Rich's father loved the cut and thrust of trying to wipe him out. Both families also attended Taunton greyhound meetings – in fact that's where they were the night President Kennedy was killed. Strange how everyone over forty remembers where they were that night, when you consider all the cataclysms that have happened in the world since.

Rich and I stayed close friends after our schooldays ended, although when Richard fell for his future wife, the bond had to be put on hold while he pursued Rosie. Forever dashing up to East Anglia and back, he wore out two sets of tyres on an E-Type

Jaguar before Rosie put him out of his misery and accepted his proposal.

Naturally, while the chase was on we had a bet on the outcome. I was convinced Rosie was far too bright, beautiful and upmarket to fall for Richard's mad existence. I could not have been more wrong. Of course I paid up, but I made the £20 up with forty old brown ten-shilling notes. Rosie came from a totally different background from either of us. She even thought a bookmaker was a person who bound books! We soon led her astray.

Rich and I shared so many jaunts and we still work on the same wavelength. We've always taken the mickey out of each other. Once, to deflate Richard's ego, I took the five-times British table tennis champion Chester Barnes to one of the Monday night relaxation sessions, introducing him as George Barnes, which is actually Chester's real name. Richard, keen to prove his skills, set off aggressively and smashed straight into 'George'. He was mystified at being thrashed by an opponent who won without ever moving his feet and with one hand behind his back. 'George' proceeded to beat Richard with smaller and smaller bats, even doing so with one the size of a ten pence piece; then, as the ultimate insult, he used a frying pan as his bat, forcing Richard to run about the table as if it were a squash court.

All three of us have been firm friends ever since – apart from one temporary dent in our relationship which resulted from another fun evening at Pond House. It was snowing hard, precluding any racing the next day, and we were amusing ourselves with games of cards, snooker and table tennis. Richard had no car of his own that day, and had been picked up by Chester, who had promised to return him in time for a Christmas party with Rosie. The opportunity looked too good to miss so I played my advantage, continually insisting on just one more game before we took him home.

It got to the point where Richard stormed out into the night saying he'd walk all the way home if we had not picked him up by the time he'd reached the end of the drive. Chester and I let him go, thinking we would let him suffer a little then pick him up a mile down the road, only to find he was made of sterner stuff than we had imagined. Richard steadfastly refused to accept the lift, insisting on walking the eleven miles home through the snow without an overcoat, protected only by a suit and shoes. He did it in two hours forty minutes and although decidedly late for the party was highly satisfied with himself, if somewhat frozen.

Following the initial half-hearted offer of a lift shortly after he stormed out of the house, we approached Rich again en route, tempting him with fish and chips, which pig-headedly the silly sod refused. Rich had gone past the point of no return and was determined to show us he was not just a joker. Realizing he would not give in we even asked the local police to pick him up, but as no crime had been committed and he was walking of his own free will, that request was declined.

When eventually he did arrive home we were cosily sitting in Rich's kitchen chatting up his wife. Admittedly it took a while for him to thaw out, literally and mentally, but when he eventually came around we all had a laugh and a drink then thought to hell with what people might think and went to the party in our wellies.

You might expect Richard to be privy to inside information after our long and enjoyable betting history as kids, but being a true friend he did not feel it right to make money out of our friendship, and for some years stuck to following four horses regularly each week. To this day, though, Richard regrets ignoring my advice in the second week of March 1981 when our Daily Express Triumph Hurdle runner Baron Blakeney was the value in the contest. If the horse had been trained by Fred Winter it would have been a 10–1 shot; coming from my small West Country stable 66–1 was readily available and should have been snapped up. Imagine the mixed emotions as Rich watched the Baron sweep past the favourite, Broadsword, to win. He will grudgingly admit that he felt a real twerp, especially as he'd sunk his money in the second. I have never stopped drumming it into Rich that betting is all about value, and that proved the point.

These days we talk every day, even if it is for just thirty seconds, going through a numerical evaluation of the horses' chances. A one is maximum confidence and anything down to ten has a better than average chance. Obviously if an owner wants to have a punt he gets the best of the market, although Rich's bets don't seem to alter the price because another mate of ours puts on for us. He varies locations and is not known to have any stable connection. You can go on milking the bookies as long as you don't try to kill them. Having said that, the time I first gave Rich a good thing I nearly blew a fuse when I found out he'd backed it in my father's Taunton shop.

Before he started riding and, later, training, Martin was considered to be a good if somewhat brave bookie. He needed to be on the ball to stay afloat at that game, and in all probability that grounding has helped him in the training game. His strategy still revolves around value, be it in betting on horses or buying them. Many's the time he has lost a potential owner by refusing to fill the order until he saw one that represented value. The more impatient newcomers get snapped up by other trainers who buy purely to fill a stable. Martin refuses to do that because at the end of the day he has to face the music if he has bought a dud.

Richard Lewis now listens to his old school mate, is selective with his bets and, as a result, is one of the few people to make his gambling pay.

Chapter 2

The Family

Martin and Carol's only child David is named after his paternal grandfather. Martin's father, however, is called Dave by everyone except his wife Betty, who prefers his proper name (and that's not just when she wants to get his full attention). They now live in a modest, comfortable bungalow, cocooned in a small copse literally yards from the all-weather gallop, where their son and Carol lived as newly-weds, when the Pipe operation on its present scale was not even a dream.

Dave Pipe is the eldest of nine children, Betty one of just two, and neither has strayed far from their roots. Dave's father Albert farmed in Sampford Moor, a mile from the twelve-house hamlet of Nicholas-hayne which over the past six years has become virtually synonymous with the name of Pipe. Working on the land from an early age, Dave learned some of the harsher lessons life has to offer and even if his schooling saw him top in most subjects it was his early working life that taught him the value of a pound. Since those days, while never moving more than five miles from his birthplace, in business terms Dave has travelled a long way. Hard work combined with a canny sense of value has made him and his family financially secure for life.

As in so many other large families in the 1920s, the job of bringing the Pipe children up was spread among relations, with Dave Pipe's formative years guided by his maternal grandfather Albert Nation.

Dave Pipe
He was a Colour-Sergeant Major, a stickler for punctuality, cleanliness and total obedience. At the time I thought I was pretty

19

hard done by. There was no such thing as television, it was dominoes or draughts. I had trouble beating the old man, so I started giving up before the game was finished. When I did this, Grandfather would snap the board shut and say – 'When you can learn to lose, you will learn to play.' I've done the same to Martin with snooker. It's an important message to get across. When Martin was still quite young we played everything for small stakes to teach him the value of money. Life is not always smooth, you have to learn to take the knocks and then evaluate why things went wrong. I'm sure those early lessons have stood Martin in good stead in his training career.

I have always drummed it into Martin that business comes first, pleasure afterwards and now I'm doing the same to my nineteen-year-old grandson David. It will all be his one day but he's got to earn it, to realize how everything was built up. It's hard to establish financial security yet so easy to throw it all away.

To this end David is currently learning the ropes of the bookmaking game, acting as my outside man at the eight racecourses where I have a pitch. His job is to keep an eye and an ear on what's happening in the betting ring and to report back to me any significant moves. He'll get to know the important faces and come to tell the clever money from the wild bets.

Looks are certainly deceptive. Dave Pipe, the real power behind the throne, could easily be, and often is, mistaken for the yard's odd-job man. On the racecourse most onlookers would think him a struggling bookie when in fact he could buy out the vast majority of owners and also fund his rivals' overdrafts.

Anonymity is a powerful cloak, especially coupled with being a good listener. Although Pipe senior does not set out to extract information from people, he has an ink-blotter memory, and all the seemingly superfluous facts it soaks up have an uncanny way of bearing fruit later.

Dave Pipe

I left school at fourteen despite always finishing top in my class in almost every subject. I wanted to work for myself, and I realized that if you want something, you have to graft for it. I've been doing so ever since. I've never felt the need to take a holiday in my life. I don't even possess a passport. And I've no intention of altering either situation.

Betty Pipe
We never even had a honeymoon, although I must add that I was under no illusions on that score from the outset. Even so, David has never stopped me from having holidays and has always provided whatever I've wanted.

My holiday companion is Ira Chatfield, the vicar's wife. In the early years of our marriage we never missed church on Sundays and regularly entertained the Chatfields to cards and supper on Tuesday evenings. David was a sidesman – I think he enjoyed handling the money – and Martin read the lesson from when he was seven. But then as the business grew it inevitably took over. On Sundays the credit punters called, either wanting to be paid out from Saturday's racing or to settle their debts. Even so, David regularly produced an enormous Christmas tree and loads of presents for the local Dr Barnardo's home. He had a good moral upbringing and had an eye for a cause deserving support.

His only indulgence was a twelve-foot boat for mackerel fishing, moored at Lyme Regis. He'd only be able to slip away after racing had finished, of course. We'd often be out all night and drop off fish to our friends on the way home, then eat the remainder for breakfast. They were the best days of our lives, without a doubt. Then evening racing came along and put a stop to our capers.

Martin was always a quiet little thing, a sensitive boy who loved his own company. He was brought up as a churchgoer and taught to share whatever he had. We were very strict about things such as ponies, bicycles, air-guns or roller skates, purely from the safety angle. There was no argument, Martin had to make do without them, but he was never at a loss to amuse himself. He has always tended to be a loner.

Having said that, he felt sorry for the boarders at Queens College, which was only a couple of hundred yards away. He was always telling the chaps there to run across the playing field, climb the wall and I'd look after them. They'd eat themselves silly, then drift off into different rooms to play while Martin would do his own thing. He's never liked crowds.

Martin respected his father and learned from him, although we had no idea then to what extent. Right from a young age he used to have a loan book documenting advances he'd made to the boarders and would tot up the credits or debits on the team bus to cricket matches whilst the other lads were thinking about the runs they hoped to make.

You couldn't call him a loan shark, though, as he never worried the boys to pay him back until they were able to do so. Mind you, he was no pushover either; the slow payers didn't get further advances until their slate was wiped clean!

Martin was openly discouraged from getting involved in the betting industry and was actually forbidden to go down into the basement of our home where his father's credit betting office operated. However, forbidden fruit is always the most sought after and it lured him downstairs when his father was away betting at the greyhound evening meetings. It grabbed him to such an extent that even when David was at home the budding little bookie – he was only about twelve – would be safely locked in his bedroom settling imaginary bets. He soon mastered the art. Years later, after Martin had quietly eased himself into the business, David described him to me as fearless, saying he'd ruin us given his head. Martin took far too many chances and, worse still, enjoyed doing it.

The betting business started when, as so often happens, fate played a hand in our future. The land David rented from the council for his 300-strong pig unit was sold for building and so the pigs had to go. It would be fair to say that my parents, at least, weren't sorry. When we were courting they knew exactly who I'd been seeing by the odour. The smell of pigs permeates even the most expensive perfume. If he was not working with the pigs, David would have been collecting the food for their swill from the nearby American military hospital at Sandhill Park. The pigs ate better than we did, and when we saw untouched produce, still packaged, being dumped David arranged for it to be kept separately for us to distribute to our families and friends. They enjoyed food that would otherwise have been wasted and to our minds that was a sin.

If accompanying him on the swill runs was the only time I could get to be with David, I settled for a ride in the lorry. Even that was fun – and sometimes much more! One evening the military police were having a crackdown on security and searching every departing vehicle. Realizing he and his accomplice were about to have their game uncovered, David leaned out of the window as we bore down on the exit gates shouting over and over again that we'd got no brakes. It worked; not wanting to be run down and seeing the urgency in his eyes they raised the barrier and we sailed off into the night with our booty.

True to his character, Dave was not idle for a minute. With the money from the sale of the pigs he married Betty, bought a flat in Taunton and set up as a bookie in 1944 at the age of twenty. His first tentative steps were taken with a stand at the twice-weekly Taunton greyhound stadium, near the cricket ground which he later purchased.

Dave Pipe

I'd been taken racing a fair bit by my father and his friend Tony Pennington and it occurred to me that too often we were on the wrong end of the transaction. The chaps on the stool seemed to be taking our hard-earned money too regularly; so I decided to do their job instead.

Nothing is quite so easy on the inside as it looks from a distance and so it proved. In the early days on the greyhounds I quite often found myself on the wrong end again. I analysed the situation and righted it by ensuring the book was never so top-heavy as to sink me if the result went against me. Taking a wage out of an evening's racing, rather than trying to grab the lot, became the object of the exercise. Initially I'd taken chances, backing my own judgement as a bookie by laying dogs I did not fancy to lose big money but in essence I was being the punter again.

Within two years of starting up I could see the way the betting industry would grow, so I opened a credit betting office in my home. Much of the business came from fun-starved workers who had been weighed down by the hardships of the Second World War, which had just ended. Can you believe, in those days the factory girls used to have tenners on? Imagine what the equivalent would be today! Like all emerging businesses after the war, the gambling world thrived; it was the betting tax that killed the job.

In the mid-forties credit betting was done over the telephone, by letter or through runners in the factories. The runners couldn't accept cash, just written proof of the bet and to stop fraud they had clock bags which had to be timed locked before the first race of the day. I paid over the odds to my runners at one shilling and sixpence in the pound commission to make sure I got the pick of the bunch.

By 1947 I'd added Exeter greyhound meetings to Taunton,

then two years later the first of my racecourse pitches saw me standing on a joint at Devon and Exeter races, high on Haldon Hill. I'd previously tested the on-course horse betting business at Nedge and Blackmoor Vale point-to-points and found I liked it. In those days you just turned up and made a book at the points but on the proper racecourse you needed a guarantor. It transpired my guarantor was skint, so it was just as well I never had to call on him to bail me out.

By the time cash betting shops were legalized in 1963 I was well established, with nearly twenty years' experience behind me. It was easy to see the growth potential in the new shops. I opened the first of what became a chain of betting shops in Canal Road, Taunton, and that one was the sole office I held on to when I cashed in my chips nine years later.

Martin was eighteen when that first shop was opened and with his appetite for the job and enthusiasm for progress the timing could not have been better. It soon occurred to me that the man with the most conveniently positioned shop would take the lion's share of any money that was about. After Taunton I added a branch in Bridgwater, then Bristol, and went on acquiring places at the rate of six or seven a year until the string totalled thirty-seven. I'd taken a decision to head south-west from base in order to keep the whole thing manageable. If you intend diving into deep water, better the pool you know than the ocean where the sharks live. In the early days you could open a betting shop for £20. Some old material covering the window to protect the non-betting public's eyes from what was supposed to be a den of iniquity, whitewash on the walls and a bundle of old cloakroom tickets for betting slips, and you were away. Looking back on those hectic days setting up the chain, it was the speed of purchase and the position of the sites that worked in my favour; then the offers started to arrive.

Even then, I could see the necessity to protect myself, along with the other small bookmakers, but all attempts to form a cartel in the West Country met with complacency. Who knows, if they had joined forces then, maybe the Western Bookmakers Association could have been trying to buy out the William Hill Organisation instead of vice versa.

Besides the chains, we also operated two fun shops outside the main business. The nearby Butlins holiday camp at Minehead had

24

thousands of regular punters trapped on their obligatory holidays simply itching to have a bet. What made it look even better to me was that the law governing afternoon closing did not apply to holiday camps. So while the kids were glued to the one-armed bandits, teenagers were chasing each other around the fun fair and the wife was taking full advantage of her resultant freedom to see a show, dad was hot-footing it between the betting shop and the bar.

The second diversification was simply window-dressing, advertising the business at the Bath and West Show. Lord Darling, a client of ours, invited us to erect a stand there. We got plenty of customers who came in to shelter from the sun or rain, but the free drinks and £200 flower bill rather took the gilt off the gingerbread.

I have to laugh now at the thought of the old security equipment in use at that time. The bets were recorded on a Photobet camera, which compared to the sophisticated machinery available now was like driving an old Austin 7.

Having built up the chain and established its financial health, the decision to sell out to Hill's did not come easily. Eventually, after a great deal of thought, I agreed terms that gave me financial security and left me the properties. For a million pounds Hill's took over the right to conduct the business in thirty-six shops, with me as the freeholder. That way, I was able to have my cake and eat it too; if I hadn't been able to get that sort of deal I'd have been happy to stay as I was.

A million pounds in 1972 is probably worth about ten million today, yet the decision to sell didn't make me want to rush out and do handsprings. Even when I had the cheque in my hands I wasn't sure I'd done the right thing. The piece of paper looked rather insignificant measured against the cut and thrust of the thriving chain I'd created. The business was something alive; by itself the money couldn't give me the same sort of motivation. In the end I settled for a long-held belief that it was far better to have my name on the deeds than on the shop front – a principle that I've since followed in the training venture.

Even these days, and despite keeping right up to date with everything that moves in the stables, I have retained enough of a link with the bookmaking industry through the Taunton office I kept back from the sell-out. The eight racecourse pitches I've got satisfy my thirst for the excitement of pitting my wits against the punter and my name's down for several other courses – although the way the system works I'll probably be dead before they become available. I'm never out of touch with the Taunton shop; even when I'm betting on the racecourses I still phone the shop after every race to keep control. If I'm going to lose any money, I like to do it myself. Unlike Martin, though, who has a mobile phone permanently attached to his ear, I always use the public telephone because it's far cheaper than the phone in my pocket.

People tend to assume that the sale of the betting shop chain financed the training venture, which is not true: I'd bought the first half of the current place in 1968, some four years before selling the bookmaking business. The moment I saw Tucker's Farm it was going to be mine. Both Carol and Martin knew that, because it was by far the most derelict of the thirty farms we had looked at. By then I had a lot of experience of buying property and knew this place could only be improved. It consisted of an old, almost derelict, house and a collection of disused pigsties, all in 130 acres. Everywhere was overgrown; but to my eyes it had tremendous potential. If you buy well at the outset you cannot lose money, even in a recession, but if you buy the finished article values can plummet.

Tucker's was not at all what Martin and Carol would have liked, though: being young and engaged for the past two years they had starry eyes for a ready-made property. I suppose they would have married then if I'd bought a smart house. As it turned out they waited another three years before marrying and moving into the bungalow where Betty and I now live.

I bought Tucker's Farm for under £20,000. My original plans for the place were slightly fluid and certainly did not run to what has grown out of the ruins. In the first place I liked the idea of getting back to my farming roots; then it occurred to us that we could train our own horses from here; and most of all, the place would grow into money if we ever changed our minds.

Obviously, the sale of the betting shops has enabled us to build the equine swimming pool and put in the all-weather gallop before results from the stable produced enough income for growth, but to be strictly truthful, the training has since generated its own profits which have been relentlessly ploughed back.

Pond House, which adjoins Tucker's Farm, was purchased in 1972, costing £40,000 for its seventy acres. It seemed expensive at the time; now that the two farms have been developed jointly into such a specialized training unit it would prove difficult to liquidate in order to retrieve anything like its worth. Personally I can't think of a single jumping trainer who could buy it, so David junior is being moulded to take over should Martin fall off his BMX bicycle . . .

It is difficult to establish a man's wealth in any circumstances; when an entrepreneur has kept a low profile while establishing his empire the task becomes even more difficult. Dave Pipe has property extending from Bristol to Falmouth covering a multitude of usages. He does admit to rarely selling and has accumulated diverse outlets, from Morelli's ice cream shop to a Taunton nursing home; and at the age of sixty-eight still has his finger well and truly on the pulse. Having sold a Taunton building site for £9 million, the estimates of his worth at upwards of £20 million do not look unrealistic.

Dave Pipe hung on to his betting office in Taunton initially to retain a lifeline; yet in instigating the record-crunching stables he has created a second forest fire to fuel.

Chapter 3

Youthful Days

By the time Martin was ready to make his way in the world his parents had realized that he would follow the bookmaking trade however much they objected: so he joined the office staff working from the basement at the family home at Cara, where Carol Tyson, his future wife, was the in-house accountant. Two years older and four inches taller than Martin, Carol remembers taking no more than a fleeting glance at the boss's weedy son until he joined the firm.

It all seems rather hazy now how they became a pair. They seem to have drifted into each other's lives, rather than falling in love at first sight.

Pipe
It was more a convenience to go out together at first. I had been educated at boys-only schools and had not come into contact with girls much. Carol freely admits to having been a tomboy, leading all the street games with dens, bikes and roller skates; she was far more interested in being one of the male mob than in any individual boy in it. Carol's strength of character from an early age made her the natural leader of the gang and even though she lived in the next street to us, she never once noticed me. If she had, she would probably have thought me a wimp. Her territory, Albemarle Road, regularly took on and whipped our Belvadere Road and although she never got the chance to dominate me then, she's made up for lost time since.

Once I'd managed to get on the payroll, we saw more of each

other; but even if Carol could see anything in the impish, innocent character I was then, even so to an eighteen-year-old girl a sixteen-year-old boy is light years away from equality.

My evenings were usually spent settling bets or helping Father at Taunton or Exeter greyhound stadiums, but we did manage to sneak some time together. Our first regular date saw us enlist in the 10 p.m. session of the Ken Jones School of Ballroom Dancing. We managed to achieve our Bronze Medal, eventually, before losing interest. What those sessions did do, though, was to establish a closer link between us: bodily contact had been made, albeit at arm's length. Both of us admit there was no immediate surge of electricity, more a feeling of security in each other's company.

When I became capable of running the credit office while Dad built up the chain of shops or bet on the racecourse, my style developed along lines he disapproved of. I was too brave – or too stupid. He used to rip into me when I laid horses to be big losers but never praised me if they won for us. In retrospect I can see his logic. If you play it safe, you can take a regular living out of the game. If you go for broke, sooner or later that's exactly what will happen. All his life Dad has kept a tight grip on his business and even though he had to get out and about to expand, he was not entirely happy to leave me holding the fort. He'd phone up from all over the countryside to keep tabs on the office with the same gruff question: Cop or blow? Quite often by then I'd copped – held on to the bet and won a few quid; other times I'd blown the day's takings. They were incredibly fascinating times, watching our fortunes change by the minute. Bookmaking is a game of nerve; you need a cool head and the ability to make instant decisions.

The credit side attracted some big punters, and a particularly successful group from Cornwall got the better of us for a while. We nicknamed them 'the Cornish Mob'. One of them was a big farmer called Bill Scott, who later had horses in training with us, but at that time it was us doing the paying as Bill went through a profitable period, quite often up about £30,000. He was becoming a definite worry.

The real concern was that there was no obvious rhyme or reason to his bets that we could see. If you can spot a pattern in a winning punter's bets it's relatively simple to avoid the hot money; but Bill

Scott's looked to be random selections. At first it just puzzled us; then things became serious enough for Dad to devote his whole attention to finding out Mr Scott's information source. He took to engaging Bill in idle gossip when he rang up to place his bets in the hope that something would be let slip. After a week of chatting Dad burst from his room one morning as if he'd won the pools. 'We've got him!' he was shouting. Bill Scott's information, it turned out, was coming from the *Sun*'s daily cartoon tipster Sunny Jim. No paper tipster can sustain such a winning run for ever and, as Dad predicted , Sunny Jim's purple patch soon faded; and with it the Cornish Mob's danger to Pipe Bookmakers passed. Dad has always been an attentive listener, a trait which has stood him in good stead whatever he's done.

As for Carol and me, we both admit we drifted into becoming an item and it proved to be an incredibly slow-moving current which eventually led us to the altar. Our courtship lasted eleven years, the final five as an engaged couple. For several years Carol prodded me into at least looking at jewellers' displays, only to be regularly fobbed off with pretty lame excuses for not actually buying an engagement ring. Then right out of the blue one afternoon in 1966 when we were on our way to buy Carol's first car I suddenly steered her into Draytons the Jewellers and did the honourable thing; I bought the ring. It occurred to me on the spur of the moment it would be cheaper to buy a ring than a car. Of course, I've since learned that that's only the first instalment. You never finish paying once you've bought the ring.

We were married on 18 April 1971. It was definitely the best wedding I've been to. The service was in Taunton, then everyone trooped back here for the reception in a red-and-white striped marquee. We had loads of bookmaking and racing friends here, most of whom thought we'd never make it up the aisle. Naturally it went on late. In fact, it was such a good party I didn't want to leave, but eventually Carol dragged me off on our honeymoon to a hotel at Bideford at one o'clock in the morning. That was on the Monday, and we were back by Wednesday for me to ride in a point-to-point at Nedge, where I ended up lying on the ground watching my mount disappear into the distance.

There's no doubt I'd tried Carol's patience often enough, and never more so than six years earlier, when I ran out of road at

2 a.m. going home from Exeter. By the time I was twenty I'd smashed up three Volkswagen Beetles, a Mini van, a Triumph GT6 and the first of three Triumph Stags. She definitely knew what she was taking on.

I learned to drive on the local aerodrome long before my seventeenth birthday and as a result sailed through the test the same day I became of age to drive. Dad has always believed in offering incentives and true to his word there was a Beetle waiting for me when I arrived home. I felt King Pin. It was my first real taste of freedom, and once I had wheels things definitely began to move.

I was now allowed to work in the Butlins betting shop in Minehead; at that time the campers had fortunes to spend, and it was a great place to be. We had a portable television in the shop and I used to take it to and from home in the car with the aerial sticking out of the window, watching programmes as I drove along. I worked hard down at Butlins and as the shop closed straight after the last evening race it was natural for us to stay at the camp for some fun. Three times on the way back from Minehead I turned the car over, always through going too fast while trying to watch the television. Once, having pulled myself out of the wreckage with nothing worse than concussion, I walked towards home, eventually hitching a lift without a second thought for the day's takings lying in the wreckage. Dad was furious. He dragged me back to the scene of the crash and luckily we found all the money intact. We towed the car home with the cash safely in his pockets, and despite my harrowing experience I was made to hitch-hike to Minehead and back for a week to teach me a lesson. Funnily enough, the episode worked in my favour as I was then allowed to stay down there. Now that was *real* freedom.

About this time I decided I would like to be a jockey and a local trainer, Eric Foster, kindly consented to teach me to ride. This was when not having been allowed a pony as a boy did prove a handicap, as Eric's idea of life was do or die. The first morning I turned up at Henlade, just outside Taunton, he threw me on to a racehorse called Clown and put me at the end of his string. In those days crash helmets were not considered necessary and cloth caps provided scant protection from injury. Within a hundred yards of leaving the stables the string broke into a trot but as I knew nothing of the signals a rider gave his mount, it was only minutes before Clown had increased his speed to the gallop and taken me across the main Taunton road, totally oblivious to the game of Russian roulette we had played with the heavy traffic.

Strangely enough, the incident failed to put me off, and although I have no proof of this whatsoever, it did occur to me that Dad had probably told Eric to make my first riding venture my last. It wasn't: lessons, if you could call them that, continued daily before work in the betting shop, with similar out-of-control endings usually the order of the day. The lads and Eric certainly got their entertainment from my morning visits. How I survived I'll never know. I wouldn't inflict the chance of galloping across a main road on my worst detractor. Later on, Eric's brother Johnny found a safer ride for me to practise on: a hunter called Moony, on whom both Carol and I had endless fun.

A far worse incident than being carted by Clown occurred when I was almost twenty and still burning the candle at both ends. I fell asleep in the car coming home from Exeter in the small hours and crashed head-on into a concrete lamp post. What was left of the lamp post ended up alongside the Beetle's gear-stick, with me pinned in the mangled wreckage. I had to be cut out of the car without knowing anything about it and remained unconscious for three days over Easter 1965. It was all of two months before I saw home again.

Mum still shudders now at the thought of that accident. I had serious multiple injuries, and she was told to get to the hospital quickly in case I failed to come around. There was a distinct possibility I might not have. I pulled through, but for quite some while it appeared as if they would need to amputate my foot at the ankle. Mum said that she never felt so helpless as when I was lying there unconscious.

I can clearly remember being petrified while my future hung in the balance. To this day it frightens me to see anyone with a leg missing, realizing it could just as easily be me. As things have turned out, it might well have made no difference if I had lost a leg, except that at the rate I have to rush around to keep the show rolling I would have worn out plenty of artificial ones. As it is, though the ankle was saved when Dad intervened and forbade an amputation, that injury and the smashed thigh I got later in a race at Taunton are the reason why I ride my BMX bike everywhere. I am simply not sound.

Naturally, being such a finicky eater I hated hospital food, but happily for all concerned Morelli's ice cream shop was close by, and the family spoon-fed me until I could shovel it down myself.

Forced to wear callipers to walk once I was up, I was sent for diagnosis to 71 Park Street, Mayfair, where the late Bill Tucker had speeded the healing process of so many injured sportsmen. Johnny Foster, the father of Martin, my second champion conditional jockey, persuaded me that as I was no more than a heap of calcifying breakages, the renowned orthopaedic surgeon was my only chance of being put back together. In pointing me in the right direction, Johnny rekindled a link with our family started years before when he rode my grandfather Albert's ponies at local gymkhanas and in races.

Tucker's reputation was so high that his books were full with world champions, and the only way to get into the place was to make out racing would lose an outstanding prospect if he turned me away. Me, a loss to racing? I could hardly sit on a stool, let alone be champion jockey. Anyway, he saw me. It puts my sheltered existence into perspective when you think that the trip to Mr Tucker's was not only my first journey to London but my first trip on a train.

Convalescence was slow and frustrating. Special square buckets were bought for the hot and cold water treatments I was prescribed; Carol administered them, which put her directly in the firing line on my frequent bad days. I vividly remember once kicking her across the room when she upset me. No matter what pain and exasperation I went through I should not have got away with such tantrums. Still, the time we spent together while I was recuperating certainly brought us closer together. Mostly we played gambling games for hours on end. So much for the Swinging Sixties! We were quite innocent, really. There was no sex for us then; unbelievable when you think I was twenty and Carol was twenty-two.

I returned to work while still in callipers as the main office was in the house. Carol says I looked so vulnerable and helpless then it was one of the few times I've ever completely been the boss. She didn't have the heart to argue with me. I was cut about the mouth and had lost most of my teeth; and I've got a peculiar nose as a result of that crash. I still have funny turns now. Carol says I've never properly recovered.

Using either the callipers or crutches, I set about strengthening my wasted arms and legs by walking up and down the streets of Taunton, refusing all offers of lifts. The townspeople were so kind then; life held far better values in the sixties. I carried weights to make the retarded muscles work much harder, a strategy I use today with horses that have suffered muscle wastages, including Carvill's Hill.

I'm an inveterate fidget; I can't keep still for more than a minute unless it's to study form. I even fell down the stairs trying to carry a large old tape-recorder while still on crutches. It was a full year before I was fit enough to throw away the walking aids, and I chose my twenty-first birthday party to regain my freedom.

Everyone says I am still a mad driver these days despite those crashes in my youth. I must admit, though, it took me quite a while to get my confidence back in a car after that last scare. Like every other human situation, it can be related to the way horses must think and that is why I give a high priority to considering animals' reactions in every circumstance. Put yourself in their position and things become clearer. After a fall, a smack with the whip may make a horse jump, but that is negative thinking. Surely it is far preferable to regain his confidence over small obstacles, encouraging him to jump for fun again. Achieving the object of any lesson by fear is the surest way to lose your pupil's trust.

It may seem as though my years between leaving school and adulthood were rather empty, but as Dad's betting shop string continued to grow, pleasure came a very poor second. I was as excited as he was and only too pleased to work all hours God sent. To create what Dad did does not happen by luck; you have to keep ahead of the game. With so much happening within the business the odd night out had to be snatched when the situation presented itself. Trying to catch up with the action may have been one reason why I was always dashing around in cars and crashed so many.

Dad gave us a Range Rover as a present at our wedding in the hope it would slow me down. Twenty-one years later that same vehicle is still in use although, on it as on me, time and abuse have taken their toll.

Chapter 4

Pigsties to Stables: Tucker's Farm

Pipe

I was twenty-three when Dad bought Tucker's. Carol and I, engaged by now, had hoped for a tidier place in the country, but we knew in our hearts the challenge of turning it into an asset was irresistible to him. Remember, it was Dad who controlled the purse strings.

Even so, those days were some of our happiest times together. Dad had just added a grocery shop to his investments with muggins here expected to deliver vegetables in the evenings after the betting shops closed. The delivery van was an old Mini which, because of my appalling crash record, provided Carol and me with our only means of transport for a while. We'd come out to Tucker's at weekends from Taunton to work on the place with a picnic, packed by Mum, large enough to feed the whole village. It was a struggle just to get into the place, the lane down to the farm having degenerated into nothing more than an old mud track. The muck engulfing the yard had long since hidden the cobbles from daylight and the surrounding pigsties lay in varying degrees of collapse. The whole family set about the place and between us we demolished the old buildings, scraped the manure off the cobbles and generally pulled the farm into some sort of shape. The house where the offices are now had a huge old inglenook fireplace where we burned all the rotten timber and trees that we felled to make an entrance and exit. That hard graft gave me an appetite like I'd forgotten existed. Imagine it, half a tree on the fire and

Mum's picnic. It was fun and laughter all day.

Dad bought an old tractor complete with an even older trailer and we'd set off again after lunch to clear more debris around the farm, with him driving and the rest of us in the trailer singing away with our legs dangling over the back. We were like gipsies, covered in muck, tired out from hard physical work but absolutely immersed in that hazy happiness of creating something from nothing.

The first horses entered the place twenty-three years ago. Dad gutted the house, then put it back into a habitable state before asking his brother Tony if he'd like to train from the stables that had risen from the bases of the old pigsties. Tony had landed some rare old gambles when riding for the wealthy Bedfordshire permit-holder Sidney Banks in the early sixties. He had quite a few owners willing to support him and, together with our handful of moderate horses started off with a dozen inmates. The idea was for me to ride out in the mornings and learn the game from the grass roots.

At the same time an old baler arrived from one of the local auctions, starting us off in the haymaking game. To this day we still grow all our own hay, only now we get contractors in to do it. We also started to grow oats for the horses and although they are now fed mainly on Ebor nuts, we still get through seventy tons of oats a year as well. Both oats and hay are tested for content and quality, and in twenty seasons they have only once failed to be up to the required standard.

When Tony started training the stables were in better shape than either the house or the driveway. Although money was tight, Dad knew he had to attend to the business end first. The day Tony and his wife moved in they had to lay sheets of tin down in order to get their furniture over the mud to the house.

Tony Pipe

We'd only got bits and bobs of horses and no gallops to speak of but it presented a challenge. Although Dave said we could gallop anywhere on the farm, no single field was big enough or level enough to get any decent work into them. I preferred to hack up to the Blackdown Hills overlooking the place. Just getting up the steep ascent made them blow, let alone working when they reached the top.

Ron Atkins, Robert Alner and John Francome rode winners

from the yard, with Old Paint, owned by Jenny Hembrow the most regular to oblige. He was not exactly the big, well made chasing type John was used to riding for Fred Winter and when he first clapped eyes on the horse in the parade ring at Warwick he said 'Oh shit, he's a pony.' I told him the horse's heart was big enough and although he did a sort of Ali shuffle before taking off at the fences, provided John left him alone to do his own thing they'd survive. Francome tried to organize the old codger at one fence down the back side after the little horse had shaken him up a bit over the first half dozen jumps. The pair of them rubbed their noses along the ground for a couple of strides but thankfully stayed upright. Francome sat still after that and got back in the race to win nicely. It probably did him some good. You never stop learning with horses.

The family arrangement lasted from 1969 to the 1973–4 season, when, in Tony's words, 'You know what it's like with brothers. We knew each other too well. Dave paid the piper but I would not always play his tune. We're both stubborn men, it couldn't last.'

Tony Pipe still lives across the road from the hive of winning activity, enjoying the more leisurely life of whipper-in to the Taunton Vale Harriers and helping his son Raymond with his blossoming fourteen-strong stable of show jumpers. There is little love lost between the brothers these days, despite their close proximity, yet Tony admits, 'They've done well. Martin could not be safely let loose near a horse when we started but he's learned through pure graft and an inquiring mind.'

Pipe
When I took out a permit to train Dad's horses in the 1973–4 season my knowledge was lacking and my experience nil. I can remember telling Dad the horses were mad fresh because it had been raining for three days. 'What's that got to do with it?' he asked, to which I indignantly said that if he knew anything about horses, he'd realize they couldn't go out in the rain! Once he'd pointed out in no uncertain terms that horses raced in the rain, the issue resolved itself.

Some well known faces cut their teeth at Tucker's Farm twenty years ago, including Ron Hodges and Jeff Pearce, both now trainers themselves. Pearce chuckles at the thought. 'I'd been working for Les Kennard getting the occasional ride until I saw I had no future there. Les promised me the ride at Taunton on a horse I looked after called Perdition, that is until it cut up to become a bad race. It looked a certainty. He warned me the night prior to the race that the owner might want a better-known jockey but said he'd try to persuade him to let me ride the horse.

'The clever old sod had no intention of letting me on board such a fancied horse but needed me to lead up two others in earlier races and did not want to be left holding three nags himself, so he strung me along. After I'd led the first two up and was about to slip my breeches on, Les broke the news that Macer Gifford had narrowly been given the vote to partner Perdition due to his greater experience. It's not in my nature to explode, but I won't be dumped on either. Clearly there was no future for me with Les, so I joined the Pipe clan over the hill.

'They were fun days. I lived with a local family called Goff who for a fiver per week provided clotted cream teas and a roast dinner every night. That may sound value today but it constituted half of my week's wages. The old man made his living as a wheeler-dealer and looked as sharp as Mr Pipe senior, albeit on a smaller scale. What with Les Kennard, Mr Pipe and then Mr Goff all living by their wits, I learned what life is basically about. What does amaze me, though, is, if they are all so clued up around Devon and Somerset, how does anyone come out on top?'

Pipe
Because we had no proper facilities at that time we did a fair bit of exercise around the lanes – that is, until we came across a flattish field, anybody's would do as long as the owner's house was out of sight. We used to be in, gallop around several times and be out again within minutes. The trick was not to poach a gallop on the same farm too often. We never got caught either. Jeff Pearce had often done the same trick following Les Kennard around the Quantocks. It must be like kids scrumping apples, the excitement of running the risk is a bigger lure than the rewards.

Everyone seemed a larger-than-life character down here then. Our blacksmith, Jorrocks, was a giant of a man, almost square in shape and sporting large McCririck-type whiskers. He had hands like sledgehammers. I bet he could nail horses' shoes on with his fist. Like most other folk in the area, Jorrocks trained a few greyhounds in his spare time. Racing twice a week at Taunton greyhound stadium, which Dad owned, proved great fun and often provided him with additional income in winning bets. They mostly won when fancied and got beat when filled up with meat pies and stout to stop them. Jorrocks was one of life's real men, one it was better to keep on the right side of too, not least because of his habit of carrying a shotgun around in his van.

Pearce agrees those carefree days were priceless. 'Martin generated fun from everything he did. He bet on snooker, darts, dogs, horses or whether or not it would rain. He was a hard man to beat. As a rider he lacked the basic ability but made up for it in guts. When I joined the team, Martin had only recently returned from breaking his leg in a fall at Taunton, yet he still wanted to continue until he had proved to himself he could win a race in the saddle. Like a dog with a bone, he refused to be beaten by anything.

'I could see his riding career ending in tears but I am not at all surprised that he has bypassed the trainers who were bred for the job. He quite liked the idea from the moment Dave Pipe elevated him from gofer to gaffer.'

Pearce left the Pipes on good terms to earn better money labouring on the construction of the Severn Tunnel before returning to racing. He is now making ripples as a Flat race trainer in Newmarket.

Pipe
Jeff is one of the few trainers I will not claim a horse off because of our distant association, although he takes the minority view that horses entered in such races are there to be claimed.

Unlike Jeff, Ron Hodges failed to partner a winner for us, although he often says he would like to be on our horses now. Ron cost us a good few quid at Market Rasen in 1975. I drove Marine Parade and Weather Permitting up in the trailer while he used his brains, persuading a mate to fly him up to the Lincolnshire track in a tiny two-seater plane. Both horses looked certainties but he managed to get ridden out of victory on Marine Parade by Richard Linley, despite my grasping at straws by urging him to object. In those days the verdict often went to the most convincing storyteller but Ron obviously blushes when telling lies.

We looked like getting our money back on Weather Permitting, who went clear going to the last only to attempt to uproot the

41

fence. Ron shot out of the saddle and ended up with his arms around the horse's neck. He lost both stirrups and while he was struggling to regain his seat gave away the lead and with it any hope of salvaging the day's expenses. It occurred to me on the long trek home that Ron had his head screwed on properly. There he was flying back to Somerset while I pulled his mounts halfway across England in a trailer.

From the purchase of Tucker's Farm in 1968 and the addition of Pond House five years later, the progress of the training establishment, and of its tally of winners, was spasmodic. For a decade the whole enterprise was little more than a plaything; yet gradually the amalgamated farms blended into the finished article of today.

True to his principle, 'If it's cheap, I'll buy it,' Dave Pipe obtained ten thousand roof tiles at auction. These were unloaded by Martin, Carol, the Irish handyman Paddy – and anyone else with arms.

Pipe

The trouble was they were not used to re-roof Pond House until two years later and constantly needed to be moved as the place mushroomed. In terms of labour and strained relationships, the original bargain paled somewhat, but it did teach me a lesson in planning. Now anything that is bought for the future is stored well out of the way.

It was during the evolution of Tucker's Farm that I smashed my leg for the second time since my devil-may-care attitude began to run riot. It was a reaction to the strict upbringing I'd had; as soon as I was free to control my own life, I wanted to taste the delights of risk, to test my nerve at every opportunity.

When Dad gathered his horses from other licensed trainers to be prepared at Tucker's Farm, he decided to keep one hurdler with Tim Handel at nearby Hatch Beauchamp. The little grey had been called Lorac, which is Carol spelt backwards. I realize now that was tempting fate. The mare was not over-blessed with ability, but she did run with enough promise several times to suggest she would win a race of some sort.

Nigel Wakely rode for Handel at that time and had partnered Lorac on seven occasions before I was given the leg-up at Taunton in a handicap hurdle on the day after Boxing Day 1972. I had no illusions as to my ability or the reason I'd been given the ride:

Nigel had been offered a much more fancied mount in the race on Drakes Gold for the late John Thorne. He started at 4–1, with Lorac given no better than a 20–1 chance.

Of the eight runners, the favourite, Baytree, ridden by champion jockey Bob Davies, looked in great shape in the parade ring. Charlie Micklam was the only other amateur rider besides myself in the line-up, while of the rest Geoff Shoemark and Peter Jones oozed the confidence of their loftier positions in the jockeys' pecking order.

It seemed to me Lorac had an each-way chance, judging by appearances. She had some potential, having managed two seconds under Nigel, and felt in good spirits when we cantered down to the start. After a mundane pace over the first mile, the race started to sort itself out with me sitting in behind the bunch going as well as anything else.

Riding rather like I drove my cars, I rushed her up the inside of the other runners the moment I spotted a gap on the rails but had not quite got through when the hurdle loomed up. The pro jocks were not having an amateur squirt showing them up so the gap was closed without any sort of warning, putting Lorac through the wings of the jump.

Amazingly the mare stayed upright as she crashed through the solid barrier, smashing me against an upright post in the process. I'd managed to stay in the saddle during the incident but fell to the ground afterwards as the pain swept over me. The ambulance staff rushed to help me and I'm ashamed to say I must have been very abusive because they jumped back from me as if I'd been wired up to an electric current. I knew I'd broken my thigh and was in no mood to be examined for verification.

I'd chanced my luck trying to nip up the inner and paid a high price. Lorac was not the safest of rides anyway, yet when you're young you'd have a go on a one-eyed horse that had difficulty seeing out of the other. Things don't change, either: our son David started off this year in point-to-points on a collection of broken-down, dodgy beasts and was pleased to be riding them.

Nigel Wakely, who had ridden Lorac prior to that fateful day at Taunton, won the race on Drakes Gold and remembers it well. 'Lorac was not the best of jumpers and should not have been entrusted to someone with as little experience as Martin. The incident grew out of the normal scrimmaging you see in races every day. Obviously the regular riders close ranks when new faces start thrusting up the inside rail. It is a blocking movement rather than malicious intent and in the vast majority of cases the horse being squeezed for room either backs off or gives as good as he gets.

'I went to see Martin in hospital once visitors were allowed. He was in a great deal of pain and looked set for a long time out of action.'

Pipe
This period in our life saw a lot of change. Since marrying the year before we had been living in a bungalow surrounded by trees at what is now the top of our all-weather gallop – which at that time we hadn't even considered. When Pond House became habitable Mum and Dad moved in there and we moved out.

Pond House came on the market several months after my Taunton accident and although the property shared its driveway with Tucker's Farm, Dad was not prepared to buy it at any price. Being as run down as Tucker's had been, it appeared to be exactly his type. Typically, in order to prevent the bidding becoming inflated, he stayed away from the auction, leaving precise instructions with a locally unknown friend as to his ceiling. He was far from pleased when learning the final bid was £2,000 above his imposed limit of £38,000. Imagine the pickle we'd be in now if someone else had bought it, though. We'd be sharing a driveway, causing havoc with the volume of traffic, and be open to uninvited guests.

Twelve months after we acquired Pond House Carol left for Wellington Hospital to give birth to our son David. On that same day the workmen moved in to start building the house as it now stands.

Pond House now has five bedrooms, four of them named after some of the better horses trained here – Sabin Du Loir, Beau Ranger, Strands Of Gold and Baron Blakeney. The names were chosen because those horses had lifted the stable from merely winning races to taking the major prizes. Now, with the list of big winners growing annually, the bedroom names will have to become removable in order to placate all the owners who stay with us overnight. Besides the usual domestic rooms there is a family area fully thirty feet by forty that houses a three-foot-wide television. I spend so much time watching races these days it seemed sensible to magnify events. Over the past five years I have built up a video library logging every race covered by SIS to complement the form book. There must be thousands of races on tape at my call. The professional race-readers who compile Chaseform are usually spot on, but I still take a visual check for myself. This game is all about opinions, and I like to form my own. With SIS showing a minimum of twelve races per day and double that number at weekends, I have almost instant access to the bulk of the Flat and jumping meetings. Besides proving useful when evaluating the opposition, the videos give us a valuable insight into prospective purchases' good or bad points prior to the sales. This saves a lot of leg work.

Adjoining the family room there is a heated indoor swimming pool thirty feet by fourteen. Mum swims twice a day but though I can swim I'm still basically frightened of water. Above the family room, the same area is used to house a full-sized snooker table, table-tennis table and darts board, although the nightly reviewing of the day's races and the incessant telephone calls mean the light relief stays idle more often than not. Carol says it would be more peaceful living in an aviary. Our kitchen leads into a large conservatory the size of a squash court, with access to the four garages.

Both Carol and I are paranoid about cleanliness; we feel it reflects a person's attention to other details. All our best staff are tidy in themselves and correspondingly fastidious in the care of their horses. When visiting other stables to look at prospective purchases or people to care for our horses out of training, I always take note of their feed house. If that area is clean and well run, the chances are the rest of the job is done properly.

Amazingly for a house that is almost as busy as a Chinese takeaway, Pond House remains neat and tidy whatever the time of day. This is indicative of the way the entire Pipe empire is run: a place for everything and everything in its place. But a glance at Martin's boyhood teddy bear sitting on a bedroom chair waiting to have his left eye sewn back in place reveals him to be as ordinary as the rest of us.

Chapter 5

Only if the Price is Right . . .

Dave Pipe
If something is cheap, I'll always look at it, and if it's worth the money I'll buy it, even if there is no obvious use for it at the time. As long as the purchase is not an animal, it can be stored for the day there is a job for it and the odds are by then the purchase is even more of a bargain.

When I bought Tucker's Farm in 1968, although the intention was to train from there, it would patently grow into money whatever happened. The place was in such a derelict state it could only be improved. I liked the space here and I could also see that the adjoining Pond House Farm, which shared our access, would also become available in the foreseeable future. Every innovation in or around the place since then has either been my idea or approved by me following persistent reasoning from Martin. Either way, once a decision to improve facilities was made, it fell to me to organize and oversee the building or installation.

The equine swimming pool was the first training aid we put in, to help overcome the lack of fitness which is the most common excuse used for horses beaten on their seasonal reappearance. At first the idea centred around the pond adjacent to Pond House which was cleared, reshaped and dredged with conversion in mind; but after long discussions we rejected it in favour of a proper pool, under cover, that we could use every day, in all conditions, not just when the weather was favourable. We inspected existing pools in Cheltenham, Lambourn and New-market, gleaning the best ideas from each to incorporate into our final plans. Jim Wilson, Nicky Henderson and Clive Brittain were all willing to discuss the pitfalls of building and using swimming pools to supplement gallops. At the time, siting the pool 200 yards from the main stable block seemed extravagant; but since then the whole training set-up has grown so far and so fast that the yawning gap between the original stables and the pool is now in full use for additional stabling, storage barns, workshop, electricity generator and the wood-pulper used to top up the all-weather gallop.

Having sited and excavated the hole for the pool, I actually had second thoughts about continuing; but I realized that if we stopped now the money already spent on materials and labour would have been totally wasted. Nothing was salvageable, and waste is not a word in my vocabulary.

The building to cover the pool proved more than adequate, having previously housed the grandstand at King's Heath greyhound stadium. I knew the huge amount of redundant space would come in useful somehow, although I could not have envisaged its current worth. Measuring fully one hundred yards, the building now serves as home to a pair of stables used exclusively for horses in need of cold running water treatment after racing to ease hot or filled tendons. Next in line is a large stable for the occasional oversized horse, a solarium, then the pool itself, a covered automatic horse-walker for eight horses, covered lungeing ring and kindergarten jumping area, storage barn and a block of twelve stables. The whole thing may have evolved more by chance than design but not entirely by accident.

Although Clive Brittain advised that horses swim with more enthusiasm in unheated water, I installed a heating plant in case I changed my thinking later. The pool is circular, designed to encourage doubtful swimmers into the unknown, has a padded entrance chute for their protection and has the cleanest water imaginable, which combine to make it one of the best equine pools in Europe.

Having established the price range of filtration plants from the regular equine pool suppliers, I set about locating one bigger and better in the second-hand market. Eventually I found a plant with twice the required capacity at half the price. For £4,000, a unit big enough to service an Olympic-sized pool was unearthed. Its sole use had been during the making of the first *Jaws* film and since being installed at Pond House, has proved just as valuable in the production of winners as it did in making the film a box-office hit.

In the mid-1970s our horses were mainly bad-legged animals whose training consisted more of swimming than galloping. Weightless galloping is how we describe swimming, which I think is important when trying to get sufficient work into horses without making them fed up. As with everything else in life, trial and error established the amount of work required in water to equate to normal exercise. Files of the daily work reveal Baron Blakeney the clear record-holder, covering 100 circuits with ease. These days the stuffier horses do up to a maximum of thirty laps, divided into two equal sessions with a rest period of five minutes in between. Most days up to forty horses are swum, depending on the time and staff available.

Quite often horses are swum as well as, not just instead of, normal exercise. Martin says swimming is enjoyable work, not arduous or stressful labour. Contrary to the popular belief that horses must be finely tuned on turf gallops, numerous horses from this stable have been trained to win straight from the water and the rest run from being trained on the all-weather strip.

As for the horse-walkers, they have repaid their purchase price a thousand times over. For the first machine we paid Frankie Durr the princely sum of just £200. At that time they had become unpopular as the pendulum swung back after the initial excitement and purchase en masse by the major stables. Opposing the anti-walker trend, we then snapped up Peter Walwyn's automatic exerciser at double the price we'd paid for the first one. When we bought it we had no immediate use for it, but sure enough when the second yard at Sunnyside evolved in 1991 the old Walwyn machine came out of storage providing a further eight-horse exerciser for one-tenth of the current price.

To those who argue against the use of such machines I am adamant that as young horses even have to be taught to walk properly, this is one way of achieving that aim while the staff do other jobs. Also, surely it is preferable for horses to be walking in the company of others than to be in the solitary confinement of a stable. Remember, we use our walkers as a supplement to normal exercise, not instead of it. If you asked the majority of human prisoners if they would like to walk around an exercise ring for an extra hour instead of being locked up, I'm sure they'd opt for the greater freedom.

Our walkers are in use most of the day, six days a week and to a lesser degree on Sundays, which is why it is essential that they are under cover. Another important reason for using them indoors is to remove distractions. With so much going on here all day it would be inviting trouble to have young horses on open walkers. In turn, that would mean staff continually leaving their other jobs to sort out the walkers.

Both the pool and the horse-walkers are monitored by closed-circuit colour television, housed in the main office. With three secretaries working there it would be odds against trouble going unnoticed, yet a further simple device ensures that it never does: angled mirrors around the office mean the pictures are never out of sight, even when the girls have to leave their desks to dip into a filing cabinet. Also linked to every building and stable is an audio system, used mainly as a music line pumping out Radio One throughout the working day. This proves invaluable in getting youngsters used to the noise they will encounter on the racecourse. It is also an excellent way of tracing Martin or passing on instructions to any of the staff. The labyrinth of passages and alleys here can make it difficult to track people down; with this system calls can be put out to staff, vets, farriers – or to me when something practical requires attention. It saves a deal of leg work. And the entire audio system came out of Taunton Greyhound Stadium, which I had bought ten years previously.

Another of my often-aired mottos is 'Let your eyes be your guide and your money be the last thing you part with'. Laying an all-weather gallop is a very expensive business and when this project came up for discussion I kept a firm grip on the cheque book despite being pressurized from all sides. I'd always been slightly doubtful of the value of galloping on an artificial surface, basically because I thought it was false compared to the turf horses raced on. But most big stables and training centres had been using them for years, which made me wonder if they were right and I was wrong. So I went to numerous all-weather gallops to investigate, mostly by invitation, sometimes without, and came to the conclusion that many of them had been spoiled by skimping on the drainage, causing wet patches to appear. That false economy destroyed the object of the exercise because in a wet period horses would run off good ground on to a deep patch and back on to good again. Even worse, in a freeze-up, when the gallop would be needed most, those wet patches would be a death-trap. The man who gave me most help in my research into all-weather surfaces was the Jockey Club's land agent at Newmarket, Robert Fellowes. He alerted me to the pitfalls they had encountered and, in time, overcome.

Having decided that an all-weather gallop was indeed what we needed to break into the higher divisions, I set about creating one better than any I had seen on my travels. Work began in December 1983 and did not reach completion until twelve months later. Quotes of up to £50,000 from Dormit had rung alarm bells in my businessman's head, and although in the end I spent that amount, the finished article was wider, deeper and boasted several additional features. Martin wanted to be able to work three horses upsides instead of the normal two or, in some cases only one. We had also noticed that even many of the better all-weathers failed to prevent drainage stones from working to the surface. The answer was simple, though it took some putting into effect. After doubling the normal depth of drainage stone, ensuring total water release, the usual membrane separating it from the artificial surface was laid completely around the stone bed then sewn up by an army of locals with mail-bag needles to form a four-furlong intestine.

Since January 1985 all our winners have been trained solely on an artificial surface half-a-mile long. When you consider that the horses are being pulled up over the last half-furlong our short, straight, all-weather strip blows long-held theories right out of the window. It is simply not necessary to have any number of lengths, shapes or gradients to make horses fit to win. Martin has also proved beyond any shadow of doubt that interval training over a short distance up a gently ascending wood-chip gallop, can and does achieve the object of producing winners. The only time his horses ever gallop on turf is when schooling over fences or when racing.

There are, of course, many very good all-weather gallops in use around Europe but I defy anyone to name a better one than ours, bearing in mind most trainers use them only for cantering whereas our horses actually do all their work on it. Both John Dunlop and Jim Bolger are leading advocates of similar surfaces for training.

For the surface itself I chose half-inch wood chips, smashed rather than cut. The rougher edges after smashing bind together much better forming a firmer surface, one much less likely to move or slide under the weight of a galloping Thoroughbred. In our opinion excessive surface movement is the prime factor in causing back problems. I happened across some redundant machinery at a farm sale which proved ideal for the job of converting wood into chippings. A bone and metal pulverizer bought for the bargain price of £300 crushed the locally purchased wood offcuts. Add to that an old grass drier to provide the belts and conveyers at a cost of £200 and the home-made wood-chip production line rolled for the price of a couple of loads of the commercial product.

Another feature of this gallop is that apart from a slight curve when pulling up it runs straight. I had been in favour of following the twisting and turning hedge boundary but Martin argued that would put undue pressure on one leg or the other, and after thinking it over I acknowledged the wisdom of his theory.

Paul Leach, our jockey when this new toy first came into use, said the worst ground our horses ever encountered was when racing in public.

When any stable expands, it needs more staff, and the accommodation you give them determines the quality of the workers you get. This came to Martin's notice on his initial visits to Newmarket when inspecting horses for sale and the point was not wasted on him. His insistence on providing proper on-site accommodation for the single staff brought to mind just the thing. You need a lot of imagination to see the end product, and when lorry-loads of wooden sections in various states of repair appeared, Martin thought I'd lost my marbles. But knowing me, he sat back and watched the erection and subsequent transformation of the building that had formerly been home to Taunton Council. The building cost £400, but we spent £20,000 on it to provide individual accommodation for twenty staff with the most modern of kitchens and a large communal television and games room attached.

The much talked-about Pond House laboratory fitted into the building housing the saddle room, feed store and half a dozen stables. Here for once I was forced to leave the buying to experts, realizing the equipment had to be the proper models in an industry where technology moves fast. Besides considerably shortening the time lapse between taking and receiving the results of blood samples, on the spot testing by our own technician halved the cost and paid for the new service in a relatively short time.

Another major training aid took shape in 1990 when, to get over the problem of the relatively few days when even getting to the all-weather gallop was too risky, an indoor ride mushroomed behind the pool area. I hate to leave odd corners; they invariably fill up with scrap and look untidy. It is the longest covered ride I have seen, purely because the dimensions were governed by the length of the old King's Heath greyhound stadium in front of it.

Once again, as much time was spent on the underground work as on the superstructure. The availability and minimal haulage costs of the local stone meant we could use twice the normal amount of base materials and, as with the all-weather gallop, it was sewn into huge membrane bags which allowed the drainage to work while keeping the stone underground where it belonged. Having covered the stone with a deep layer of wood chips, it struck me that the application of tar on top would both protect it from rotting and also form a sounder base for the sand surface.

But after I had sought estimates for the work, which varied from £165,000 to £200,000, I dug my toes in. We'd managed to do the job up to that period without luxury. Having sown the seed, however, it became too difficult to get Martin off the subject and eventually by buying direct from the steel stock-holders and using sub-contracted labour we put up the building for £40,000.

Initial use showed there to be far too much dust in the air from the sand surface, which itself required a great deal of harrowing, simply because we were using the facility much more than we had originally envisaged. I sat down with a sheet of paper and a list of the problems to be eradicated and within an hour came up with a design to do the job. Most things are simple when you take the time to work backwards from the problem. A three-ton roller the exact width of the covered circular track puts back the surface while a tank sitting above it supplies a constant stream of water to an ordinary pin-pricked hosepipe across its width. This smothers the dust with fine water, and a single row of metal tynes harrows the finished surface. The complete contraption, made from odds and ends, cost next to nothing.

At the opposite end of the financial scale I bought our first helicopter for Martin's use in 1988 – but still at the bargain price of £60,000 from the South West Electricity Board. Having bought it right via an employee of SWEB, we duly made a £30,000 profit on the transaction when part-exchanging the helicopter for the current Bell jet-powered model. Training is Martin's job and the hours he spends here are the most important; the chopper helps him get the most out of the daylight hours. My friends find it quite amazing that I have never flown in either machine. Nor do I intend to.

Even Dave Pipe, though, occasionally gets it wrong; racing is a game of chance as well as skill, and even the canniest wind up on the receiving end from time to time.

One evening I was sitting in Martin's conservatory waiting for the family and troops to return from Taunton races, where the stable had pulled off a double with Dan Marino and Tom Clapton. Martin, Carol and Chester Barnes were first home, full of champagne, followed ten minutes later by son David, who had been assisting his grandfather laying the odds at the course. In answer to Martin's inquiry as to his father's whereabouts, David cheekily replied, 'Having laid Dan Marino at all prices from fives out to eights only to watch him bolt in, then backed our Nordic Delight and watched speechlessly as Tom Clapton the lesser fancied runner in the same race won at 9–1, if Grandad does come in it will be straight through that wall!'

Those racegoers who think it unethical for the champion trainer to have a practising bookmaker for a father can rest assured he comes to his own conclusions and is definitely fallible!

Chapter 6

Friends and Allies

Pipe

When I smashed my thigh at Taunton in December 1972 it left the workforce at home short on the riding front, opening a door for the then sixteen-year-old Ron Treloggen. Ron, a dairy farmer's son from Street, near Glastonbury, had decided to ignore the school careers officer's advice to make his living as a farmer instead of pursuing his dream of becoming a jockey. Realizing self-help would be the only leg-up he was likely to get, the keen youngster devised a way of getting himself known. Having followed racing since his Pony Club days, Ron knew that during every afternoon's sport horses could be seen galloping around riderless after falling or unseating their jockeys, often avoiding capture for some time and causing havoc. With this in mind he set out to catch loose horses and ride them back to their owner or trainer, specifically to gain introductions rather than thanks.

The first attempt worked like a dream. Local trainer George Small was not only grateful to the boy who prevented his loose horse from doing itself any harm but impressed enough with his riding to comment on his tidy style. Unfortunately, this promising beginning had no sequel as George had no openings on his staff. Nevertheless the idea not only held promise, it came to fruition on that dank December day in Taunton when I, an equally keen amateur rider claiming a riding allowance of 7lb, went through the wing on Lorac. Treloggen, oblivious to my problems, had only one thing on his mind – the capture of the loose horse. After a brief, determined tussle with a groundsman, who had his sights on a few pounds tip for delivering the horse to its connections, Treloggen won the day, vaulted into the mud-caked saddle and hacked Lorac gently back to the waiting trainer, Tim Handel. Suitably impressed with the horse catcher's enterprise but unable to make room for him in his stable, Handel promised to recommend the ambitious boy should a vacancy arise elsewhere. Two days later Dad, left holding the fort, contacted the youngster on Handel's advice to offer him the job of work rider while my broken thigh precluded a return to the yard.

While lying in hospital I had plenty of time to reflect on the reasoning and actions Ron Treloggan employed to get his way. I realized then you have to make your own luck and that lesson has stood me in good stead ever since.

At the time all Dad had in were four point-to-pointers, a couple of broodmares and some of their offspring. Even so, the place offered a start in racing for the farmer's son who desperately wanted to break into his chosen career. Ron Hodges was kingpin in the area at the time among the amateur riders, leaving precious little for the lesser lights, let alone a boy with no experience at all. Still, Treloggen's ingenious method of attracting attention earned him the craved-for initial education in the arts of work riding, schooling and race tactics during my hospitalization and convalescence. Four months to the day after engineering a job, Treloggen got his chance to take the long-range plans a stage further when given the ride on Weather Permitting at the Taunton Vale point-to-point. Starting odds-on, the combination failed to justify the bookies' confidence by the shortest of short heads. Ron blamed his inexperience for the defeat, and although Dad agreed with the jockey's assessment he had not backed the short-priced favourite, so shrugged off the defeat.

In those days the horses simply fitted in and around the bookmaking business. Weather Permitting had been purchased with form at Ascot Sales, but the others were odds and ends. Bobo's Boy, bought the same day for no better reason than to act as travelling companion on the journey back to Somerset, proved to be a lunatic with dodgy legs. Clock Corner only made up the numbers; but it was this one which realized Ron Treloggen's dream, winning at Clyst Honiton, a small course opposite Exeter airport, a year after his first ride.

The next season my leg had mended sufficiently to allow me to resume my spluttering riding career. I was more careful when picking my mounts now, which enabled Ron to grab more chances; in that season, his third, he secured two victories within a week on Bobo's Boy. On the second of these Ron was entitled to allow himself a satisfied grin when beating me on the safer Clock Corner at Minehead. In all he managed sixteen mounts in point-to-points and four under Rules during his spell with us, which gave him sufficient experience of the riding game to reconsider his future. Certainly he loved the riding as much as he had hoped he would, yet his initial three-year stint brought home to him the difficulty of eking out a living as a jockey, even with a great deal of luck. Having decided to return to the home farm and ride for fun, Ron moved on to partner horses for Alf Stewart and Max Churches, notching up eleven winners from Maester Max and Panmure in a single season. Now, at the age of thirty-seven, he's still going strong and rode no fewer than twelve winners in 1992 on the grey Brunico.

When he left us in 1975, Ron Treloggen thought we had reached our intended level in the racing game. A few patched-up cast-offs to play with in the mornings before the main purpose of the day started in the betting office – that looked like the beginning and end of it. Yet it was just at that very time that Ray Alford introduced Len Lungo to the yard with the express intention of injecting knowledge to match our plans to expand.

Farming with his father three miles away from Nicholashayne at Culmstock, Ray had aspirations in point-to-pointing, and these naturally threw me and him together, although in terms of background and riding experience we were worlds apart. Ray rode as soon as he could sit upright, feeling more at ease in a horse's saddle than on a bicycle. While my growing years saw me sheltered from normal boys' toys and games and my horsy interests revolved around the racing results in newspapers, Ray learned to be of use around the farm and machinery at an age when I could not, nor would be allowed to, knock a nail into a piece of wood. Ray was a skilled man long before his time, while I was no more use than a gelding at stud.

Our first contact with the Alfords came through our need for gallops. Dad asked them to construct a mile circuit high above Nicholashayne under the shadow of the Wellington Monument, which is plainly visible from the M5 between Junctions 26 and 27. The ground proved too stony after ploughing and reseeding, causing more injuries from cuts and bruises than it was worth. We religiously commandeered anyone capable of walking to help with the stone-picking after every morning's gallops. Not only was the work back-breaking, it was exasperating. No matter how many stones were picked up, there were just as many laughing at us the next day. Fruitless as that proved, the exercise provided two valuable lessons that have since served us well. I needed no further proof that stones really could grow. The number of stupid injuries incurred through horses treading on stones also made me aware of the value of removing every possible alien item before a disaster, not after the damage has been done. These days, no matter how busy or behind schedule, I fastidiously get out of my vehicle to pick up paper, drink cans, plastic or any other rubbish the general public discard around the place. Horses are their own worst enemies: even if they manage to avoid standing on sharp objects they will almost certainly shy away from other rubbish, inflicting injuries on themselves and other horses. To this end I am almost paranoid about everything being put away after use.

Ray Alford and I quickly became easy in each other's company; despite – or probably because of – our totally different ways of looking at things, we laughed at everything. My Triumph Stag definitely elevated me in the social pecking order, until it blatantly revealed my ostrich-like tendencies. Ray could not believe my way of dealing with the ominously loud knocking noises emanating from the engine. My reasoning, that because by turning the car radio up I could drown the sound there was nothing to worry about, was alien to everything he had been taught. Twenty years on the situation is much the same. I value technology without wanting to understand what makes it tick, and even less how to put anything right. 'Ask Dad' is my answer to every problem which doesn't involve horses. Ray and myself have shared triumphs and disasters, ridden for and against each other, done reciprocal favours, pulled strokes and covered for each other when the need arose.

I think my saving grace as a jockey was determination, backed up by bravery bordering on stupidity. The horses were always mad fresh from too much food and too little work. I fell off more times than I stayed on, yet doggedly refused to let go of the reins. I hardly ever escaped without grazing hands or face, and quite often both. As for race-riding, I admit I lacked the basic skills, although I got quite good at falling, which is hardly surprising considering the experience I got. A horse called Sailor's Warning pulled me over his head six times in succession and each time we parted company somehow or other I landed running.

Ray Alford revels in the memories of those happy go lucky days. 'Strangely, despite not having a clue about the job himself, Martin worked things out in detail when letting others ride his old screws. I had been given the doubtful honour of trying to revitalize the sour old Mayumbe down at Totnes, only to see the tents blowing across the road as we pulled into the car park with the trailer on the back of the Range Rover. The meeting had already been abandoned due to the gales. Aborting the day's sport didn't worry me as the tactics decided on by the budding trainer on the way down had been to make the running on the leery old gelding to keep his mind off refusing. The logic of that failed to grab me.

'Not to be denied his sport, though, Martin decided to make a dash back over Exmoor to Williton, where Mayumbe was also entered, and dispatched me in a friend's car to go on ahead to make the declaration deadline. The other runners looked like leaving the parade ring by the time Martin pulled into the box park, but the tack was slung on in time for us to join them on the way to the start. Knowing better, I ignored the order to make the running, instead contenting myself with the sensible course of dropping in behind the leaders. Mayumbe tried to refuse even as he instinctively became airborne from self-preservation, causing all sorts of havoc. At the second fence he won the battle of wits, digging his toes in and instigating a pile-up. On reflection, perhaps Martin did understand horses then, he simply could not implement the theory himself.

'Another example of the man's thinking surfaced at Tiverton when he gave me the ride on Bobo's Boy. Convinced the animal would run out at one of the invitingly open island fences, he insisted that if this happened, instead of pulling up I should carry on, missing the other fences out, to get a gallop into the horse to put it right for the following meeting at Nedge. Even if things went wrong there was a plan to salvage something out of the day.

'We had shared numerous disappointments before Martin rode his solitary winner on Weather Permitting at Bishopsleigh. Like the majority of the Pond House inmates, this one also bordered on the mad side and I still smile at Martin's coolness with victory in sight. He came past me saying 'Whoa boy, whoa lad', as if he'd ridden hundreds of winners. Never having grasped the basic art of giving a horse its head by slipping the reins when they overjumped or stumbled on landing, Martin was completely oblivious to the fact that instead of breaking his duck, he'd be pulled out of the saddle if the horse so much as coughed over the last two fences. If ever a man deserved a winner it was Martin and, confirming his astuteness, he retired from the saddle there and then.'

Pipe

Six years later, just four days after I took my first major race with Baron Blakeney in the Daily Express Triumph Hurdle, we went to Nedge, where Ray persuaded the reluctant Mayumbe to win a modest point-to-point. Then, half an hour later, still fired up by his success, he broke a leg when David Pengelly's Orchard Mist fell heavily to remind me just how unpredictable horse racing is.

We are still close today. Ray keeps sick, lame and lazy horses for me during the winter and was only too willing to supply a safe mount in February 1992 when I felt the need to get away from the constant demands of training such a large string of racehorses. We chose to have a day with the Taunton Vale Farmers Hunt, the first such indulgence for me in ten years. Turning the clock back came easily enough, despite the incredible change in my lifestyle during the intervening period. Although I wanted to wrench myself away from the at times all-consuming daily routine, it required brute force to separate me from the portable telephone that has become my Siamese twin.

A further link between us is Gail Harrison, my senior secretary and Ray's constant companion. She and head lad Dennis Dummett provide the continuity so necessary in such a fluid business. Everything is open to instant change here and with people and horses constantly needing attention Gail runs the office and Dennis the yard. Gail is well educated, polite to the point where pushy inquirers want to scream, and possesses enough personal experience of riding and training her own horses to know what she is talking about. She seems to have been made for her current position. She is the daughter of a Devon vet, and trained good winners from her home in Buckfastleigh before moving to the heart of the steeplechasing world with Fulke Walwyn in Lambourn. Several years there observing the diverse methods employed by the big names in racing at least satisfied her that the grass is not greener on the other side of the fence. After a short breathing space back home Gail answered an advertisement in March 1984 for a secretary to the forty-horse stable we ran just over the border in Somerset. We were far enough away from home to provide independence yet close enough to enable her to retain family links. The previous season the stable had topped twenty winners for the first time and looked assured of bettering the thirty mark that term. Signs of progress abounded, including the addition of the short uphill all-weather gallop; but it was our quiet assertion that we wanted to emulate Michael Dickinson which convinced Gail that we were her kind of people.

Obviously, life moved at a gentler pace eight years ago. Gail had time to ride at least one horse at exercise each day and when we needed spare riders she rode as many as three before attending to her office duties. She has seen the quality improve and the quantity increase, and has watched us enjoy the incredible highs and somehow cope with the awful lows. When you consider the dramas spawned by such a huge enterprise, it comes as no surprise to learn that the apparently immovable Gail has handed in her notice on three separate occasions. The inevitable problems generated by the turnover of two hundred plus horses a season, eighty staff, an army of owners and the press home in on her like flak on a bomber. Having run the heart of the operation with strict efficiency Gail earned the nickname 'The Headmistress', which following the *Cook Report* has been replaced by 'Geoffrey Boycott' as nothing gets past her. Such is the strength of Gail's loyalty even the triumvirate of Carol, Dad and myself come up against a stone wall if any of us tries to extricate information about any of the others. Firmly, with respect, she diverts inquiries to the source. Basically Gail is the valve to the heart of the establishment, deflecting the dross and passing the essential.

If I have painted a picture of a characterless automaton, that is wrong. Away from the confidences she so avidly protects, Gail is a fun-loving country girl. Admittedly, living within a six-minute drive from Pond House does leave her vulnerable to our pleas for help outside working hours, but I suspect it is the close proximity of home that keeps her lid on in times of stress. There are occasions when all hell is let loose around her, but Gail finds that chaos strengthens her resolve to remain calm in the eye of the storm. Her sternest test came when realizing it was solely her error that all fifteen intended jumping entries for a bank holiday had missed the deadline. To face me with the dreadful news, knowing how carefully I had planned the entries, took every scrap of her courage and prompted the second of her resignations.

Gail still shudders at the agonizing minutes spent making up her mind to deliver that news. 'All of the horses possessed live chances and had been trained to the minute which set the scene for a bonanza. I really thought he would blow his top and having seen others on the end of a roasting, did not relish the prospect. Mr Pipe [she refuses to call him Martin except when socializing, and then never in the company of owners], a man of constantly changing moods and full of surprises, took the blow with no more reaction than if I'd just given him a bar of chocolate. He actually felt sorry for the agony I'd put myself through and said, 'Oh well, we'll have to content ourselves with the couple of Flat race entries you did manage to make.'

Gail knows her boss's idiosyncrasies, can judge his temperament and instinctively reacts appropriately according to the situation. 'I admire him tremendously. He possesses incredible depths of determination and drive. Few people running multinational conglomerates would have to face such regular, intense pressure. When he is tense I keep a low profile, other times I have to harass him for decisions. Either way I do enjoy the constant action and am always able to cope, safe in the knowledge he will back me up.'

Of her eight years at the helm, Gail cites the *Cook Report* attack and the 1986 and 1992 Cheltenham Festivals as the lowest points in the extraordinary Pipe saga. 'The Cheltenham incidents drained Mr Pipe in totally contrasting ways. Corporal Clinger fell at the fifth hurdle in the 1986 Champion Hurdle, injuring himself and the jockey. Paul Leach's broken wrist meant finding replacements for the stable's remaining runners, but that problem paled into insignificance beside our concern for the horse. Going down under the field's hooves while the bulk of the twenty-three runners were still grouped meant Corporal Clinger was kicked and trampled by several horses going at racing pace. When the helpless, haemorrhaging horse gained then lost ground in his fight for life, Mr Pipe became oblivious to everything else. He had to go home not knowing whether his gallant little hurdler would survive the night at Bristol University veterinary hospital, where he underwent major surgery to stop him bleeding to death.

'The second day of the Festival saw him supervise his unplaced runners almost by automatic pilot. He took little or no notice of Strands Of Gold's promising second in the Sun Alliance Chase or Omerta's easy success in the four-mile amateur riders' Challenge Cup. Both horses were destined to join him in the future, adding a Hennessy Cognac Gold Cup, a Jameson's Irish National and a Kim Muir Chase at the 1991 Festival to Mr Pipe's clutch of big-race victories. But then he was too distraught to pay them any attention.

'Gold Cup day dawned with news of Corporal Clinger's life being out of immediate danger, though it was doubtful whether he would ever race again. Lifted by the news he perked up a bit and thoughts of Roark taking a second Triumph Hurdle saw a rejuvenated trainer bouncing back. A classy, handsome acquisition from Dick Hern's Flat stable, Roark had bolted in on his only start over hurdles at Wolverhampton by an impressive ten lengths under Paul Leach. With Jonothan Lower booked for the stable's less fancied Ninattash, Phil Tuck came in for the job of steering the heavily backed favourite. After avoiding the usual scrimmaging caused by the inevitable big field, the chestnut looked poised to join the leaders at the top of the hill when those watching closely witnessed the first tell-tale signs of trouble. Roark's white face was bobbing up and down in time with his desperately shortening strides as his main flexor tendons tore apart. Momentum, racing instinct and body-weight forced the lame Roark to gallop downhill, fighting his desperate rider and undoubtedly compounding the injuries before Tuck was able to pull the gelding up approaching the second-last hurdle. The tendons had ruptured so badly it looked odds-on he would never see a racecourse again nor even be of use as a riding horse. Two such blows in forty-eight hours weighed appallingly heavy on Mr Pipe's head. As it turned out, both horses survived to race and win again. But at the time there was no thought of that, and the hurt he felt for them shook his belief in racing.'

Gail feels it is this type of private grief, Martin's reaction to it and his deep care for his horses, not just the statistics, that the press and the wider public will never see. Weather Permitting died in July 1992, aged twenty-three, having enjoyed a happy retirement along with several other old equine friends on the Alfords' farm. Examples of Pipe's compassion and humanity would certainly have been a big vote-winner when his methods were so arbitrarily challenged by the *Cook Report*, but the naïvety of the Somerset trainer prevented him producing such evidence.

None of us knows what the future holds, but Gail Harrison is adamant she intends to be associated with Martin Charles Pipe in some shape or form whatever her future holds.

Chapter 7

Why Us?

Each year since 1989, as January has come around Martin Pipe has found comfort in his position at the head of the trainers' table with the buffer of fully 100 winners already in the bag. His facilities are geared to allow the horses' daily exercise to continue whatever the winter has to throw at him and he is excited at the thought of the major races to come at the Cheltenham Festival and the Aintree Grand National meeting. January 1991 looked no different – until what started as a few spasmodic inquiries to several of his patrons regarding dissension, injury and even death multiplied to epidemic proportions. Reports filtering back to the trainer indicated he was under investigation – but by whom?

Pipe
The odd whisper from loyal owners and friends who had been approached by an unnamed journalist quickly swelled to a flood. To start with I reacted casually, then annoyance turned to anger and finally to panic when I realized the furtive investigator must have substantial backing. Not knowing why or by whom I was being scrutinized was bad enough, but thoughts of where it might all lead were deeply unnerving. One thing was for sure, I would not just sit around wondering if and when a direct approach would be made. I decided to talk personally to everyone who had been questioned and as a result we formed an Identikit picture of the dirt-digger. At least we had unmasked the stranger and

would know if any of the staff were quizzed in the pub or at the races.

Once his anonymity was destroyed it only took us ten days to put a name to the face and establish he was freelancing for the *Cook Report*. At the time that meant nothing to any of us. How that changed. When we found out the programme specialized in exposing crooks and frauds we were all shattered. Why us? we kept asking.

Attack being the best defence, I informed the Jockey Club, hired lawyers and set about forming a dossier on every horse that had been mentioned by name at the interviews. Ever since I started training in 1974 I've kept meticulous records of every horse and every employee who comes under my care. At times my insistence on maintaining details has raised a few eyebrows, but now their worth quickly became evident. If we were going to be tried publicly on television we would need facts to defend ourselves, although at that stage no one knew what the charge against us was. It has always been my policy to keep photographic evidence of a horse's condition when it joins the stable. We take shots of it from every angle, including individual limbs, with the date verified by the inclusion of that day's *Sporting Life*. Another safeguard I insist on is a detailed inspection completed by three staff who each fill in and sign a comprehensive form.

By now Cheltenham was getting ever closer and we could have done without the extra pressure of a war being waged against us. Horses I knew; television tactics I did not, so after making discreet inquiries I decided to hire the expertise of John Stoneborough, who had worked with Cook and knew his methods and weaknesses. I hoped he also knew how to combat them.

John advised me to use the press to take the sting out of the programme by informing them of developments as they materialized. I had been through an anti-press period and this tactic did seem rather two-faced; but why pay for advice then ignore it? As John pointed out, we had nothing to hide. He strongly advised me to appear on the programme if given the chance, but at that time I was a million to one against going on. All the racing media men I spoke to advised me of the dangers of what can happen to recorded interviews. Clever cutting can change the impression radically. But if I did appear, I wanted to be ready. I took expert advice, turning this time to Fran Morrison, the former television reporter and newsreader. To simulate the grilling I would get from Cook, she fixed up a mock *Cook Report* here, complete with lights and cameras, to produce the proper effect. Rather like taking a driving test, it would seem much easier the second time.

Fran warned me that she would be nasty, tricky and goad me into losing my temper. She was true to her word. Halfway through I remember thinking she was a bitch. Nothing was further from the truth; but she acted well. It was a nerve-racking session but as I could answer everything she threw at me, my confidence was boosted. Fran admitted she thought Cook would not be as hard on me as she had been, went through the questions again and pronounced me ready for trial by television. Yet despite her assurance, I was still a non-starter in my own mind.

The team tried to enlist Carol's help to persuade me to go on to defend myself. But she said no, it was a personal decision and if I appeared against my will and it went wrong, I'd be hell to live with. It was only on the day before the programme that I decided that if they were going to hang me out to dry, I'd have my say first. Our team consisted of myself, Carol, Peter Scudamore, Barry Simpson, who runs the racing club, Lindsay Moffat, our solicitor, and Bruce Borthwick, one of our vets. We purposely left out Fran and John Stoneborough as their presence would have been a red rag to a bull. If Cook had seen them he'd know we'd been well primed – which, of course, we were. We'd gone to war. We'd been attacked, and we had protected ourselves. Dad was absent as well, for two reasons. Our advisers, who had encountered him already, thought he'd get too heated; and they decided it would only cloud the issue to bring in the father/son, bookmaker/trainer relationship.

The interview was done here in our sitting room and to say the atmosphere was tense is something of an understatement. Funnily enough, the one person I did not fall out with was Cook himself. His team were still researching names, dates and facts in our kitchen before filming started, confirming what we'd been told, that Cook would not be armed with in-depth research. That gave me a lift; but I was acutely aware that he had the advantage of surprise with the actual questions.

Peter Scudamore's additional television exposure during a

ten-week absence from race-riding while injured also helped us. He knew the techniques of television and overrode me when I agreed to what are called 'two shots' and 'noddys'. Peter knew that the seemingly harmless nods and shakes of the head could be attributed to any question the producer wished in the edited version. We also decided to sit Barry Simpson behind Cook, within my sightline to enable him to give me hand signals indicating how the interview was progressing from a viewer's standpoint. A single thumbs up half way through the twenty-minute session boosted my spirits and kept me going.

The only occasion on which I could not answer a question was when Cook asked me how many horses I still trained that were with me in 1986, five years earlier. I could not answer that one accurately without recourse to the records, but as this was a one-take job I said I did not know. Had I guessed at ten, he might have had facts to contradict me, which would in turn have weakened the validity of my other replies. If I'd refused to reply, that would also have damaged me. So I told the truth, which was I did not know.

We had done our best; then we had to sit and wait until the following night to see what they had come up with. Remember, we had no idea what else they had to throw at us and were aware our contribution could well have been lying on the cutting-room floor. It was 6 May 1991, a day that will remain engraved on my mind long after I've forgotten my last winner. We asked lots of friends to share in our misfortune and there was plenty of champagne to ease the tension. The greatest anxiety that remained concerned their assertion that they had a leading jockey to spill the beans. None of the genuine riders could testify against us as we had nothing to hide, but the threat was real enough that a sacked employee, loosely labelled 'a jockey', might have been tempted to make a name for himself.

There was no jockey, real or otherwise, but we still felt sick watching it. It was dreadful. When the music at the end of the programme died down we were drained. Then, within seconds, all the phones in the house started ringing, with everybody saying the whole thing was empty if you knew anything about racing. The messages were comforting, even though we realized the majority were from friends. It is at times like that that you get to know who they really are. We also received tremendous support from other trainers – and I thought, goodness me, I can't claim a horse from any of them from now on! To some of the wider public, though, I must seem a dubious character. Still, if they stop to consider that only hostile witnesses were given air time, they might realize how slanted the whole programme is. I firmly believe the whole concept of the *Cook Report* is devalued by that approach.

Cook tried to establish stories of blood doping and an excessive mortality rate among our horses. He posed the question, 'Did I get results by asking too high a price from the horses themselves?' The blood-doping theory developed because we built our own laboratory within the main stable yard, complete with a qualified technician to provide instant results to avoid the normal delay via the post. Strange, though, when you consider the noted Flat trainer Guy Harwood never once attracted similar accusations when he set up his own lab years earlier. Perhaps they thought Guy had too much money and power for them to mount such an attack.

We are able to laugh about the idea now when asked innocent blood-related questions at racing forums. We explain how difficult it is to make sure the same amount of blood is transfused into each leg, or admit to a secret extra lab under the stable yard, and this breaks the ice. Blood doping has been successfully used on human athletes before being outlawed but a half-ton horse is a very different proposition from a twelve-stone man. A horse requires eighty pints of blood; how would you store the amount of red cells needed to boost performance? It would be difficult enough to service a single horse in this way, let alone attend to our 166 inmates. And then there's the human element: in such a large gathering of mostly single young staff, there will often be disenchanted workers who would spill the beans if there were any to spill.

The programme used images cleverly, too, without backing them up with reasoned argument. Cook's use of the slamming stable doors to illustrate that seven out of ten horses trained here fail to return the next year was calculated to leave a powerful impression, bolstering an otherwise unconvincing case.

To give the programme weight, Jenny Pitman and Ginger McCain were brought on to evaluate my method. Neither added much substance. Mrs Pitman merely pointed out that she trained a very different type of horse from me; hers, being young, raw stock, needed time and education over a period of several seasons to get them into a condition to run regularly. Mine are mainly already hardened from Flat racing and after winning several races in their first year for me are too highly handicapped to merit retaining. Mrs Pitman did phone prior to the show, half-heartedly apologizing, but she has long played television outlets to her own ends and certainly knew the wide audience that would be watching.

As for Ginger, he loves to pontificate; and he expressed surprise that Cook had chosen the selective clips he eventually used from the extensive interview he gave them. Having been involved with television people so much during his days of prominence with Red Rum, surely Ginger should have worked them out by now?

I was far more hurt by the vitriolic attack from trainer Alan Dunn, whose public-school confidence carried conviction when relating how one of my horses ran three weeks after finishing lame. Racegoers, though, know that the vets and stewards inspect runners in the parade ring and on the way to the start and would have stopped a lame horse from running. Another small-time trainer trying to make a name for himself made out that two horses that came to him from me were in a terrible condition. What he fails to understand is that neither a horse nor a man needs to be fat to be healthy. Our horses carry no extra flesh as a result of regular exercise and a controlled diet, but I defy anyone to prove they are in a bad condition. They are fit, and true fitness requires good health.

As for the man who bought one of ours in the mandatory auction after it had won a selling hurdle, only to find the poor thing had broken down in the race, simply made a fool of himself in public. In a situation like that the trainer has no power to prevent the sale going ahead, but if a horse is so obviously lame after a race no one bids for it and it is retained.

The programme, born of bar-room gossip and sour grapes, should never have seen daylight. It cost our family over £30,000 to defend ourselves to a television presenter of whom the best that can be said is that he may have believed his own crusade. Imagine the outcome if someone unable to find the resources to fight was opened up in public in this way: the damage would be unthinkable. In the long run I do believe that, unsavoury as the trial was, it has not done us lasting harm, although a section of the non-racing public will probably always consider me an unscrupulous man.

Every trainer has casualties; the larger the string, the more horses drop out. There cannot be a person training who would welcome a similar public examination. Pipe's horses receive the best of attention; he cares for them and is never blasé about even the smallest winner. That his success should have engendered such suspicion hurt this quiet, private man and although he has bounced back he will feel the effects for a long time yet.

Chapter 8

'Martin will never train a winner!'

Pipe

When Len Lungo, the leading jockey on the West Country circuit,
met me at Taunton races in 1975 the introduction had been
specifically engineered by Ray Alford. Realizing that once
something had interested me, I wanted to excel at it, Ray rightly
thought a few words of advice from a respected source would not
go unheeded. He probably considered he was too close to me to be
taken seriously and, of course, Len had a track record that would
impress me. I soon saw that I could glean sound advice from Len,
whose successes for local trainers Les Kennard and Gerald
Cottrell gave him an insight into the diverse methods they used to
produce horses to win. A well-spoken, smartly dressed Scot, Len
had ridden twenty-three winners the previous season which to
me, without a solitary victory to my name from almost three
seasons with a permit, meant the big time. Len accepted the
invitation to appraise our string of three. Marine Parade, Hit
Parade, and Weather Permitting were the only heads over stable
doors and, to the jockey's practised eye, the heads were by far
their best attributes. Choosing his words carefully, Len suggested
where improvements could be made.

Len Lungo clearly remembers that day, seventeen years ago. 'I did
not want to offend Martin, but neither did I intend to butter him up
as that would have been a thorough waste of time. All three horses
were far too fat, their mangers had food in them long after feed

73

time and their legs showed distinct signs of wear and tear.'

Pipe
Len's first piece of advice concerned feeding. He explained that once horses have more food than they need, they start to leave oddments in the manger, eventually leading to lethargic eating habits. They know there is always food in the pot so they see no need to clear up each meal.

To encourage them back to efficient feeding he suggested I simply threw the *Daily Express* into their mangers for two days and let them do no more than read about food. I didn't take him literally; but the practice of leaving horses hungry for a while, then feeding slightly less than the norm never fails to sharpen up the appetite. Once the horses are shouting for their feed whenever they hear the buckets rattling, you're back on the right track.

With only a month of the season to run it looked obvious that Weather Permitting would not get the soft ground he needed with his action, so a holiday at grass looked best for him. Marine Parade's legs would not have stood another race on the prevailing ground, so that left only Hit Parade to knock into shape in an effort to net that elusive first winner.

Len had actually ridden Hit Parade to finish third at Wincanton several months before, but that had been a one-off engagement with no more contact between us than the briefest of chats in the parade ring and unsaddling enclosure. This time the liaison looked as if it could lead to something more substantial.

To back up his advice, Len invited me along to Gerald Cottrell's stables to see for myself the vastly different appearance of horses which were winning races. You should generally be able to see the last two ribs showing when they are ready to do the business. I watched Gerald's horses work and was only too aware that mine were getting neither enough nor the right sort of exercise.

With little time for me to play at trainers, a crash course in dieting and sweating was prescribed for Hit Parade, whom Len exercised for me in the late mornings when he had finished at Gerald's. Two wool rugs under the saddle and endless cantering saw the weight dropping off the tubby gelding and within a fortnight he faced the acid test. The last chance selling hurdle at Taunton that season presented us with the ideal race to get me a winner, although the hard underfoot conditions that prevailed in May that year made the task more difficult.

When the ground is baked, the hurdles do not give when horses hit them. Len, besides riding him in one race, had also watched Hit Parade attempt to demolish the obstacles on several other occasions. Altering things in his favour seemed prudent to the little Scot. 'Having walked the course well before racing started it was obvious the hurdles would come off best if it came to an argument, so I simply loosened the second section from the rails in each of the eight flights we would be jumping. This only works if your race is the first over the course that afternoon and if you intend to make the running. If your race isn't the opener, the ground staff will have driven the hurdles back into the earth before you start, and if you're not making the running you're liable to be met by the loosened hurdle swinging back towards you after the preceding horse has clouted it, which is even worse than the original problem.

'The selected race offered an ideal opening, provided the changed eating habits, weight loss and extra work had improved Hit Parade. I thought they had and put my neck on the line by telling Martin and his father they would have their elusive winner that day. Martin accepted my assurance but Dave, still smarting from almost two winnerless seasons, thought for a moment or two, then said, 'I intend to lay the horse to any punters who want to back it with me. Mark my words, Martin will never train a winner!'

Backed down from 2–1 to 13–8 favourite, Hit Parade made all the running and won easily by seven lengths under a confident ride from Len Lungo, snug in his secret knowledge that the second hurdle from the inside rail would bow to his wishes. Martin recognized the part his jockey played in achieving his first winner by giving him the entire first prize of £272 instead of the statutory 10 per cent. The jubilant winning trainer passed his father driving off to bet at the evening greyhound meeting. Financially, neither was any better off as a result of the victory, yet the flashing headlights and frenzied cheering said it all. Martin Pipe was on his way and, as luck would have it, the timing was perfect. Up to that point Dave Pipe had had serious doubts as to the future of Pond House as a training establishment.

Pipe
The 1975–6 season saw the inmates double to six, including the home-bred Carrie Ann, who four and a half years later landed a

monster betting coup at Haydock Park. Len Lungo's advice was held in high esteem with us, although it took many long hours of reasoning and persuasion to get me to accept his suggestion that I paid over the going rate to attract Dennis Dummett into the fold as head man. Having listened to Len's well argued advice I wanted to dissect the reasons and explore other avenues, query the worth of established ideas and pose hypothetical situations. On this point, as on any other, I'd never let go until I'd exhausted every angle, even on seemingly unimportant issues. Of course, I saw the wisdom of employing a man of Dennis's knowledge but such a small operation hardly merited a head man and paying him enough to secure his experience seemed an unnecessary expense. Dennis had been looking to move from Gerald Cottrell's stable in order to better his income, either within racing or in some other job. Once he'd agreed to come here it became obvious he was exactly what we lacked, a top stockman.

With Len and Dennis on call we naturally talked a lot before, during and after work about my ambition to become a proper trainer and if it was wise of me to try to establish myself in the West Country. We could see that the emerging motorway system would let us out to raid distant racecourses but at the same time would encourage many more established trainers to compete on our home patch. I learned fast from Dennis, watching, copying and cross-examining everything the new font of information divulged.

The same fanatical urge to squeeze out every last scrap of worth from the horse husbandry side also applied to race-riding. I'd go over and over every race Len rode in, or for that matter any others we watched, seeking the reasons behind jockeys' tactics.

Living with us as he did at this time, Len was a captive audience, but our sheer enthusiasm kept him on a high rather than boring him. Having listened to the reasons for different happenings, I quite often came up with strong counter-arguments without entirely grasping the merit of attaching them to the right horse. Eventually I could see that horses' temperaments played as big a part in their performance as their physical fitness and that I should leave tactics to the jockey, despite having to fight the instinct not to do so. Hit Parade's win had given me the push I needed to start plotting and planning with the half dozen horses we'd got to play with. Seeking out suitable races months ahead gave me as big a shot in the arm as anything else. I thoroughly enjoyed the scheming.

With Dennis and Len both on the payroll we were overstaffed when I insisted on doing everything with them, but the only way to know how theory works is to watch it put into practice. The pair of them thought I was a complete joke; the galling thing is, they were probably right.

My inbuilt urge to turn every situation into a betting opportunity backfired on me when sorting out fifty sheep for market from the 200-strong flock. Herbie the farm hand selected the gradable ewes and passed them to me to wrestle them towards Len to isolate in a second enclosure. At a moment when my attention was all concentrated on Herbie, Len playfully slipped one ewe back into the main flock, enabling him to query the final number with some degree of confidence. Counting sheep is an art; they constantly move around and look so alike. It came as no surprise to either of them when I confidently backed Herbie's judgement against Len's to the tune of a fiver. Being a bad loser I insisted on fully ten recounts before parting with the cash, and berated the hapless Herbie for days.

That initial winner in the dying days of the 1974–5 season leapt to five in 1975–6, with Hit Parade contributing three of them. Taunton again provided the first opening; no one bothered to bid for the horse in the subsequent auction. That was not the case next time out, when we ventured further afield, to Towcester. After that race I went to 800 guineas to retain the horse in the mandatory auction.

It was a clever move that got us to Towcester that day. Dennis, Len and myself had initially set off to race at Folkestone the day before, only to realize soon after sun-up that the meeting would be cancelled because of frost. Our three-man team could hardly believe the bad luck: Folkestone's turf lay under a glittering blanket of impenetrable frost while the rest of the country wallowed in weather unseasonably warm for December.

Ten minutes spent with my nose in the form book convinced me our modest selling hurdler could win the opener at Towcester the next day. The gelding was declared by telephone and the Range Rover, trailer, horse and men trekked off from Folkestone through London to Northamptonshire. Being away so long and spending most of that time in the trailer, Hit Parade needed to have some work to stretch his legs and clear his windpipes. In those days there was no provision for overnight lodgers to gallop, so we got up just before dawn to pinch a sprint in a field adjacent to the racecourse stables. The hoofprints left in the dewy grass were incriminating enough, but before we could get off the land the farmer turned up. He didn't mind too much as it turned out, and in fact looked pleased when I told him to back the horse that afternoon. He won well.

By the time our tired little gang drove back into Pond House we had been away three days, covered the best part of 500 miles to win £300 and been forced to spend £800 to retain the horse. On the face of it the venture had been a costly affair; yet to me it was another winner on the books. Then, as today, I realized that every point counts in a game where statistics are logged, dissected and used daily by the national and racing press.

If that venture had been little more than a public relations exercise, Leopardus's victory at Taunton in April showed a profit. The seven-year-old, who had done many good turns for Gerald Cottrell's stable either side of serious leg problems, was exactly the sort I loved to get hold of.

Leopardus had enough winning form for me to gauge his true mark and was cheap to buy due to a well known history of tendon strains. This was the type I cut my teeth on and have never been able to resist to this day.

His first three outings of the new term, twice under Neil Kernick and once under John Jenkins, saw the hard-pulling staying hurdler make much of the running only to fade when it mattered. It was obvious he needed settling, so Len and I decided to alter that by initially switching the gelding off at home then continuing the lesson twice on the racecourse. By mid-April, with the gnarled old legs showing only spasmodic signs of heat, the right race materialized for Leopardus to earn his corn. There was only one horse who posed a danger: the former point-to-pointer, Dance Again. Having gone through the form book for us, Roy Hawkins, our form expert, decided he had the beating of us – and so, apparently, did his connections, who backed him down from sixes to 7–2 second favourite. Len was the only one who remained adamant we would come out best; he was convinced Dance Again would pack it in the moment he got a bump or made a mistake at a hurdle. He'd done it before, and he'd do it again.

In the final analysis Dad and I sided with Roy, who thought we'd need luck to win, and halved our intended bet. Len still insisted we would win because if the general unfolding of events failed to destroy Dance Again's enthusiasm he could give the old horse the bump it required himself. We were quite shocked to learn such gamesmanship went on in races and were not entirely convinced it was proper. It was agreed Len should keep hold of Leopardus's head on the firm ground to nurse his battle-scarred legs, win if he could but not knock him about if patently beaten.

In three-mile-one-furlong contests at Taunton the field passes the grandstand three times. On the first occasion, due to the insanely fast pace, we were trailing Dance Again by fully forty lengths. At the same place a circuit later nothing had dramatically changed and I could sense Father's eyes boring into my skull wondering if Len had gone crooked on us. But watching from the grandstand is worlds apart from the feel of things on a horse's back. The breakneck early pace could not be sustained to the finish and, provided Len could creep near enough without working too hard, those vying for the lead were sure to collapse in a heap and give Leopardus his chance.

When a rider is going through a good patch plans unfold to order, confidence is transmitted between him and the horse and everything drops into place effortlessly. This was one of those days. We won by three lengths, without Len having to give Dance Again the threatened nudge as he pulled out to challenge.

Funny thing though: Dad, having thought Len was pulling the horse for himself during the race, then became suspicious he had put all his friends on Leopardus because he'd been so bullish about his chances before the race. It was a touchy fortnight until Dad accepted he was straight.

Len only stayed two seasons with us, before the lure of making a home with his Exeter-born fiancée drew him back to Scotland. It had been a good partnership for both of us; we understood each other. We have remained firm friends ever since. The only time we came near to blows was when I insisted on ruffling Len's well groomed hair before a date. Len was always immaculate: clean shoes, sharply pressed suit, crisp shirt and never a hair out of place. After I'd ruffled his hair half a dozen times he grabbed the bait, turned on me and for a moment looked likely to put me down. Len admits he had risen to the goading but only needed to put 'the cold eye' on me to stop the nonsense. The same treatment on young jockeys works wonders, too.

Fortunately, Len had not left for Scotland when I rode my solitary winner on Weather Permitting.

Of that memorable victory Lungo reflects: 'By his own admission Martin was moderate. He simply did not have much experience; but having said that, he definitely had his head screwed on. He stuck rigidly to the plan and although in a position to go on from over a mile out he stayed cool, timing his winning burst of speed to hit the front halfway up the run-in. There is no doubt Martin was not even a distant relative to a pro, but he certainly thought like one. Had it not been for his injuries, I'm sure that dogged willpower he's shown since would have made him half useful in the saddle too.'

Pipe

Len came to me ten years too soon. In 1976 he was ready and good enough to take a top job. Sadly, there were none free and our little set-up still needed miles on the clock before expansion. Len and I had agreed the facilities needed completely updating to attract more owners but I knew the results would have to be more reliable before Dad would commit the kind of money it would take to do the job properly.

Perhaps it all fitted into Fate's grand plan. After a year riding in Scotland, Len took the plunge in no half measure. He married Barbara and bought The Stag in Dumfries. After five years' graft the pair bought a second property, turning it into a disco bar and in 1984, just as we laid our all-weather gallop, the Lungos added a snooker hall and an imposing businessman's residence to their string.

Well entrenched in the local community, Len now has a 320 acre farm where he is in his third season as a trainer, handling sixteen horses for people who can – and, far more importantly, want to – pay their training bills. Financially secure and independent of racing, Len Lungo has the best of all worlds. Who is to say that would have been the case had he lingered longer driving an old Triumph Spitfire around the racetracks of south-west England?

Chapter 9

Dependable Dennis

After a week observing the most expensive of his employees, Martin Pipe realized Dennis Dummett would prove to be by far the best value. He could do what was necessary to achieve the results which up to that time had been conspicuous by their absence. A jack of all trades and master of most of them, Dennis represented everything Martin was not, especially in the arts of feeding and recognizing signs of leg trouble.

Like any head man worth his salt, Dennis is married to the job, which has proved too heavy a load for both his wives. On leaving school forty years ago, the youngster found employment helping Cullompton farmer Gerald Cottrell on his 500 acre holding, a two-year absence doing his National Service proving no more than a temporary nuisance. On returning to the farm after his military service, Dennis answered negatively to Cottrell's enquiry regarding riding experience. The fact that he'd never sat on a horse made precious little difference; the first day back at work Dennis was put up on the family's good point-to-pointer Royal Sun and told to walk him around for an hour or so. He grins at the memory. 'It was as simple as that; one day farm hand, the next exercise rider. Gerald had another top horse called Judy Jones and it wasn't long before he had me riding one and leading the other around the Devon roads. There wasn't a bad thought in either horse's head. In fact, I'm convinced they took me around the routes they were used to rather than me guiding them. After I'd proved I could stay on top, Gerald quickly elevated me to the cantering stage by putting me in a field and shutting the gate. Sometimes he'd forget I was there for hours on end.'

Of his many attributes Dennis is most valued for the ability to make horses eat, something the layman would take for granted. Dennis picked up the art through nothing more than observation, watching intently every time Cottrell fed his racehorses. 'He'd always weigh the various feedstuffs for each horse and then weigh any leftovers in the manger. He was meticulous. In those days it was much more of an art, with individual feeds made up from oats, bran, beans, barley, maize, chaff, linseed mashes, oils and vitamins. These days the feed firms have got it down to such a fine art that if you can read, you can feed. Horse nuts contain everything an animal requires to keep it right and on the back of each bag they display the ideal amounts to be given according to an animal's size. The one thing you can't get off a bag, though, is probably the most important: the feel a good feeder develops for each of his charges. That only comes with time, and sometimes not even then. Horses are like kids, they're all different, and to get the best out of them you must know them inside out.'

The farm work decreased for Dennis as he became more useful to Cottrell on the training side of his business, with a leaning towards their care rather than riding. Although pleased to have survived the do-or-die method when learning to sit on the racehorses, Dennis became utterly convinced it was not his forte when asked to gallop two and a half miles around the Devon and Exeter course in a four-horse full-scale trial. Fit and hard as oak from years of physical work, Dennis experienced the helpless feeling as the legs turn to jelly and exhaustion creeps up through the body when those muscles, awoken only under stress in extended gallops, go into spasm. He decided there and then to concentrate on horses' welfare rather than a life in the saddle.

After fifteen years with Cottrell it was nothing more than money that lured Dennis away. 'It's a job to live and I could see the potential at the Pipes'. A bigger wage attracted me, but I was sorry to leave Gerald.'

Pipe

Dennis started at Pond House on 21 July 1975, two months after Hit Parade provided me with my first winner under Rules. The stable diary states that as my new head man settled in on Sunday morning, I rode Weather Permitting out for thirty minutes. There were just seven horses in training which from the next day could be exercised in two lots by Dennis, Ron Treloggen and myself, with

Lorac led out on his own for a pick of grass. I well remember telling Dennis to watch what went on for a fortnight then take over. After just two days Dennis couldn't stand it any longer, elbowed me out of the way and assumed command of the feeding and general care of our motley string.

You must realize that then the horses were only pleasure for me and Dad; the betting office was our living and as soon as we'd ridden out and tidied up, I was off to Taunton. Things carried on that way for some years. The diary states that in December 1979, four years after Dennis joined us, the string had only increased to nine horses; but we'd had some fun from the twenty-odd winners that we'd produced. Thinking back, Vengo provided us with one of our most satisfying training feats, several months after Dennis joined the firm.

'Every dog has its day' was the *Chaseform* comment after Vengo won at Devon and Exeter on 11 October 1975; they were right without knowing the half of it. I bought him for a couple of thousand pounds, which in 1975 represented a fair amount. By the Derby winner Crepello, this one was intended to put me on the map. Instead, he put me on the floor.

Stupidly, I could not wait to jump on him to get a feel, a bit like a kid with a new toy I suppose. As soon as we got home from the sales I led him out into the middle of an open field where Dennis threw me on board. I simply did not know any better in those days. Vengo weighed me up in two seconds, took off flat out across the field, dumping me within a few strides, and charged riderless straight for my Granny Whitmarsh, who had been dragged out there against her better judgement to see the wonder horse. See it? The thing galloped right at her. Nearly frightened her to death.

Vengo was a really exasperating horse, the type to try the most patient of men. He would stand for an hour refusing to go up the gallops or, if in a really foul mood, to go back home either. Dennis found the answer: I rode the horse with him chasing us in the Range Rover, honking the horn and cracking a Long Tom whip out of the window. We tried it with Dennis on top and me in the vehicle, but I'm so utterly useless at practical things I couldn't drive, honk and crack the whip at the same time.

We ran the uncooperative Vengo on the second day of the 1975–6 season, trying to nick a race before the more competitive horses came out. He refused to exert himself, eventually finishing out with the washing. Five subsequent outings showed no hint of improvement; on two of them he was even pulled up. He would no more gallop on the racecourse than he would at home. He really was a useless article, and embarrassing, to say the least. We eventually found the world's worst race at Taunton – but again he proved too clever for us, casually pulling himself up when they raced past the stables on the second circuit.

Dennis suggested a change of rider at home, as much to give us a rest as anything else. The short straw fell to a lad called Michael, who rode more like a cowboy than a jockey. Strangely enough, Vengo reacted to the different feel of the rider by condescending to go straight on to the gallops, working right up to the top with Michael flapping about. There was no sign of the nonsense he got up to under the rest of us. I then got him to jump our makeshift hurdles from the landing side to make him think about the job; anything different to change his mind.

We decided to give the unwilling creature one last chance in October at Devon and Exeter, where he had bottom weight in a bad selling hurdle under Ron Atkins, who was having his first ride for us. To make full use of what looked like being a wasted day, we decided to give Carrie Ann, who hated travelling, some education by taking her to the races for the ride. Things started badly when the mare refused to follow Vengo into the trailer and quickly got worse when she even turned her nose up at the pony Boris.

After an hour Dennis lost his rag and started to bellow at Carrie Ann, and I can tell you, he could start an avalanche when he lets rip. Poor old Vengo, who'd been patiently standing in the trailer all the time, started to climb the walls when Dennis hollered. It was the most reaction we'd ever got out of him. Anyway, by the time we got the mare loaded we were very late for the races and only arrived in time to drop the ramp and go straight into the parade ring. Vengo's eyes were still out on stalks, his nostrils were flared and he was in a muck sweat. He must have thought war had broken out.

It further embarrassed me when some people standing in front of us in the grandstand said 'What's Pipe running that screw for? He pulled up last time out in just as bad a race. He must be an idiot.' They were right, of course, and naturally we did not back Vengo. He started slowly and sulked around behind the other thirteen runners until at the second-last hurdle Ron got fed up with the lack of cooperation and decided the horse needed galvanizing. Running towards the stables with Ron riding at his strongest, Vengo flew for the first time in his life and got up in the last strides to win by a short head at 33–1. The chap in the stands was right; we were all idiots, except for Michael the cowboy who had put his last £6 on Vengo. He took home £200, which was probably as much as the horse was worth.

Basically, we had upset Vengo's comfortable routine with all the noise while trying to load Carrie Ann, then when Ron decided the gelding was pulling his leg, the world changed for old Vengo. No one wanted him in the auction afterwards so we sent him back to the Ascot sales. We were pleased to see him go. But they were right in the form book; every dog has its day.

A glance at that day's diary shows me experimenting with extra wide racing plates on the runners with a view to spreading the load. Even in those days I was trying to look beyond the obvious, to find the advantage.

The next week when Hit Parade ran at Folkestone everything else ground to a halt. The diary states: 'Left home 9 a.m. Monday, horse finished third on Tuesday, arrived back home on Wednesday after 500 mile round trip leaving Herbie the odd job man to look after the horses at home. Nothing done for three days, horses mad fresh!'

We got up at 5.30 a.m. in those days in order to finish in time for me to get to the betting office before racing started. Nowadays the early stint is Dennis's domain and is without doubt the most important period of the day. He feeds the hundred horses in the main yard in little over forty-five minutes with two helpers to open and shut stable doors before and after him. In the thirty seconds Dennis spends in each stable he evaluates the horse's well-being by observing the way it moves to the manger, takes note of any feed left from the previous night's meal, then runs a hand down its front legs for tell-tale signs of heat or swelling. He is then in a position to report to me anything that needs a second glance before we decide whether to work them or not.

Dennis scurries around on the dawn shift tuned into any signs of change, reasoning: 'Horses are creatures of habit. From the moment I open the feed house door they react vocally. As I come out with the first horse's breakfast they start up the equivalent of the dawn chorus. One starts to whinny with anticipation and it immediately sweeps through the barns. I say to them, "Speak to me my beauties" and they do. The day they are only half-hearted, I know there is trouble afoot. Funny, for the first month of the 1991–2 season the horses were slightly muted in the mornings but by September they were greeting me with loud excited roars. I was happier then.'

Of the valuable instant messages to the brain via his fingertips, Dennis says: 'The first reaction is always the best. If you need a second feel, you're definitely in trouble. It means there is something to consider, perhaps to rectify. During evening stables I have another leg inspection which signals what, if anything, to anticipate overnight.'

As for the facilities, Dennis was appalled on arrival. 'I only went up to gallop on Culmstock Beacon once before disapproving totally. It may have looked the part in photos and to the Jockey Club inspector, but the amount of stones in the grass was sure to cause problems, outweighing any good the exercise would produce.'

Pipe
I had a few small levellish fields to canter around up the top of the farm where the existing all-weather gallop now ends. They were by the bungalow where Mum and Dad now live and although a far cry from what Dennis had been used to at Cottrell's, they got half approval from him. At least we then had sound horses to work with.

When I mentioned to Dad we needed more room, hedges were taken out before the week was over. It's been the same ever since. Dad is the mover and shaker; I never know things are being built until the bulldozers move in and the foundations are laid. When things happen here, they grow overnight like mushrooms.

Dennis is the dependable rock in a movable operation, he relentlessly pursues his duties and apart from one period when he left for fifteen months, has run the yard for seventeen years. Things grew here to the extent he seemed to be working all day every day. I assumed he was content without actually asking him. For me the increased workload represented my future, but it's not quite the same when you are breaking your back for someone else, is it? We never really talked about Dennis's situation. I took him for granted, so he left to go back on the farm and then back to Gerald Cottrell's. There were no hard feelings between us and in fact I was forever phoning Dennis to come over to blister legs or clip a troublesome horse, which he was happy enough to do.

In those days I still did a lot of the manual work myself; it was only six years ago that things started to go through the roof. Nowadays neither of us has time to do other than our specific duties. It's probably because we've both done everything ourselves in the past, though, that the current procedures have been able to evolve. There are plenty of people around the district who have tried to copy our methods. It seems to me that they implement one or another of the things we do, but the results must come from the combination of them all adding up to the right recipe.

Dennis has been too busy to clip a horse for a while now, but that doesn't mean he's forgotten all the little tricks. You can imagine that with such a large string to clip here each winter, we get our share of ticklish or awkward horses. Once, while he was away at Gerald's I gave Dennis a shout to come over to finish a flighty chestnut mare who'd had enough when she was only half clipped. Like everything else, the answer lay in common sense. The mare would not stand any more messing about, even when he turned her loose in the stable, until something caught her eye outside. That was the distraction Dennis needed. While she looked out over the stable door and pricked her ears at whatever it was she could see, he whipped the remainder of her coat off before she realized he was doing it.

As for betting, Dennis simply does not have the time to think about it any more, although he used to love a touch like everyone else at Pond House. Amazingly, no newspaper, bookmaker or punter has ever tried to use him as a mole or information source, despite his proximity to the heart of the action. Needless to say, though, anyone trying to buy him would quickly find where Dennis Dummett's loyalty lies. He rightly feels proud of the structure he has undoubtedly helped create.

After fifteen months of recalling him on spasmodic visits to Pond House, I realized Dennis's worth could not be counted in pounds sterling and likewise he admitted to himself that his future lay in the expanding stable. He has never been sick nor sorry and has only once been hurt by one of his charges when a colt stood on his foot.

Right up until last year Dennis only took a week's holiday. This has mainly been due to our policy of training each season's early runners even before the previous term has finished. Obviously he took payment in lieu of the rest of his statutory holiday, but it was as much Dennis not wanting the yard to be run by anyone else for a whole month as there being too much work to do for him to go. He might try to relax, but he would only have worried. Dennis admits that the one snatched week was spent sleeping day and night as his body claimed its due. I suppose we are birds of a feather really; I hate holidays too. Under pressure from Carol and those closest to me, most summers we have spent a week in Spain with Bob Wheatley, one of our owners. Once we ventured to the Bahamas for eight days, which nearly drove me to drink. What with the Flat horses and the August jumpers in full training, I was never off the phone. On checking out of the hotel I was amazed to find the phone bill of £1,500 cost more than the holiday.

I find it quite unbelievable that no one has tried to persuade Dennis to move on. In any other business key personnel are head-hunted remorselessly. If owners like Peter Bolton are prepared to lay out millions of pounds in building costs at Whitcombe and then offer a reputed £75,000 for a trainer to run the place, what value would the holder of all my secrets be worth to ensure a return on the investment? I suppose the reason is simple. Few people, even our owners, know the head man from Adam. Visitors to the yard rarely meet Dennis as his regular workload precludes idle chatter or even the luxury of passing the time of day. The horses never swim without Dennis being on hand nor gallop without him supervising when I am engaged elsewhere.

On the subject of the well used pool, Dennis agrees swimming makes horses think and work. Obviously there are lazy swimmers, but not many. On the gallops plenty of horses doss about, whereas in the pool they have to work to stop themselves sinking. I like Dennis to start every new inmate off in the pool himself in order to evaluate its capabilities and thinking. He has never yet lost one nor come across a horse who did not take to swimming eventually.

I notice that, almost without exception, horses swimming for the first time don't take a breath until they've gone at least three-quarters of the way around the pool. It is an enormous change for a horse when it first takes a dip. People say horses are natural swimmers but it is only from self-preservation, not from the love of it, and they need care and understanding to adapt. We never ask them to go around more than one lap to start with; if it becomes arduous or tiring, the element of fun will quickly disappear and much of the point would be lost.

The workload is such that Dennis only ever gets to the races for Taunton evening meetings, a fact of life he accepts with a resigned shrug. 'I did go up to Aintree for the Grand National meeting when Baron Blakeney won over fences, but there's too many people there. They push and shove, I had to fight to get a drink then be equally tough to get to the gents afterwards. In any case I never stopped worrying about the horses back home, so the whole day was anything but enjoyable.'

Pipe
Although we have a resident vet in the yard, Dennis does all the blistering at the first indication of minor leg trouble, reasoning that if it's done properly blistering saves a lot of horses breaking down. When he does it Dennis shaves all the hair off the area and rubs the blistering gel in with a brush until he's sweating. It's no good half doing the job, and that goes for everything in our line of work.

Another important function Dennis instigates is the immediate removal of a horse to stables several miles away the moment its temperature touches 101 degrees. Although that is only half a point above normal, it is a definite sign something is amiss. It could, of course, be a result of temperament but it's far more likely to be a harbinger of illness. Instant removal of a carrier saves a multitude of work and remedies.

Dennis and I sometimes look back to the good old days when the job was more personal and much more fun, knowing full well they can never come back again. Between us we have created a monster that can only get bigger or perhaps more efficient, but the job thankfully still has its rewards – especially when we manage to win with a very moderate horse.

Of his numerous proud moments over the past seventeen years, the one Dennis holds most dear is the curious achievement of having finally taught Martin the difference between oak, ash and sycamore, turning the townie into a true countryman. He would ideally like to train thirty horses in his own name but knows it will never happen now. 'I'm ten years older than Martin but I dare say I'll still be up to my share of the job for as long as he can take the strain of his side of it!'

The master of Nicholashayne watches his horses on the gallops in the early morning. (*George Selwyn*)

ABOVE: The sun shone on Carol on her wedding day in 1971 and has continued to do so in the intervening years.

TOP LEFT: A day trip with Mum to Lulworth Cove in 1956 aged eleven, but only the knees saw the sun.

ABOVE LEFT: Martin's first set of wheels 1961.

LEFT: While recovering from his smashed thigh in 1973, Pipe went through a hairy phase. David was a big boy, even aged six months.

Lorac cantering to the start in 1972. She came back with Ron Treloggan in the saddle and Martin in the ambulance.

In 1975 Weather Permitting recorded Pipe's sole riding success, prompting his immediate retirement. With his arms at full stretch, any slight stumble would pull him out of the saddle; but otherwise his style is good.

Dave Pipe in his Taunton betting office, the only one he kept after selling the chain to William Hill. (*George Selwyn*)

The humble beginnings of Tucker's Farm in 1970, two years after Dave Pipe bought it. The house has been renovated to provide room for three offices and the first of the barn stables has been built on the right.

ABOVE: Pipe and his
assistant Chester Barnes
(in the moth-eaten fur
coat) looked mugs when
backing Carrie Ann at
Haydock Park in 1980.
But they had the last
laugh and shared over
£50,000 from the
bookies.

RIGHT: Weston Bay and
Kay Rees prove home
gallops to be unreliable,
having comprehensively
beaten more fancied
stable companion
Cherchez La Femme in
1982.

ABOVE: Baron Blakeney (second from left) is well behind Broadsword at the last in the 1981 Daily Express Triumph Hurdle. (*George Selwyn*)

BELOW: But he came storming up the hill to catch Broadsword and gave Martin Pipe his first major success – the one that put him on the racing map. (*George Selwyn*)

Baron Blakeney displays his scope over fences under Paul Leach before retiring to stud in 1984.

Mr and Mrs Bob Wheatley present a cake to Martin at Taunton in 1985 after their horse Carado has provided the trainer with his first half-century of winners.

RIGHT: Martin and Chester have seen more good times than bad; they are great friends, as well as working colleagues.

BELOW: Cat's Eyes (Paul Leach) jumping the last to win at Aintree in 1985. Cat's Eyes was one of Pipe's most prolific winners. (*George Selwyn*)

Eddie Buckley leads the string after galloping while the trainer checks on the horse's fitness by monitoring its breathing. (*Gerry Cranham*)

Some of the string file past Pond House en route to the gallops. (*Gerry Cranham*)

Constant use of the weighing machine confirms when the ideal racing weight is imminent for each horse. (*Gerry Cranham*)

Strands Of Gold, monitored by Wendy Labbe, exercises on a treadmill designed to simulate a twenty per cent climb. (*Gerry Cranham*)

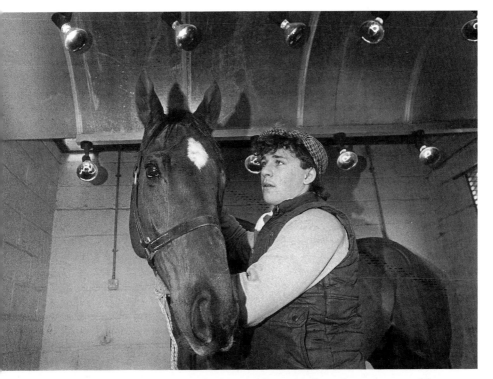

Corporal Clinger enjoys the solarium while Jonothan Lower, a working jockey and invaluable member of the team, looks on. (*George Selwyn*)

ABOVE: Beau Ranger winning the Mackeson Gold Cup in 1987. Beau Ranger was one of many horses whose careers were dramatically revived by the move to Pipe's stable. (*Gerry Cranham*)

BELOW: Beau Ranger is led into the winner's enclosure with Pipe after the Mackeson. (*Gerry Cranham*)

ABOVE: The ups and downs of National Hunt racing . . . Strands Of Gold, with Peter Scudamore the unfortunate jockey, falling at Becher's second time round when well clear in the 1988 Grand National. (*Gerry Cranham*)

BELOW: Strands Of Gold (Peter Scudamore) winning the Hennessy Gold Cup in November 1988. (*Gerry Cranham*)

Martin likes to see what goes on at both ends of the gallops.
(*Gerry Cranham*)

Owners are welcome to watch their horses work. Pipe believes that
constant observation is the key to a horse's well-being. (*Gerry Cranham*)

Pipe watches as head man Dennis Dummett, helped by Melanie Cross, introduces a first-time swimmer to the pool. (*Gerry Cranham*)

Much of the homework is done in the bleak winter months. Left to right: David Pipe, Martin Foster and Peter Scudamore tell Martin their views after schooling over hurdles. (*Gerry Cranham*)

The all-weather gallop has destroyed the long-held belief that horses need variety. Pipe's horses canter here six days a week, pulling up as they start the right-hand turn at the top. (*Gerry Cranham*)

Chapter 10

The Inquiring Mind

In the early 1980s Martin decided it was time to confirm or disprove the knowledge he was gathering from the increasing number of experts he listened to on every subject from exercise to nutrition.

Pipe
I've always had an inquiring mind, reading articles in the trade press then spending hours reasoning their opinions through in my own mind. While I was browsing around a jumble sale in Taunton I spotted this old book called *Modern Horse Management* by R. S. Timmis. A quick flick through it convinced me it would be good value at £2, and so it proved.

The title is a bit misleading as it was written in 1890, but what was correct then still stands close inspection today. The book looked daunting at first, and the language was obviously dated, yet once I'd become accustomed to the different terms, it fascinated me and held my interest better than any novel. The author listed all the requirements to ensure the digestive system worked efficiently and went into great detail about healing or curing the million and one things that cause horses to perform below their best. What immediately grabbed my attention was the fact that a 15.2 hands high horse requires sixty times the dose a human needs to put right any given ailment. That told me that even the proper cure for a problem would be next to useless if administered in insufficient dosages.

Our family had been friendly with Taunton chemist Harry

Adcock for donkey's years, so I took the book to him for advice. At first a lot of the suggested plants, herbs and veterinary concoctions seemed to be obsolete, but on further research Harry realized that in many cases, while the names had changed, the products remained the same. He made up tonics for us for years and really set us up on that front.

The book proved invaluable and I still refer to it today. Spurred on by what I had found, I looked for other similar sources of knowledge, alighting on *Veterinary Notes for Horse Owners* by Captain M. H. Hayes, published in 1952. Once again, the advice on the basics of getting a horse's body to function to its maximum provided information gleaned from years of experience which I did not have. Having re-read both books, I looked for others to take the learning process further, moving on from the basic care of the horse's welfare to the specific art of training them to run faster than their rivals. Two books, both called *Training The Racehorse* and written respectively by Lt P. D. Stewart DSO and Tim Fitzgeorge-Parker, set the ball rolling in that direction.

Both writers believed eradicating dust from the environment to be of paramount importance. This was something I had already thought to be important from a common sense angle. When we first started here Carol and I used to empty every sack of oats as we needed them into buckets, then tip each one into other buckets ten times, leaving the feed as dust-free as was humanly possible. Later, when we progressed from oats in sacks to a storage bin, they were, and still are today, sieved before being fed to the horses. The week before Baron Blakeney won the Triumph Hurdle, a lorryload of oats was being tipped into a hopper with a strong wind driving the dust straight at Baron's stable. I went mad at the men, who must have thought me round the bend. They stopped unloading but that started a row with Dad, who rightly pointed out it was our facilities that were at fault, not the men. Re-siting the storage bins away from the stables and filling them by augers means a dust-free operation.

On the subject of feedstuffs, I have to admit to being a jackdaw, only it was oats, nuts and hay that attracted me, not shiny objects. Our policy of buying Flat-race rejects for instant returns gave me access to all the leading Newmarket stables on sales day as trainers walked their horses to Tattersalls from their own boxes for the allotted sale time.

They were fun days. For the price of a catalogue anybody could get into the most successful yards in the country. I used the opportunity to observe everything, comparing their methods and if they were different from mine quizzing the grooms about the reasons for them. In every stable I visited, I made a point of wandering into the feed house to snatch a handful of oats and nuts which quickly disappeared into my pocket. Before leaving I'd add a wisp or two of hay as well. As soon as I'd left the premises the samples were popped into individual plastic bags, labelled for identification and dispatched for analysis. If the top yards had certain standards I meant to match them. I've still got packets of samples at home from Henry Cecil, Michael Stoute, Geoff Wragg, Clive Brittain and a dozen other stables.

Ironically, fifteen years later Bob Champion bought Vagog out of a seller from our stable with the express purpose of analysing its blood to establish what levels we had decided were ideal. I was quietly chuffed that he should consider us as a yardstick but that did not stop me buying Vagog back when it won for Bob. Pride, I suppose.

Never having worked in another trainer's yard, I had nothing to compare my ideas with at that time. Buying horses was the main reason for being there, but observing what went on gave me every bit as much satisfaction. I didn't know who was doing things best – they were all having winners; but some were attaining better ratios of winners to runners, and that interested me.

I would love to have worked in a proper stable. Henry Cecil, Fred Winter and Vincent O'Brien are my heroes. The trouble is that in 1973 I did not have the confidence to approach them and now there is just not enough time. What stamps the likes of Winter and O'Brien as truly great trainers is they ruled the roost without the help of modern-day science. People write glowing reports about what has happened here over the past six years, but when you stop to think back, Vincent O'Brien sent out multiple Grand National, Gold Cup and Champion Hurdle winners before doing the same in the Classics on the Flat. Now he really does have something to crow about.

It would be a dream come true to spend a week or two with Vincent O'Brien just joining in and watching what he does. I might not agree with everything, but I would be fascinated to be party to the workings of such a great man. I honestly think I'm still lacking somewhere, missing out really. Perhaps if I went to a top stud in America where no one has heard of me, I could satisfy the need to see at first hand the age-old proven methods.

Looking back it does make me blush to think that for years I hadn't a clue about the points of a horse. Tendons, quarters and muscles did not feature in my vocabulary, let alone what went on inside them.

In 1979 we won a weekend on the *QE2* to France with friends, and I got split up from the rest after spotting an old English horsy book in a shop window. Eventually they realized I was missing and retraced their steps to find me still browsing around the bookshop. I'd come across an encyclopaedia relating to training the racehorse in 1800 and amazingly the problems were exactly the same then. It said breakfast time was the worst period of a trainer's day, with the news of one horse coughing, another with a runny nose, the best horse entered that week has broken a blood vessel on the gallops . . . and that was almost two hundred years ago. It's just the same now.

A month later one of our French party phoned to congratulate me after two of our horses had won in the same week, which was unknown in those days. I told her that it really was amazing as I'd only got as far as the third page in my book on how to train.

I'm still learning the names of different internal organs. It fascinates me, and of course you never stop learning if you have an inquiring mind. What I am convinced of, though, is that God created the horse right. He knew what he was doing. The way the limbs work together to produce acceleration, suspension, shock-absorbers and a system for pumping blood to and from the extremities is nothing short of brilliant.

Dad has benefited over the years from his ability to extract useful information from people during normal conversation, and urges me to do the same when buying a horse. I do listen to advice while reserving judgement. If the methods employed to train an animal have not got the best out of it, surely a new approach is advisable. After all, I buy a horse because I think it can perform better, not just run up to its previous mark.

When we bought Le Dauphin for seven or eight hundred pounds at Newmarket sales, his trainer explained he was a wild little thing who needed practically no work, cortisone between races, at least a month off after running and a whole list of veterinary preparations to keep him sound. I'd never heard of cortisone or most of the other things he was supposed to live on, so I took him home, gave him loads of work and no medication and won three races with him in the space of a month. I'm not into asking trainers what to do with their horses if they have not won with them. What's the point?

This season I've been running the horses with special cushions under their racing plates to counteract the increasingly firm ground they now face. To this day Peter Scudamore does not know his mounts are wearing the aid. If you know something new is being used, it's human nature to imagine side-effects. So far, he has not mentioned feeling anything different; I'm waiting for him to report positively or negatively on the feel he is getting *without* knowing something is different. When Takemethere fell at Devon and Exeter's final fence I was worried Scu would report the gelding had slipped because something was different, would say he felt wrong. It immediately flashed through my mind that the horse could have slipped because of the new shoeing arrangements. In the event, Scu said nothing that could be linked to the cushions, but had he known we were trying them out his mind might have been subconsciously prompted to associate the fall with the trials. I am convinced the cushions are preventing injury or at least helping the horses to cope with the faster ground. There have been far fewer leg problems since we started using them.

I first tried a similar experiment soon after we started training, but made the mistake of telling our jockey Ron Atkins what was happening. He thought the device made the horses move badly and advised stopping using it. In those days I was aware I didn't know enough to stick to my guns so I capitulated. Prior knowledge can do as much harm as good. If you are told you look ill, you soon feel ill.

I now ask vets or back specialists to examine horses without alerting them to what we think is wrong. Made with an open mind, the diagnosis can then be pooled with our information to find the solution. Several years ago a back specialist always found trouble at the points we had told her to check. Then we slipped one in we knew to be a hundred per cent healthy and suggested where she might find a problem. Sure enough, the expert confirmed our suspicions, pronouncing the horse to need treatment.

Martin used this same theory on me in September last year. He told me to ride Paul Green's latest French purchase Funambulien to see what I thought. Three pieces of work up the all-weather strip and two canters down it gave me all the information I needed. Well balanced, still short of race fitness but possessing a powerful engine which reacted immediately to the signal to go up a gear. 'I'm relieved to hear that,' he said. 'The horse you rode was Granville Again.' Six weeks later the gelding took the first of four straight victories before falling when favourite for the Champion Hurdle.

Pipe
In order to make correct decisions I need unbiased reports and that includes from myself. Quite often I keep the morning's work list in my pocket purely to put myself on the spot. When one hundred and fifty horses gallop past me in a morning in twos or threes, it takes a lot of concentration and alertness to catch the signs that tell me if a horse has worked well or perhaps is showing a respiratory weakness. I don't want to know which horse is which, I just want to soak up what my eyes and ears tell me.

The idea can be applied to other people's horses too. Last season Carol and I studied every runner in the pre-parade ring before a selling hurdle with a view to filling an order to buy a cheapie for a man who wanted a quick return. I felt none of them had any future but in the event one came home a distance clear of the rest. Our customer got excited and wanted us to bid for it, but as I explained, they all look good standing in the winner's enclosure. I had not taken to it before the race and the fact that it had won told us nothing new except that it was the best of a very bad bunch. You have to have an opinion in this game. During our serious bookmaking days we thrived because our opinions were right more often than not. It is the same now with training. Guesswork can go in your favour but is far more likely to go against you in the long term.

* * *

Attracting, and keeping owners is vital to any stable. Some trainers can call on family and friends, others may take over a going concern; well established assistant trainers often cream off some of their former employer's contacts. Twenty years ago former window-cleaner Ken Payne quickly established himself as a trainer by keeping a high profile socially in the casinos and nightclubs where moneyed people gathered. In Pipe's case there has been a combination of factors. His father provided a rather motley bunch of horses as a nucleus and bookmaking or punting friends tested the water too; but from the very start it has been Pipe's own energy and enthusiasm that have ensured owners' enjoyment and earned their commitment.

'No matter who comes here, they can't help but be swept along on a tide of involvement,' says Carol. 'There's always a buzz of excitement, something's always happening, even if we only bet between ourselves. Martin makes things swing, he generates some sort of buzz. Often he gets the owners geed up to have a crack at the Tote Jackpot or Placepot. That way they're involved throughout the day.

'On other occasions he lets them know what horses we are watching with a view to buying or as dangers to our own. Everyone feels part of the team, as indeed they are. When he starts bidding after a selling hurdle, our owners have fun watching the plot unfold and if we secure a horse from a seller or claiming race, it's off to the bar to celebrate. Martin creates interest where there was none. Sometimes I get a bit fed up, but after half a day of quietness I'm ready for some action again. It's in Martin's nature to fire on all cylinders. He simply can't keep still.

'People are strange, though; no end of our owners phone daily to know what to back. They would rather back losers from duff information than miss winners that have surprised us.'

Chester Barnes adds his thoughts on why the operation works so well. 'Everything here is so simple. It's like Liverpool Football Club. Nothing changes radically now the system has been formulated. Like Liverpool in the glory days, we promote from within in order to maintain the equilibrium. The only observation I would make is that the establishment has grown too big. In the end Martin will find it hard to take the strain of holding it all on his shoulders.'

Whether he curtails the operation or not, Pipe is still thinking ahead. Besides trying proven methods, such as heart-rate monitors and treadmills, he is intent on finding ways to evaluate how much benefit different horses get from the same exercise. Whether swimming, on the horse-walker or cantering, they derive vastly different degrees of advantage according to their nature.

Pipe
Watching horses at work stimulates my mind. The movement and coordination is beautiful to observe. I often stand and study them on the horse-walker, which has led me to consider all sorts of possibilities. You can easily determine horses' mentality when watching them on the walker or in the pool. As they get no interference from riders in either situation, it poses the question: Would they be better off trained unridden?

I suppose people will laugh at me, but I'm convinced one day there will be a way to gallop horses without riders. My gallop is only half-a-mile long; it wouldn't take a genius to develop automated conveyor-type cages where horses worked free up the strip, walked round a ring for several minutes, then hacked back down the hill to do it again.

In Ireland they have developed much bigger horse-walkers than ours. Victor Bowens' string do much of their work on his enlarged machine, reducing the groom/horse ratio to one person to every six horses. I'm not advocating this idea to reduce staffing levels, rather because horses are more relaxed without a rider on top and definitely do less damage to themselves when riderless.

Letting my mind run away slightly, if purpose-built stables were sited with this in mind, there could be a way to open a stable door electrically with a magnetic hitch to another conveyor escorting the horse to the gallop and then back to his box. The whole thing would be operated from the computer room. Of course it's all pie in the sky, but I am so certain that horses benefit from riderless exercise that I am convinced this aspect will be developed in the future.

Pie in the sky today, perhaps; but tomorrow, who knows? Pipe has built his success by not letting his mind be dominated by other people's methods. Forward thinking is paramount, always aimed at how to improve the set-up. Yet, at the end of every season, Martin and Carol express the recurring fear: 'What if we have lost the knack?

What if we can't produce winners again next year?' I would like to find someone to lay me 6–4 about that.

Chapter 11

The Form Man

From their very first winner in 1975 until the middle of 1991 the Pipes relied a great deal on the advice of their neighbour, friend and professional punter, Roy Hawkins. Whether in buying horses, deciding which race to run in or going for a gamble, Roy's skill in evaluating the true worth of form proved invaluable.

For the past forty years, since leaving school at fifteen, Roy has quietly nibbled away at the bookmakers' profits, thriving in a world where few others have managed to survive for even a fraction of that time. His position as form adviser to the Pipes dovetailed smoothly with the work he needed to carry out for his own betting purposes, until the training operation grew to the present monster proportions.

Hawkins
My outlook on life is to enjoy it while it lasts, a philosophy that was eroded in proportion to the expansion of the string I had to monitor. With a capacity for 166 horses between Pond House and the Sunnyside complex, the seasonal turnover could reach above 200 horses.

I became attracted early on to walking the financial tightrope, pitting my wits against the odds when betting at the local greyhound meetings before being called up for my two years' National Service. On being demobbed I felt horse racing offered a wider choice of openings; I was now determined to make a living from betting, escaping the constraints of bosses, unions or

101

rules. As most horses bred for jumping emanated from Ireland I decided to acquaint myself thoroughly with their early performances – information which in 1960 was less widely available to the public in Britain than it is today. A weekly subscription to the Irish form book put me ahead of the game.

Roy enjoyed a winning run on the West Country bookmakers, including a healthy raid or two on Dave Pipe's satchel, and became of increasing interest to Pipe the bookmaker when relieving him of large amounts of cash for little outlay on Tim Forster's Fiddler's Flute at Newton Abbot.

The gelding had decent form in Ireland which received scant attention in the English trade papers. Roy, knowing the majority of Forster's horses needed a run to sharpen them up, watched Fiddler's Flute run with promise at Chepstow on its British debut then availed himself of the 33–1 Dave Pipe offered next time out. Seeing his money reduce that price to 25–1, Roy again backed his judgement before the gamble became infectious.

Hawkins
Fiddler's Flute did the business all right, followed by another long-priced winner for me the same afternoon; the two hits compounded Dave Pipe's losses on the day's transactions. Strapped for cash, he offered to pay me, his biggest creditor, by cheque, giving him the opportunity to engage me in conversation. From this chat Pipe learned that I was far more than a casual or lucky punter, and decided that this was something he could put to use in his quest to make his son into a trainer.

A tour of the stables convinced me that the training operation, then spluttering into life, would grow enough to make it worth my while to help select and place the horses. I assure you it was not money that motivated me – the pleasure of helping to develop such an intriguing business provided sufficient bait.

From their point of view the Pipes had all the proof they needed that I could take the guesswork out of placing horses in races where they held the best chance and also advising which horses should be bought out of claimers. This left Martin to concentrate on getting the horses fit.

As a result of my first piece of advice Dave Pipe bought Hit Parade for 1,050 guineas after it had won a seller for Gay Kindersley. Besides providing the stable with its much sought-after initial success, the inexpensive purchase continued to cement our relationship by taking three more first prizes the next season.

The basis of my success in making betting pay also formed the foundation for Martin's rise through the ranks as a trainer. Find the openings where no matter how large the field only two horses at the most can realistically hold sound claims. Backing or running horses in their own class, or preferably below it, dramatically reduces the odds against defeat. Today both Martin and Dave Pipe insist that evaluating the opposition is crucial. Once you've done the homework there, it is quite easy to find a horse within the stable to win the race.

When a Pipe-trained horse held two or more engagements, my brief entailed going through the credentials of its rivals – often up to sixty of them – in order to pinpoint the best chance. Often the options boiled down to a straight choice between one event in which I reckoned Martin's horse would come out top, but with maybe six others holding strong claims, and another contest in which his runner looked second best but with only one possible danger in the rest of the field. In these cases my advice was to ignore the race where he came out the winner on paper, as trouble in running or a jumping mistake could give the edge to any of the several dangers. Conversely, in the race where the Pipe runner had only one serious adversary, its chances of error were the same as ours. Nine times out of ten that principle worked in our favour.

An inherent danger to racegoers looking for future winners is the false impression gained when noting fast-finishing placed horses. Often they are running through beaten rivals, benefited from educational tactics or were only put into the race after the principals had flown. Many horses look impressive in those circumstances, then are found lacking on their next outing when asked to get in the thick of things. I could cite numerous cases of horses which if they'd fallen when well clear at the last fence would have gone into punters' notebooks as winners without a penalty in future contests. Throughout the season horses jump the last obstacle with an apparently unassailable lead, only to fold up in a matter of strides. Garrison Savannah's gallant defeat by Seagram in the 1991 Grand National is a good example. What might have been and what was are often very different events.

Having been deceived in my early punting days by setting too much store by unimportant late flurries instead of solid facts, I have long since relied on the form book as the definitive guide to unravelling each day's puzzles. I read *Chaseform*, use a daily paper then cross-check interesting horses in the *Raceform Notebook*. Their comments are pertinent, devoid of padding and reported by race-watchers who know their job thoroughly.

One instance where the Pipes and I differed as to the merit of a particularly unlucky faller proves the point. In winning his third novice chase of the 1988–9 season My Cup Of Tea benefited from the fall two fences from home of David Barons' Danny's Luck at Newton Abbot. Pipe's horse had made all the running until the New Zealand-bred challenger took it up after the eighth fence going like a winner. Two fences later Danny's Luck fell with My Cup Of Tea in what looked like vain pursuit. The eventual twenty-five-length gift victory materialized out of apparent defeat in front of the world and his wife and you can be sure everyone intended to back the unfortunate faller next time he ran. Not surprisingly when the two met ten days later over the same course and distance, again on firm ground, Danny's Luck was deemed certain to take his revenge, starting at 8–11 with My Cup Of Tea a 5–2 shot – an exact reversal of their odds on the previous meeting. It was obviously going to be a steal: Danny's Luck would have won with a clear round then, was better off at the weights this time and must have improved from his seasonal reappearance. All three points were not lost on the Pipe clan who did not see the value of wasting a run when there were numerous other openings for novices during the first few months of the chasing season.

For my part I argued fiercely enough to get my way – eventually. Ours already had three wins to his name, proving his jumping to be safe enough, whereas Danny's Luck's fall might have made him think twice about jumping with any degree of confidence. We were also assuming he would have stayed on stoutly to the finish had he stood up, but more certain winners in the past had stopped to a walk. Also, the other six runners could not beat us if they started the day before. This would be a value bet, 5–2 about an even-money chance.

The two rivals got a good lead from the hard-pulling Gustavus Adolphus until the second last, where My Cup Of Tea took it up with Danny's Luck on his tail in second place. The expected surge of speed that had so easily disposed of My Cup Of Tea ten days before simply never materialized, and the favourite's fate was sealed when he belted the final fence. He was eventually beaten five lengths. Yet again, the tried and trusted guidelines that have kept me afloat in a business that sinks most who embark on it had come good. The situation is so obvious in the cold light of the next day; it is working the puzzle out in advance that wins the bets.

Couple stories of incidents such as these with some of Len Lungo's stories from twelve years before, and you could be tempted to conclude that the Pipes have clawed their way into racing's stratosphere on the backs of cleverer men. Instead, look at the situation from another angle. They have risen from total ignorance of the age-old art of training racehorses to their current lofty position by recognizing talent in others, digesting everything they have seen, heard and read about, then decided which bits to utilize or discard and worked, incessantly, on the basis of their new expertise. Never content to be drip-fed, Martin and his father have systematically syphoned off the experience amassed by experts in every facet of the game. What's more, they have subsequently been uninhibited enough to delve beyond the boundaries accepted as fact by their predecessors and the majority of their rivals.

Pipe
In line with our thinking on everything else, we also observe rival horses in the parade ring and note their condition before the jockeys mount. Roy will have evaluated them on past performance but I want to know which, if any, will improve for the outing. Each rival will attract at least one comment ranging from 'fat' to 'fit'. These remarks are stored back at the office to be referred to when any of them next takes on one of our runners. As this practice became noticed I became aware that several of

my colleagues tended to smirk, although the cleverer among them took note of our horses too, and compared their condition to their own.

While I'm assessing the physical condition of the runners, any relevant activity in the betting ring is noted and relayed back to me so I can alert my jockey as to the horses he should keep an eye on. Time has taught us that money usually talks.

Roy's invaluable assessment of the actual worth of a performance has consistently pointed our owners in the right direction when buying horses. From that initial advice to purchase Hit Parade in 1975 up to recent times the results have shown his reasoning to be far from guesswork. Roy's last two selections were The Blue Boy and Primitive Singer, who between them clocked up nine wins within three months of their purchase.

Hawkins' rich Somerset burr quietly unearths endless successes, with most satisfaction from the cheap buys.

Hawkins

Too many inflated prices have been paid for horses off the Flat. Owners naturally want to go to the big meetings if they spend a lot of money, but by the time their hopes have been dashed the attraction of winning a little race at a gaff track has paled somewhat. Martin briefed me to look for horses that would be capable of mopping up several smaller contests before attempting to go upmarket. That way if they don't prove good enough to set the world alight, at least the owner will have got some pleasure and some money back rather than tilting at windmills from the word go.

Mayumbe is a good example of a cheap buy that proved to be worthwhile, although for a time after its purchase at Ascot sales Dave Pipe tried to convince me I had been wide of the mark. 'It's absolutely useless, it can't even beat Carol's hack up the gallops. There has got to be something wrong with Mayumbe, you've made a proper mistake this time,' he castigated me.

After weeks of fast work up the rotavated earth gallop, Mayumbe still showed nothing to convince either Dave or Martin that the horse possessed any ability. Neither could they uncover anything wrong, medically or mentally, and the plain truth seemed to stare them in the face: the horse was just extraordinarily slow.

The only option left was to run him in the hope that the racecourse would galvanize the gelding into action. After drifting ominously in the betting market on his hurdling debut at Devon and Exeter towards the end of November 1976 under Ron Atkins, Mayumbe ran on, a little one-paced, it's true, to finish a creditable third of the ten runners, offering a ray of hope that something might just be salvaged from the purchase in the future. The team had won with Carrie Ann an hour before and in those days a victory plus an unexpected third from the small stable was more than satisfactory.

Mayumbe showed little or no change in his home work, prompting Martin to have another look at the gelding on the racecourse. He pitted Mayumbe against well tried novices in a twenty-five-runner event at Chepstow the week before Christmas. Lack of stable support saw him again drift in the betting. Not surprisingly, Ron Atkins chose to ride the Windsor winner James Three, leaving Pipe's horse in Jeff King's capable hands. The race went to Fred Winter's St Cadwaladr from the favourite Escapologist; Mayumbe finished a pleasing sixth, some way ahead of previous winners. King reported back that the horse needed further than the minimum trip and felt at home on the soft ground.

Pipe had now got his enigma's measure. He chose a wet Monday at Leicester in January to test the theory in a three-mile novice hurdle that attracted so many hopefuls the race had to be split into four divisions to accommodate them all. Jeff King naturally retained the ride and a few hundred quids' worth of half-hearted gamble reduced the horse's chances to second favouritism. He ran out a five-length victor, vindicating the judgement of jockey, trainer and, more to the point, me, having advised the original purchase. It may have been insignificant to the few hardy faithfuls who braved the elements to watch the eighth race on a mundane card, but to those closest to the result it confirmed the pattern that has held us in good stead over the past fifteen years.

Another outing at Ascot over half a mile less saw Ron Atkins back on board for a fair fourth behind the subsequent Cheltenham Gold Cup winner Master Smudge, confirming yet again the horse's proper mark. Once established, the pattern is glaringly obvious. A huge drop in class, back to his right distance and the money spread about at lowly Plumpton on his next start and our plans were smoothly executed once again.

Martin gets it right far more often than not, although I would not presume for a moment to suggest he is infallible. The following season Mayumbe's niggling leg problems kept him off the course until the last day of January, when he actually broke down at Chepstow. He was only seen out another three times in the following four years, drastically turning the original profit into a thundering loss. The one saving grace about such losses in racing is that they are taken in instalments, not all at once.

In those days no one took any notice of Martin's runners although bookies have been well and truly stung in the intervening years. They take few chances these days with Pipe horses but there is still value to be had if you're selective and don't mind letting the bulk of the short-priced winners run unbacked. People still ignore a horse that has been off the course for a year or so, yet Martin has won with so many of this type that it ought to be obvious by now that he is a master at producing them fit to win, no matter how long the absence. In recent years Omerta at Cheltenham, Balasani at Sandown Park, Strands Of Gold and Chatam's victories in the Hennessy Cognac Gold Cup all illustrate the point – and Martin's handling of Barry Window to win at Newton Abbot in January 1992 after an absence of three years and nine days underlines his aptitude beyond doubt.

I have never sought the limelight, preferring to go about my business quietly. I have stayed afloat on the strength of a photographic memory, aided by the ability to evaluate beaten horses. Too many watchers are deceived by horses flying through a moderate field; everything in its class is the cardinal rule.

Having brought up a family of four from punting I am living proof that it is possible to earn a livelihood from betting; but it is a full-time job, there are no short cuts. The rules I've religiously obeyed to dodge the numerous pitfalls that dog attempts to make a living out of the betting ring will not have been lost on the Pipes and, like the majority of people who have been on their bandwagon, I've enjoyed the ride.

Chapter 12

The Cockney Kid: Chester Barnes

In 1979 the Cockney kid who at fifteen years of age became the youngest ever British table tennis champion – a record he still holds – struck up an immediate though unlikely friendship with the then small-time trainer Martin Pipe.

They met through a mutual friend, Malcolm Zadel, with whom they frequented Flynn's Restaurant in Torquay, enjoying endless boys' nights and days out together until Malcolm's premature death from cancer in the late 1980s. Martin found in Chester a man who lived and loved life one day at a time, an approach refreshingly different from his own strict upbringing and the rigid business thinking drummed into him by his father. He relished the diversion.

Chester's real name is George but incessant bawling as a young child earned him the nickname Chester after the comedian Charlie Chester. A comedian is exactly what he has become. He is a master of the one-liner, loves sending people up and has survived three marriages without showing any visible scars (coincidentally, all three of his wives have been school-teachers). Jane, his wife now for twelve years, bowed to Chester's passion for racing in agreeing to name their son Lester.

Barnes
My table tennis career got under way when I won the *News of the World* championship at Butlins Holiday Camp in Clacton aged thirteen. Butlins and the paper lapped it up. There was a lot of publicity because of my age; they sort of adopted me, with the

109

paper's sports writer Johnny Leach promoting the job. Two years after the first holiday camp victory my parents entered me in the British championships as a birthday present, more as a treat than as a serious challenge. But I won it; and that unexpected success was followed by a further four championships.

You see it so often when a youngster hits the headlines: sudden success and a few quid in the back pocket and the sense of reality goes out of the window. I rapidly became the Hurricane Higgins of the table tennis world. I was cocky and confident. The press loved me because I always spoke my mind. When there were bad decisions I'd say 'F— the officials, he's a prat.' They all used to ring me up for quotes and articles, including Julian Wilson's father Peter, 'The Man They Cannot Gag'. I was for ever being suspended or banned; I had shoulder-length hair which prompted writers to call me Beatle. I suppose the whole thing was anti-establishment. I was a kid from West Ham and wanted the world to know you did not need to go to Eton to get on in life.

I wrote my autobiography aged seventeen and four instructional books after that. Books are not so easy as they seem. I had 45,000 words to write but when you've told the story in 5,000, it makes you scratch your head a bit. In the end I cottoned on and was pleased to be ghosted. The racing photographer Gerry Cranham did a revolutionary shot at that time which we staged on the Surrey Downs in pitch dark to get the effect he wanted. They were great times, though like all youngsters I failed to appreciate it then.

Like the tour of China at the age of sixteen. We flew into a military airport and there's me, just a kid, inspecting a long line of pilots and officials as if I was the Prince of Wales. As you can imagine, I made the most of that. They expected me to look them all up and down, so I did. We were protected from every possible danger, treated with kid gloves as they didn't want anything to go wrong in case of bad publicity. We were the first party of Brits to be invited from a sport the Chinese excelled at.

I tell Martin Foster, one of Martin's conditional jockeys, now not to take what's happening here too much for granted. It's an era that will be looked back on with amazement in years to come.

After retiring from competitive playing I made a good living from exhibition matches, swopping horses from Butlins to

Pontins holiday camps. These days, table tennis doesn't play a very big part in my pay packet. I do 70,000 miles a year as assistant to Martin, plenty of them during the two-month break between the jumping seasons. That's when the best bargains are to be found in the numerous claiming races on the Flat. Funny really, when I was competing I used to get annoyed by the amount of racing coverage on the telly when table tennis got none. Now I'm eaten up by racing and think there's not enough of it on.

When I first visited Pond House there were only a dozen horses in training, most of them owned by the family. The first piece of advice from my new-found friend was never to own one, simply get my kicks by tagging along to the track whenever I had a spare day. That in itself made me twice as determined to have a horse. Pig-headed, I suppose. We selected one from Bruce Hobbs's stable, called Manrico. Bred to win the Derby, it had started odds-on the three times it had run for him, so obviously it could gallop; but it turned out to be nothing more than a morning glory, working like a good horse on the gallops but with enough brains to avoid exerting himself on the track.

In those days Martin was always plotting to beat the bookies, which sounded exciting to me. He would run them not fit, over the wrong distance, on a course or on ground that did not suit them. It was not a case of stopping horses, rather, of running them where they could not win. This kind of plotting grabbed my imagination. Anyway, I insisted on getting involved and bought Manrico for next to nothing at the horses-in-training sales at Newmarket in December 1979. We ran him a week later at Warwick in a novice hurdle. He started at 33–1 and finished sixth of twenty-four runners. Well, as you can imagine, we were rubbing our hands at the thought of dropping him into selling class on good ground. It was simply a case of putting the money down, then picking a lot more up from the bookies: but we were not ready yet. Next time out the public's money made him second favourite in a seller only for him to fall when going well.

The bookies were taking no chances when he next ran a month later, sending him off at 7–4 for a trip that was too long and on ground that was too soft; he finished fourth. Another outing on heavy ground saw him a well beaten third before, on similar going at Chepstow, without a shilling of our money riding on his back, he just got touched off by Parton Belle. Seven days later, racing for the first time on the good ground he needed, we went for the touch we'd been planning since the day I'd bought him. For once given everything in his favour the horse, bred to pass racing pigeons, refused to go fast enough to keep himself warm. We were gutted, to say the least.

And, as so often happens, we took no heed of his next run, at Hereford ten days later. Martin decided to leave the rogue in his stable for thirty-six hours prior to his race and we didn't have a penny on him, so we could only watch in amazement as he bolted in by four lengths. What's more, at the subsequent auction there was no bid so we were left with the enigma. The date? 1 April. He never won again.

Another one that went wrong at that time was Andsome, ridden by Tim Thomson Jones at Lingfield Park. It was a certainty. Martin told the jockey to put it in front only twenty yards from the finish. What did he do? He hit the front two furlongs from home and got beaten in a photo. Martin was furious, to say the least, and I was getting slightly disillusioned.

In those days we still used to drive the horses to the races ourselves. Raging at Andsome's defeat, Martin set off with the trailer and horse bouncing along behind, far too angry to touch any of the food his mother had packed. I dived into the sandwiches only to find they was just bits of bread: no crusts, no butter and no fillings. It was the first time I'd ever been to the races with Martin and although I thought it strange, being hungry, I ate them just the same. When he cooled down enough to want some food he spat the first mouthful out. His sandwiches were buttered and that is one of several things he cannot stomach. Neither his dad nor his grandfather ate butter. I'd eaten Martin's sandwiches and left him the picnic his mother had made for me. We stopped to get him something to eat, and all Martin would accept was the white of an egg, processed peas and straight bananas. He only eats straight bananas, which set me off in howls of laughter. It was a peculiar start to our friendship, yet we clicked; we had the same sense of humour.

In the first few years I knew Martin the dozen or so horses at Pond House allowed him enough spare time to enjoy other interests. We played a lot of badminton in the barn which is now the helicopter hangar. Naturally there'd be money on the outcome, which led to foul play when either of us was stuck in a losing run. The favoured ploy was hitting the shuttlecock up into the rafters; no shuttlecock, no result. The action would then move up into the games room and some lengthy tussles on the snooker table.

Once Martin took me on at my own game. This happened under very suspicious circumstances on New Year's Eve after our usual get-together at a smashing place called Deer Park. We'd enjoyed more drink than is good for the head, but as we were staying there overnight it didn't matter. At the stage where the gaps in conversation had become lengthy enough to suggest that going to bed was the only logical step, the little bastard challenged me to a table tennis match. I was so tight I could hardly see the table, let alone the ball. In fact, I could barely talk or walk; yet he happened to know the staff had a table in the attic. Martin found an old bat with no rubber on for me then produced his own match bat from his jacket. He just happened to have it with him: such was the feeble excuse the next morning. Martin dispatched me all right and has never stopped crowing since.

Though Manrico had let me down when the money was on, any nasty taste had been more than washed away by the mouthwatering touch on Carrie Ann. Hooked by the intrigue and excitement of setting up another coup, we often discussed plans which in the cold light of day were discarded in favour of the tried and trusted methods of preparing the horse in races it could not win.

My second blunder into ownership came in the shape of a chaser called Three of Diamonds, bought in Ireland for me by Taunton farmer Tim Handel, who bred and trained Royal Toss to win the Whitbread Gold Cup in 1971. Most people may dream of winning the Derby; we centred all our thoughts on landing a gamble in a selling chase at Fontwell Park.

Tim wanted us to put the horse out to grass for a couple of months to let it acclimatize. Not us; we were fired up with a plan. We would give Three of Diamonds an outing at Newton Abbot soon after we got him – no chance of him winning straight off the boat and as fat as a pig. With the ideal selling chase two months later winking out of the programme book at us, we had enough time to make the bookies think the horse was useless. The orders to jockey Mark Floyd were quite simply to go out and enjoy himself. In our minds the horse was just not fit enough to win. It won unbacked at 33–1 in a £4,000 race, qualifying it for the Grand National, no less. There we are, trying to set up a gamble in the worst race in history, and all of a sudden we've got a National runner in the stable. It could never win a race like that unless the others all whipped around at the start, but the crack appealed to us and he'd more than paid for himself by then anyway.

It was an exciting episode all round. I was writing a column for the *Sun*, who sponsored the Grand National then, and they put me, Carol and Martin up in the Adelphi Hotel with tickets for their special lunch and viewing box looking out on the winning post. So many of our mates and the stable's patrons came up to Aintree to support us, we decided to give them a good time. One of us would go out every now and then and pass the other's entry badges to a friend; all these friends then boldly marched into the sponsors box, one by one, to wine and dine in style. The sports editor did mention he thought the box was overcrowded, to which I naturally agreed and told him it was a disgrace!

In the race itself, as the horse had no possible chance we let stable jockey Paul Leach ride, knowing full well he couldn't do the right weight even if he chopped a leg off. I hate to think what strokes Paul pulled to put up only 4lb overweight. That 1981 Grand National had several possible fairytales as an ending, although ours was not one of them. Bob Champion had conquered cancer to ride Aldaniti, himself returning from injury, while fifty-four-year-old John Thorne was bidding for victory on Spartan Missile, a horse he'd bred himself from a stallion and mare he had also owned. And Geraldine Rees had a 66–1 chance of making history on Cheers as the first girl ever to complete the course, let alone ride the winner. The whole build-up got us going, and by the time the horses arrived at the start we'd already had our money's worth. Imagine the noise our entourage made when the runners cleared the Chair at the end of the first circuit with Three of Diamonds still on his feet. You'd have thought we'd won the ruddy contest. Anyway, they got to the twenty-fourth fence, the second Canal Turn, and Three of Diamonds negotiated the ninety-degree bend like a good horse. The only trouble was, Paul didn't and was unseated, bursting our bubble in the process.

After the euphoria of the National died down Martin told me the horse was too saleable to keep. He was no good for a punt now he was fully exposed. He'd won us £4,000 on his debut and would be attractive for the 1982 Grand National. He was right. Pat O'Connor bought him for £7,000, giving us a healthy return on the initial outlay of £1,200.

Up to that point the Pipes had never sold anything. Dave Pipe continually increased his property holdings, never trading in one house to buy a bigger one; he simply kept the smaller house and purchased the bigger one as well. The Pipes are natural hoarders. Old horses are dotted about in numerous paddocks eating their heads off in case someone rejuvenates them. The same went for every car they ever owned. All previous Pipe cars are lying around the place wrecked in case they happen to come back to life.

At that time the staff was minimal and everyone who could ride, did. Even Malcolm Zadel, who had a couple of horses in the yard by then, Lucky Louis and Le Dauphine, got the call to join the fearsome team of Martin and Dennis Dummett as work rider and schooling jockey despite weighing fifteen stone. It still creases me up thinking of those days, especially when they legged Malcolm into the saddle on Lucky Louis, who turned somersaults when you tried to get on him unless he was on the move. Imagine Martin hobbling down the yard hanging on to Malcolm's outstretched leg as Lucky Louis increased his speed. More often than not they'd still be pushing or jumping in opposite directions after leaving the yard. Somehow, one way or another, Malcolm always ended up in the saddle.

When Malcolm, who always looked incredibly healthy and robust, got married and joined his wife's firm, he had to undergo a medical in London as part of the job conditions. They asked him back for further tests. Eventually they told him he'd got cancer, then hit him with the worst news anyone could ever get: he had only six months to live. He was still a healthy fifteen stone, and we refused to believe the worst, until, visiting him after a ten-hour operation on his cancerous liver, we could see he would not live. We took his son Matthew up to the hospital, then, soon after we got home, had a call asking us to visit him again. Naturally we went back in the morning; he died later that day. It all happened so quickly, from having the time of his life

115

riding out here to death within months. That sort of time-scale mercifully precludes too much suffering, but it still hurts those left behind. We often laugh about things we all did together; it helps to keep his memory alive.

These days Chester Barnes looks quite at home saddling Pipe-trained horses at the races in his capacity as assistant. He learned this most important of jobs by watching Martin do it his way and, as with every other aspect of working for Martin, if employees stick to the guidelines, the trainer will take the blame if things go wrong. Saddling horses was not always top of Chester's list of favourite jobs, though.

Barnes

First of all I wouldn't go near the horses, either at the sales or in the stables. There is absolutely no doubt I was afraid of them, and I'm still not happy with them now. Horses have a knack of hurting you for no reason. Deep down, though, I wanted to have a go at riding and as I was starting to become an authority on jockeys and race-riding, it seemed right to throw my leg over a horse.

Mart thought it prudent for me to have my first attempt when no one else could see the outcome. It had to be the safest bet of the week that I would end up on the deck. We waited until the lads had gone home before I sneaked into the tack room to try on the crash helmets for size. Sod's Law: Jonothan Lower saw me with the one I'd picked, but although he must have guessed something was afoot, he wisely kept quiet.

The beast Mart selected had the apt name of Fighter Pilot. He was by the stallion Warpath and just to keep the joke alive I was told he was bombproof. Mart tacked him up and rode the 400 yards to the gallops. For me, still safely in the seat of the Range Rover, it felt less of an adventure and more like a forfeit the nearer we got to the gallops.

I'm not joking, there was none of this gently gently stuff with Martin; he'd learned by the do-or-die method, so it had to be good enough for me too. The horse, give him his due, stood motionless while Mart somehow pushed me up and over the saddle then ran around the other side to stop me falling off before he'd even taken a single step. Mart told me just to sit

116

there for a while, get comfortable and relax. Relax! How the hell could I relax? My heart thought it was being tested to determine its upper limits. I made the mistake of looking down. I'd never realized how high horses are when you're on them. It's totally different when you're on the ground looking up. I thought: if I fall off now I'm really going to hurt myself, but before I could do anything about it Mart shouted at me to keep my hands down low, tuck the knees in and hold tight. Pull the reins if and when I wanted to stop.

That said, he leapt into the Range Rover to come upsides me, which Fighter Pilot took to mean time to move himself. I'd never sat on a donkey before, let alone a huge horse whose sole objective seemed to be breaking his own speed record. Amazingly I stayed on board, albeit by means of hanging on to the reins and mane like grim death, but by halfway up found myself quite enjoying the thrill. As the gallop is dead straight, applying the brakes was the biggest worry. As the end of the gallop loomed up Mart shouted out of the car window to pull on the reins, which the horse, for some inexplicable reason, took as a signal to go faster. I suppose I did it wrong. Anyway, with the big hedge at the end of the gallop getting too close for my health and Mart tearing along beside us, he shouted in desperation to let go of the reins. I did that, then grabbed the front of the saddle as the horse pulled up of his own accord to the relief of his trainer and, much more, me.

Mart imagined that had put paid to my riding aspirations, yet perversely the opposite turned out to be true. Once safely halted and still intact, a feeling of achievement, no, exhilaration swept over me and all I wanted to do was gallop again. All told, Fighter Pilot and I went up the strip seven times. He was definitely pleased to pull up by the end and, would you believe it, I got cocky enough to start crouching down low in the saddle like Lester Piggott while looking at my shadow for confirmation of my style.

After the horse had stopped blowing, Mart fetched his son David to come upsides me on another quiet horse. They go faster in company and the closer together they are the more it encourages them to quicken. I'm not sure if young David had orders to frighten the shit out of me but he did his best with tales of falls and jockeys in agony while we went up and down the gallop. David pointed out to me where he got bucked off, the horse dragged him right across to the fence and he thought it would be curtains for sure. But it had no effect on me; I thought I'd mastered the riding game.

Although I was stiff as blazes, I nevertheless insisted on learning to jump the next day and by then couldn't care less who watched. If walking was agony, when Mart threw me on board I could have screamed as the insides of both thighs felt like seized up shock-absorbers. Still, the pain would be well worth the thrills I expected jumping would provide.

Ever heard the saying 'pride goes before a fall'? How true. Let me at 'em, I shouted, where's them jumps? Everybody looked bemused except Mr Pipe senior who leaned over the gate effing and blinding because I had no helmet on and all the lads had come out to see the rising star.

My mount Fingale had the reputation of being blind or perhaps stupid, but as the jump stood barely eighteen inches high, it could have been fun for him as well as for me. It wasn't for either of us. He took one look at it, imagined the ground would open up beneath him and refused, throwing me onwards and upwards. The natural, and wrong, reaction is to put your hand out to protect yourself, which promptly snapped the wrist like a twig.

The lads were falling about laughing until I got up; then they saw the wrist had broken. The worst thing was, all this happened before a contracted table tennis exhibition at Weston Super Mare. I could hardly tell them the truth, so I rang up to say I'd stopped on the motorway to have a pee and had fallen down the bank. Mr Pipe didn't half rip into Mart and me, saying we weren't fit to be let loose together. He was right. Thus ended my race-riding career after only two days.

I harboured thoughts of a further attempt once I gave up playing exhibitions altogether, as the sensation of galloping had remained top of my list of enjoyable experiences. But in the end those pulsating memories remained just that, with my questionable wrist carriage a stern reminder of the other side of the job.

Being assistant trainer in my case means representing the stable most days at the races, as once things are really under way we often have runners at several meetings with Martin, Carol and myself heading the different teams. On other occasions it may be more prudent for Martin to stay at home concentrating on the horses being trained there while I do the business on the course.

The huge amount of miles I travel for the stable includes some helicopter trips, which naturally are a bonus. Or are they? The chopper certainly proved its worth in November 1991. It was one of the days when Mart stayed at home. We dropped Carol off at Stratford then flew on to Huntingdon, where we ran Sabin Du Loir against Desert Orchid and Norton's Coin. Naturally all the jumping enthusiasts flocked to little Huntingdon, jamming all the roads. From the air it was an incredible sight; even the tracks leading to the course were flowing with people. To me it looked like arteries pumping lifeblood to the heart, which in this case was a field in the middle of nowhere.

Sabin beat Dessie for the third time in a good race with the bulk of the crowd trying to melt away as soon as their hero went back to the racecourse stables, oblivious to the fact that there were two more races. We lifted off and had cleared Huntingdon in minutes, whereas a mate of mine who left at the same time by car took an hour to get out of the car park.

I'm not absolutely happy buzzing about the sky like a giant wasp, though. We've crashed twice already – well, had frights at least. The first time showed our mettle – we didn't have any! It was in the original chopper; we'd just taken off from the back garden and had reached the height of the house when it simply stopped. It dropped like a boulder and before it had stopped bouncing Mart and me were sprinting over the lawn. The pilot, Mike Perry, stayed seated, as calm as you like. I've heard of the captain not deserting the sinking ship but that was ridiculous. When he eventually joined us he quietly put it to us that he definitely would not have wanted to rely on our bravery in the trenches during the war. You can imagine, though, we thought it would be like *Hawaii Five O*, exploding on impact, showering the place with burning debris, including bits of us . . .

The other time, although less dramatic, could have been lethal just the same. We were at Cheltenham races soon after Mr Pipe had bought the jet helicopter. It had been a winning day, and a fair amount of champagne had been swallowed – in fact it was only our party that was keeping the bar open. It was almost dark when Mart phoned the pilot, who popped the chopper down next to the winning post. There were four of us passengers, all in that sort of silly, merry state a couple of wins and a couple of drinks generate. Carol was really giggly; but not for long.

The pilot flew down the track before veering off to circum-navigate the buildings and town. In doing so he unfortunately took the wire at the three-mile starting gate with him. Imagine the clatter as the dangling wire banged against the fuselage; worse still, if it had touched any electric cables or become entangled in the rotors David Pipe would have been the youngest trainer of a major string. No need to tell you we landed at once, piled out on to the dewy grass and thanked our lucky stars. Initially we refused to get back in after the wire had been unwrapped from the runners. Then Mart and Brian Jennings, one of the owners, succumbed while Carol and I insisted we'd get a lift home. Of course everyone else had departed long before, forcing us to capitulate – but only after the others had proved the vehicle's soundness with a five-minute test flight.

Those mishaps apart, the helicopter is a boon. It means the most important job, training the large majority at home, gets the attention of the man who makes the decisions. Remember, the horses actually racing on any given day cannot be helped further by the trainer; his job has been completed before they leave home. The chopper also enables us to use our stable jockey at two meetings which would otherwise be out of reach.

Lots of people think my job as assistant amounts to little more than that of court jester. The lads and girls would unques-tionably lose me regarding knowledge of the horses' make, shape and health, but I'm catching the best of them up fast. They take the mickey a bit because I don't ride and am obviously cautious towards horses, yet most of the staff are wary of me too, knowing full well how close I am to Martin. The newer ones who don't know my background or lack of horsy experience are quite respectful! None, though, take liberties. This is big business now, and I have other uses, even if it's only to keep Martin sane.

Generally, he takes the enormous pressures well. Imagine the demands of monitoring 166 horses, eighty-odd staff, hordes of owners and, not least, the press. He barely has a minute to himself and yet, because of his bookmaking upbringing, he refuses to ignore a ringing telephone. No matter what else he is doing, Martin Pipe is a slave to the phone. That's why his Monday evenings with the Lewises are important. He can lark about, be boyish if he wants, or simply chat away to people who want nothing more than his company. And no one can get at him.

The daily five-minute break around 11 o'clock is also a must, although increasingly those are interrupted by people wanting decisions. I do sometimes wonder if anyone can stand up indefinitely to the intensity of pressure Martin imposes on himself. Having said that, though, he is such a workaholic that I wonder whether anything less than what he's doing now could keep him satisfied. It's got to the stage where reverting to a smaller string would not stretch him enough, but keeping up the present productivity level could prove too much to shoulder.

Once or twice in the twelve years I've been involved here the whole thing has got to him. Once I got a call from his mum to say Mart had locked himself in his office in the house and refused to budge. Naturally I drove up there to put my oar in, but it took a couple of hours to talk him out. That incident made Martin realize he must force himself to relax, which is why he bought the flat in Brixham. He and Carol often nip down there after evening stables, spend a quiet night away from the incessant phone calls and are able to be back on duty by 7.30 a.m. the next day. It's not much, but it's enough to keep the lid on.

The *Cook Report* undermined Martin's confidence more than anyone could possibly have realized. He felt he was fighting for his professional life when he shouldn't have needed to. He could not understand why he was on public trial, what he'd done wrong. It cost a fortune in fees to defend himself. Why should he have to? They were even filming with a telephoto lens from behind hedges into the kitchen. We had them moved on, only to find them filming through the open garage doors into the conservatory. If that's not enough to make you jumpy, I don't know what is.

Occasionally Martin does moan about the demands of the job, then after watching the news on television we agree we've got it made compared to all those unfortunate people in the Third World with nothing to live for. He is a very sensitive person, and few people ever see that side of him.

Don't get me wrong, it's not all downs. Most of the time we're on a high; laughter is our strong point, we thrive on humour. And then, of course, there are the morning gallops to cheer us up. In the summer months, standing up the top of the strip in T-shirts watching the horses work while the skylarks are singing way above us we know this is the best job imaginable. It's equally enjoyable in the winter when it's frosty, with the horses steaming and their breath visible in the cold air. I look around thinking how marvellous it all is.

Then there is the fascination of watching horses come on as they get fitter. We often nudge each other when one has improved a bundle; planning a gamble keeps the blood flowing around the veins better than any pills. Horses go from being useless to looking distinctly decent with proper training. It's very satisfying.

The rise through the training ranks has happened so quickly that it's not surprising Mart has found it difficult at times to cope with the public relations side. Quite often he's misquoted in the papers, which causes no end of aggravation with the owners. When you think back, it is only since 1987 that he has lifted the roof off training boundaries previously thought impossible. He so wants to please owners that he turns himself inside out for them. Those who make it known they want real involvement certainly get more from Martin than most other trainers. He even changes gallops mornings around to suit their plans. We were earwigging Michael Dickinson at Haydock one day after an owner said to him he would be at the stables the following Wednesday to see his horses gallop and Michael replied, 'They work on Thursdays.' Mart's come from the back of beyond to being famous, yet in himself he's not changed a bit, although by nature he is always on the defensive.

Being totally immersed in racing leaves no time for other interests, which in turn makes him unaware of news or people in the rest of the world. Peter Shilton, the former England goalkeeper, phoned up the other Sunday to see how his horse was. Mart put his hand over the mouthpiece and asked the assembled company how many goals Shilton had scored the day before. We fell about laughing; he hadn't a clue what position Peter played. It was the same with England captain Bryan Robson when we went to Scu's *This Is Your Life* programme.

Martin was chatting to him when I heard him say to Bryan, 'It's lucky for you your dad's the manager of the England team, isn't it?' Bryan looked at me, smiled and said 'He's got a wicked sense of humour, hasn't he.' Honestly, Mart hasn't a clue about things outside racing and definitely would never set out to bullshit folks.

His meteoric rise has obviously dented other trainers' pride, and with the number of animals transferred to him from rival yards improving or regaining long-lost form, there is little love lost between the Wellington Wizard and many of his colleagues. They all chat away to me, yet few of them will talk to Mart. After Chatam had won the Hennessy Cognac Gold Cup at Newbury, David Barons approached me to say well done. He was at the last fence and couldn't believe his eyes as the horse was still running away. Brilliant training performance, that's terrific, he said, and he seemed genuine enough; but he would not speak to Martin.

I just think he's not one of their sort. He's not grown up with the horsy set, he's not one of them. It's been said several times that he's made them all look amateurish. That's not true, of course, but Martin has definitely removed most of the former excuses for losers. They are not amateurs – well, some of them are – but he has turned the game upside down. It used to be quite a cosy set-up, jobs for the boys; the Lambourn clique had things to themselves.

Quite a few trainers sent their head men down to have a look around on our open day. Good luck to them. David Nicholson actually asked to have a guided tour when Scu left him. Martin did so willingly; and only a couple of seasons ago he let him off the hook after David had threatened our young jockey Martin Foster. The stewards sent for Martin and Carol who decided not to pursue the matter, thus defusing a potentially explosive situation. The stewards thanked them afterwards and Nicholson, realizing he had been wrong bullying the kid, apologized. That is Martin, though; he would help anyone rather than harm them.

There is little doubt that Chester Barnes plays an important part in the Pond House set-up, and it is equally certain that he would not fit in as readily with any of the more traditional trainers. Yet as a sounding board to Martin Pipe I cannot think of anyone who could fill the role better. The cocky Cockney may have had his feathers trimmed when Fingale taught him what the Thoroughbred can really be like, but happily Chester rose above that adversity as he has done over many others. He's good at bouncing back.

Chapter 13

Buying Right

Over the last few years the pattern of Pipe's string has changed dramatically, with quality supplementing quantity at Pond House. But for all that, bulk victories still give the trainer a lot of pleasure, particularly when they come from sows' ears turned into silk purses. From the outset Martin's operation has revolved around cast-offs, runts, problem horses and rogues. Now he has graduated to a better class of Flat-race cull at the Newmarket Tattersalls horses-in-training sales, and has relentlessly farmed the growing number of claiming races to obtain well bred instant runners. These races are framed explicitly to provide an opening for trainers to handicap their horses by the value they put on them. The higher the trainer's valuation of his runner, the more weight it will carry. Astute handlers can win and at the same time sell a horse on at an acceptable price. Another opportunity they provide is for trainers with limited funds to spot the horses they can improve. Pipe works both avenues.

Pipe
The diminutive and apparently moderate My Dominion is a good example of the way I think when looking for horses to improve. Chester and I stayed at Doncaster the night before the 1984 October sales to examine the early arrivals on our list of six possibles. We had selected these from a catalogue of three hundred or more and picked them initially on racecourse performance.

A pre-sale reconnaissance provides ample time to examine,

observe and form an opinion of prospective purchases before the crush on sale day. Several on our list did not arrive until the morning of the auction, but at least by then we had crossed off three of the possibles on the grounds of bad conformation or suspected problems. With only two horses to evaluate on sale morning, we were able to devote all our energy and time to them. If they met our requirements the most important job was to price them correctly. I do give myself some leeway as regards the worth of any horse, but not much. This stems from my bookmaking upbringing; sticking to value will always pay dividends in the long term.

In My Dominion's case it was his athleticism that attracted us, rather than his form or conformation. Small, workmanlike and from a sprinting family, the colt had already been sold twice before, as a foal for 3,500 guineas and as a yearling for 4,100 guineas. He had not been sighted in five starts from Peter Easterby's stable as a two-year-old, including selling plates. Despite that, I loved him. He strode out like a real athlete, and the moment I clapped eyes on him I told Chester he'd be mine provided the bidding went no further than 1,500 guineas.

No one seemed the least bit interested in him in the ring, which prompted the auctioneer to plummet to what I thought was the minimum bid of 500 guineas. Just as I started to raise my hand he asked in desperation for only 300 guineas and he was mine for a maiden bid. My first reaction was dread. Something must be missing. Did he have all four legs? I must surely be drastically wrong for no one else to fancy him, even if only as a child's pony. Chester compounded my sense of woe by immediately declining the offer to take half of my purchase for £150, saying I must have been totally mad to have bought it. I scrutinized at length the little colt I was now lumbered with, but could find nothing amiss; likewise when the horse arrived at Nicholashayne.

I gave My Dominion a year out at grass, then tried in vain to sell him to my friend Michael Beard. When that avenue closed there was only one course of action open to me: to race the horse myself. As he had cost me so little I had nothing to lose by running the horse, and if he turned out to be absolutely useless as a racehorse, he should make £1,000 as a girl's hack now that he had grown a little.

First time out in August 1985, the horse ran at Newton Abbot with Jonothan Lower on board starting at 25–1 – the same price as another of our debutants, Miss Kewmill, ridden by Mark Pitman. The third stable runner in the race, Preordination, under Paul Leach, went off 2–1 favourite, having already won six days earlier. The favourite won easily enough from Miss Kewmill, with My Dominion finishing in the next parish without having been asked a serious question. Reading between the lines, one of the regular West Country bookmakers congratulated me as I scuttled to greet the winner, adding out of the corner of his mouth, 'I should think you'd also be delighted with the one that finished nearly last.'

A week later My Dominion ran in the world's worst selling hurdle at Devon and Exeter, in which I again fielded three of the five runners. This time Lower rode newcomer Kilcha Girl, with Leach on The Bru and Pitman on My Dominion. All three were told to do their best, although none was expected to beat Jimmy Frost on Optimosa. Mark held up My Dominion in the early stages, joined the issue at the final flight and went away to beat Kilcha Girl by two and a half lengths. Not surprisingly, no one bid for the winner and none present then, including me, the owner–trainer, could have forecast the improvement to come.

Beaten favourite in another seller under Leach next time out and a modest fourth at Worcester in similar company gave little indication of what was to come next. My Dominion won five of his following six outings, escalating in class from a Fontwell seller in which he showed wayward tendencies, dodging to both right and left on the run-in, to the competitive twenty-three-runner Tote Credit Hurdle at Newbury, worth over £10,000 to the winner. He also ran with distinction at the Cheltenham Festival and then finished third at the big Aintree meeting. In all, the 300 guineas purchase won over £20,000 that season, and was sold to the sport's emerging big spender, Terry Ramsden, for £20,000.

Working the Japanese securities market meant Ramsden kept odd hours, making contact difficult at best and impossible at other times. He surrounded himself with a team of minders headed by a personal bodyguard who weighed in at twenty-four stone. Unable to get past the human deflectors to my new owner, who had already made it quite clear he wanted to win the Tote Credit Hurdle at Newbury with the Wilf Storey-trained Santopadre, I drove all the way to Doncaster racecourse specifically to persuade Ramsden to allow me also to run My Dominion in the valuable contest.

Twenty-three went to post with Santopadre starting as 5–1 co-favourite with Wide Boy, ridden by Peter Scudamore. My Dominion went off at 7–1 under his then regular partner Jonothan Lower, who still claimed the 7lb riding allowance. Scu showed prominently on Wide Boy to the first hurdle but after that was never in with a chance. Santopadre moved through to lead three hurdles from home, then retreated as quickly as he had challenged as My Dominion rallied after the final flight to go away for a two-and-a-half-length victory.

I remain proud of that win for several reasons. It vindicated the 'feel' I initially had when first setting eyes on the horse at Doncaster sales. My evaluation that the seemingly useless two-year-old looked like an athlete had been proved correct and I had improved the horse throughout the season. Finally, and probably most important at that stage of my career, that win, after I had put my head on the chopping-block by insisting he run justified my confidence and vindicated my judgement.

Carol's assertion that I only bought the horse because the girl leading it around at the sales winked at me was naturally refuted.

Ramsden sent his purchase to Matt McCourt the following season, when he showed little form against a clutch of good horses before finishing last of twelve at Lingfield in December. A leg problem kept him off the course for the rest of the term and when he next appeared in public eleven months later, it was for another of Ramsden's trainers, Rod Simpson. My Dominion ran thirteen times during the winter of 1987–8, recording a solitary success at Kempton Park for Tom Kemp, his fifth trainer in four years. One outing the next season and four the following campaign saw the little chap once more in the sales ring at Ascot. This time he attracted a bid of 1,400 guineas. I did go to the sales to buy him back, but that price seemed rather too much for retirement. Happily he went to a good home; although I do feel responsible in some way for my old horses, you cannot keep them all.

Another example of the phenomenal improvement horses can make is that of the sprint-bred Cat's Eyes who, unraced on the Flat, fetched a mere 1,000 guineas at Doncaster's 1983 August sales to a bid from Iain Campbell. No worthwhile form from four juvenile hurdles in 1983–4 saw the gelding demoted to selling class at Devon and Exeter in November after falling on his seasonal reappearance at Fontwell Park.

In winning the Rabbit Novices Selling Hurdle easing down by thirty lengths the winner naturally attracted a deal of interest at the subsequent auction, eventually being knocked down to Les Kennard for 3,400 guineas. Les, who was still training at the time, acted for me as my selling race purchases were attracting too much interest from other trainers, which inflated the price. I in turn was filling an order and passed the greyhound-like gelding on to Pauline Fasey.

Cat's Eyes had impressed me so much when beating that admittedly very moderate field that I knew there were better things to come even if I could not improve him. What's more, he could go on straight away, which eliminated that interminable and costly education period we have to go through when buying unbroken horses. At the very worst Pauline would not need to wait long to know the truth about her new purchase. As it turned out she only had to wait three weeks. Cat's Eyes enjoyed five more wins from only seven starts for his new connections that season, netting almost £22,000 to add to the incalculable thrill of winning. Victory came at such diverse courses as Newton Abbot, Devon and Exeter (twice) and Fontwell Park before he lined up in the final of the Malden Timber Hurdle at Aintree. He was asked to shoulder joint top weight of 11st 10lb, and still won, under a copy-book ride from Paul Leach, going away by two lengths. On the two occasions Cat's Eyes suffered defeat from our yard that season his performance could without a doubt be put down to racing on a faster surface than he liked.

The majority of regular racing folk seem to be superstitious to some degree and I am no exception. I have an aversion to green, though this means forgetting how successful the predominantly green colours of Jersey-based owner Brian Kilpatrick have been with the likes of Sabin Du Loir and Aquilifer. So when Pauline Fasey turned up at Newton Abbot to see Cat's Eyes run from our stable for the first time, I was aghast to see her wearing an emerald green suit. Knowing Pauline well enough to tell her my fears, I asked if she would go back home to change.

It is hardly surprising that my superstition was reinforced

when Cat's Eyes bolted up by twelve lengths to be greeted by a jubilant Pauline, resplendent in a mainly blue dress. Obviously there is far more to training winners than avoiding a particular colour, seeing two magpies, a chimney sweep or a load of straw, wearing red socks or shirt, crossing a bridge while a train is going under it or standing in the same spot in parade rings before races (just a small selection of the superstitions of our leading trainers), but if these little foibles help us keep calm before a race our being indulged can only be a good thing.

Cat's Eyes continued to hold his form, improving physically as he aged. As a six-year-old he filled the bridesmaid's spot in Ireland's biggest timber race, the Sweeps Hurdle at Leopardstown, finishing six lengths behind Bonalma. Staying with hurdles at the age of seven, the gelding visited the winner's enclosure at no less a course than Cheltenham when taking the Spa Hurdle. Put over fences at eight, he rekindled the winning spirit in no uncertain fashion, taking first prizes at Taunton, Fontwell, Uttoxeter and Chepstow, as well as finishing second on his only other three starts. A game second at the Cheltenham Festival marked the last public appearance of this former selling hurdler. He died at summer grass at his owner's farm.

All trainers prefer to buy the horses they are to handle, yet of those sent to stables by breeders or owners none but the scrag ends will ever be refused, as winners come in very different guises. My view on this subject is clear cut: I don't mind how moderate a horse seems to be, I'll have a go at winning with it as long as the owner gives me freedom to place it in races of my choice. In fact, I still get a lot of satisfaction from winning with a bad horse. Last season I was asked to take three horses from other yards that had finished seventh, eighth and ninth in a nine-runner selling hurdle. It's a challenge to try to improve horses. Still, the problem of pride is sometimes a hard one to get over. I buy a horse because I think it will do a job, and so does everyone else. They are our babies, we automatically assume they will turn out to be good and find it hard to accept when they do not live up to expectations.

Brian Kilpatrick is my idea of the ideal owner to work with. Most of his horses came to me from other stables, having lost form or with leg problems. There was no pressure in that situation. More recently he has sent lovely untried young horses bought from the renowned talent-spotter and breeder Jeremy Maxwell in Northern Ireland. One of them, which he called Terao, is the biggest and heaviest horse I have trained, and that includes Carvill's Hill. Obviously this type of animal is totally different to the sort I have most often worked with. Instead of the fit, battle-hardened horses off the Flat ready to go on, these huge purpose-bred chasers need plenty of time to grow into their strength. They alter amazingly quickly when nature decides it's time, which leads me to think that all the stories you hear that such and such a youngster had been galloped and found to be useless as a three-year-old are rubbish. Terao weighed 620 kilos when he arrived. We were all excited; he was the sort you associate with proper trainers, not me. By Furry Glen out of an unraced daughter of the good racemare Grangewood Girl, he is bred to win a Cheltenham Gold Cup and if he steers clear of injury he could well do so.

Such heights looked very remote when he started working seriously. He was the slowest boat in the yard and, believe me, we've got a few. I told Mr Kilpatrick to forget he even owned this one and that if and when he eventually showed us he could go fast enough to get out of his own way, we'd take him to the races. For the life of me I could not hazard a guess when that would be.

For most of the 1990–1 season I kept moaning to his handler Dawn Foster that her charge was useless, too weak to get on the course. Then, during the second half of March, Dawn repeatedly told me Terao felt as if he was getting stronger. I replied that if he was, it did not show from where I stood. Within a fortnight the gelding had come on sufficiently to take to the course without disgracing me or embarrassing the owner. A National Hunt flat race at Uttoxeter on 2 April presented the ideal opening. The company was not too hot, the track with its long straights was right for a big horse, and Uttoxeter was far enough from home to prevent my friends from seeing him if he did show me up.

I told Mr Kilpatrick that Terao had no chance of winning but that the experience could only do him good. As we were also running John Fairbrother's Rastannora up there, the transport cost would not be too high; in fact, everything seemed to fit in well. With more pressing things to attend to among the mass of horses at home than the pair at Uttoxeter, I listened to the commentary on the phone in my living room.

As Terao turned for home, leading the rest by ten lengths, I looked at Carol and said, 'He'll stop now, the sharper sorts are probably happy to be getting a lead from him.' Quite the opposite happened; my overgrown baby galloped on strongly to win by twelve lengths with the other dozen runners strung out over several hundred yards. I honestly had a job to believe it. This horse is the sort most of the top trainers have bought for years, but to me it is only the start and quite different from the sort I have made my name with.

On the subject of body-weight I hold very definite views. My horses carry no excess flesh and are not asked to race until they are fit enough to win, except in cases of immaturity where a backward youngster needs the harsh reality of a visit to the racecourse to wake him up. My methods of cantering every day, regular swimming and total control of the feed intake ensures the equine athletes carry only muscle, not fat. I consider it bad management when people allow horses to put on as much as 60 to 100 kilos during their summer breaks. It is the same as letting me loose in a chocolate factory, I'd eat myself silly just for the sake of it. It's madness to let horses put on huge amounts of weight; it simply puts undue strain on their legs, heart and lungs, costing the owner a great deal in training fees to get the horses back to the condition they were in before their holiday.

Of course horses need breaks to thrive, like we do, but it can be achieved without letting them gorge themselves. Rationing the time spent on lush grass or turning horses out in the modern movable wiremesh playpens has the effect of mentally resting them while restraining their grass intake.

Another reason I have against the usual three-month summer period in a field is the inordinately high injury rate when they are turned out. Certainly more serious injuries have happened to mine in the field than anywhere else.

Chapter 14

Baron Blakeney: Now We Belong

When the 66–1 iron grey colt Baron Blakeney outran the 7–4 favourite Broadsword to snatch the 1981 Daily Express Triumph Hurdle at Cheltenham, it surprised everyone except the winner's connections. This victory started Martin off as a trainer of big-race winners; it seems incredible now that it was only the forty-second winner of his seven-season career and his eleventh of that term. Those statistics put Pipe's supposedly meteoric rise to the top into perspective; and it would be another five years before the big push to an even higher level.

As is so often the case with good horses, Baron Blakeney found his way to Nicholashayne through a sequence of events which can best be described as fate.

Pipe
Chester Barnes, who had just tasted the initial pleasure of ownership and was still glowing with the comfort of having his Carrie Ann coup winnings accumulating interest in the building society, had his mind set on buying Ravens Tower at the Newmarket December sales. This colt, trained by Bill Marshall, had won as a two-year-old then been placed eight times on the Flat over a mile the following season. Trevor Taylor, the six times Commonwealth table tennis champion who plays exhibitions with Chester and spends all day buried in the form book for his £2 bets, had noted the colt's consistency and suggested I bought it for Chester.

It's a long way from Brixham to Newmarket and when you spend all day waiting and watching only not to have enough money to reach the horse's reserve price in the ring, you've got to have a crack at the owner afterwards. Chester, himself a Londoner, knew of Bob Wheatley, who owned pubs in the East End and nightclubs in Essex. When we found him in the bar Bob, shadowed by a minder, was arguing with his trainer Bill Marshall. Chester dived straight in, introduced himself and asked if we could do a deal about Ravens Tower. Fired up by his row, Bob at first ignored the request but then asked if he'd already got a trainer. Chester proudly told him that I trained horses for him in the West Country, to which Bob said I could have Ravens Tower and another one called Baron Blakeney to train for him. I needed no second invitation, told the new owner my stables were near Bristol, which was stretching a point slightly, and clinched the deal.

Weighing up the changing situation I grabbed Mark Reeves, the horse transporter, removed two of my own earlier purchases and went around to see the two unexpected additions feeling all of twelve feet tall. Baron Blakeney in my book was a proper racehorse rated 78 by the official Flat handicapper, higher than any back at home. As soon as I entered the colt's stable I saw that the dream horse was lame, but determined not to be sidetracked or risk losing a new owner, I contented myself with a signed note from Baron Blakeney's attendant stating his condition and hightailed it home to Pond House, a good sixty-five miles south of Bristol.

As it turned out, I was right to move with speed. When Bob Wheatley got back to London his friends wound him up, saying I was Bill Marshall's cousin who trained from a row of tin sheds in the middle of nowhere. Bob was on the phone before I got home to say he'd be down the next day to inspect the place. At that time, December 1980, the facilities were a far cry from today's; even so, Pond House was built and the main yard boasted recent coatings of black and white paint; it was more than enough to put Bob's mind at rest.

Baron Blakeney's lameness turned out to be a general morning stiffness, wearing off as exercise progressed. He was also a box-walker, a horse who continually walks around his stable instead of resting, often only stopping long enough to grab a mouthful of feed in passing. This can be detrimental on two counts. First, the animal can put extra stress on one leg if continually going in one direction; secondly, it may sap its energy so much in its nervous state that it runs out of steam in its work. Sometimes introducing another animal as a companion can calm a box-walker down. Sheep, goats, small ponies, even white rabbits have been used to settle worriers. My approach, however, is based on exactly the opposite belief. I think horses develop this condition because it is inherent in their nature, and to change it can rob the horse of its character, perhaps including the attribute that enables it to win. I arrived at this conclusion after attempting another well-tried cure with Baron Blakeney, namely filling the stable full of objects to restrict the inmate's movement and to give it something to occupy its mind. Footballs dangling from strings, a tree trunk or several lorry tyres placed on the floor combine to make a horse think instead of relentlessly pacing the stable. Having tried this, as well as various methods, on the colt, Baron Blakeney looked so dejected that I feared I would destroy the colt's will to race. I felt very sorry for him and as a result came to the overall decision to let horses express their characters.

It's the same with those who try to run away with a rider; fighting them simply uses up valuable energy. Naturally you have to attempt to control a runaway, but without a direct battle. We've generally found horses settle better in front than being strangled behind the pack.

The Bob Wheatley pair's initial outings produced differing results. Ravens Tower turned out to be a lunatic with no brakes or steering. Prior to joining me he went berserk at Ascot then broke loose, all but knocking over the Queen. Ron Atkins came in for the unenviable task of riding him on his hurdling debut at Wincanton where, forewarned of his suicidal tendencies at home, he did not try particularly hard to prevent the colt running out at the first flight.

That incident led directly to Paul Leach getting and grasping his opportunity with us, lured by the chance of getting on Baron Blakeney if he first accepted the task of wrestling with Ravens Tower in public. The less attractive part of that deal came at Leicester in January; the pair at least completed the course without injury to themselves or anybody, though Ravens Tower patently failed to stay the trip. The colt never did manage to win over hurdles. For Chester, this removed any lingering regrets he may have felt at not having acquired the horse, and for Paul it meant a passport to better things. For Bob Wheatley and myself, it was merely a dent in the relationship. Baron Blakeney had already performed with credit on his hurdling debut at Devon and Exeter when second under Mark Floyd, encouraging, if not exactly cementing, the new owner–trainer partnership.

It was a partnership, incidentally, for which I had cause to be grateful a few years later when on 23 May 1985 at Taunton we reached for the first time the total of fifty winners in a season. We'd got to the forty-nine mark the evening before at Newton Abbot with Bob's The Liquidator and he would not hear of any other horse than Carado being number fifty. Unknown to me, he arranged for a local bakery to decorate a huge cake in his colours congratulating me on the win with his mare, phoned the Western Daily Press to alert them to the fact that the milestone would be reached, and told all our friends to make sure they attended the meeting.

All these arrangements went on behind my back and although Carado was a certainty, a mistake two hurdles from home saw Paul Leach unable to make his challenge until a few strides from the finish to win by an inch. If the race had been a bit shorter or the mistake worse, Bob's cake would have been left to melt on the back seat of his Roller!

As it was, he presented it to me in the winner's circle and everybody cheered us, pleased to witness our pleasure. There was no jealousy in those days and as we shared our celebration with everyone in the bar the whole thing went down well. Can you imagine the comments if we pulled a similar stunt now? 'Big headed' would be one of the more repeatable! I genuinely miss those days . . .

Bob has strong views on where and when his horses will run, so the occasion of his birthday on 1 January presented as good a reason as any to watch Baron Blakeney flex his muscles on the course. I had been emphatic that the colt was some way short of race fitness and after this good first attempt felt we actually did have a racehorse. 'Hope springs eternal' is every owner's motto, and Bob has always possessed a double helping of that. A second in a hurdling debut at Devon and Exeter would not usually merit dreams of a Triumph Hurdle victory, yet to this owner long-held convictions were being well fuelled.

The grey ran nine days later at Sandown Park, at that time an unusual venue for one of my horses. I went to saddle Carrie Ann at Haydock, entrusting Carol to represent the stable at Sandown. In those days, like everyone else we held our runners up in mid-division to challenge from two hurdles out. Ron Atkins replaced Floyd on the grey, who jumped brilliantly and gained lengths at every obstacle, only to forfeit that ground as Ron pulled him back into his designated position. Eventually Baron Blakeney faded to finish a creditable ninth of the twenty-two runners.

An hour earlier at the same meeting, Broadsword had won the more prestigious Tolworth Hurdle, confirming his position at the head of the Triumph Hurdle ante-post market. On the face of it, our dreams of a Cheltenham victory were no more than that, until Carol reported that we should ignore the Sandown result, Baron Blakeney having thrown away as much ground as he had been beaten by. It was decided there and then to make more use of him in future. With the benefit of six weeks' swimming and on other occasions being ridden out up to four times a day, the stuffy colt was able to turn around that January performance completely.

Remember we had started out with a lame animal only three weeks prior to the horse's first outing. When he next appeared after Sandown for his third run for us at Wincanton he was a very different proposition. The colt was ridden by Paul Leach for the first time, his reward for taking on and mastering the wayward Ravens Tower. In winning the modest Mere Maiden Hurdle, worth just £414, the colt hardly posed a live threat to the market leaders for Cheltenham. A week later, though, under a 10lb penalty, he comprehensively overturned the odds-on Lutanist at Worcester, at least earning his place among the best of the juvenile hurdlers.

For Nicholson and Scudamore, both of whom were experiencing a barren run at the Festival, the 7–4 favourite Broadsword looked the ideal saviour. Baron Blakeney, on the other hand, was freely available at 66–1. As the Triumph Hurdle is always contested by a big field of horses culled from Flat racing, there is invariably a strong pace on from the start. This consideration prompted me to alter my recently adopted front-running plans, and I instructed Paul to bide his time before joining the action up the famous Cheltenham hill.

The rider had little difficulty obeying orders. A large bunch of horses still had pretensions two hurdles from home, with the Irish fancy Mansky marginally in front of Tie Anchor and Fledge. Broadsword maintained relentless progress on their heels, looking likely to justify favouritism. At that point Baron Blakeney also had an ideal position to strike from, yet long-priced horses do not pose the same threat in the eyes of spectators unless they are in front with only yards to run. It is a human failing among the majority of racegoers to be influenced by price instead of their own eyes and intuitions. After all, a horse's odds are the general consensus of bookies' and punters' opinions, and they may not be in possession of all the facts. This race proved a prime example of the bulk of the industry being blinded by fashion. At that time I rated little in general equations and even less in championship races. As I had told my confidants, Baron Blakeney would have started at far shorter odds if trained by Winter, Walwyn or Gifford.

Having said that, though, as the principals headed up the hill 7–4 looked quite generous about Broadsword having taken the leader's measure on the run to the last flight. Our horse continued to improve his position, albeit under pressure, some three lengths adrift, with Paul forced to dig deep into his basic riding skills to see him home having lost his whip shortly after the second-last hurdle. Riding with hands and heels Paul slowly overhauled Broadsword to take our first major race by a convincing three-quarters of a length. Paul, aware a whipless second would not have been greeted with much enthusiasm, was the most relieved man at Prestbury Park. For supporters of the anti-whip campaign, this win is valuable evidence of the velvet glove, admittedly not intentional, gaining the day over the iron fist.

To win this major contest gave us a whole new sensation. We felt at last we really did belong, we could do what our heroes did given the same material. Now we were, by our own definition, 'proper trainers'. And besides boosting the stable's confidence, that victory laid the ground for the increasing number of winners that were to follow.

Baron Blakeney had been a consistent performer on the Flat, winning over a mile and a half at Leicester as a three-year-old under Lester Piggott before running well over longer distances in soft ground. His breeding suggested he should have been a better horse on the Flat than his Newmarket sale tag of 7,800 guineas suggests. That figure is misleading, as he had in fact been bought in by Bob Wheatley, whose reserve valued the colt at 20,000 guineas. The advantage of buying horses with proven staying form in soft ground was suddenly very clear. At best they did the job, provided they jumped, in a very short time, being fit and hardened to racing. At worst, they quickly showed further investment was pointless and, as we all know, the first loss is the smallest. Turnover has long been my policy, which in 1991 seemed to be the one thing the *Cook Report* successfully hung on me, choosing misleadingly to label it as 'wastage', which it certainly is not.

Baron Blakeney met six of the Cheltenham runners again at Aintree on his only other start of the season in the Sean Graham Hurdle. On a tighter, easier track with faster underfoot conditions and with the added blessing of a weight advantage, it was no surprise to see Broadsword again favourite. This time his supporters recouped their losses. Staying on to the death to fill third place, Baron Blakeney lost nothing in defeat, stamping himself as an above-average hurdler a fraction short of Champion Hurdle class.

Following such a good season over timber, the colt reverted to the Flat, where he took Epsom's two-and-a-quarter-mile Great Metropolitan Handicap under Steve Cauthen. I felt like a schoolboy employing a headmaster when giving the American his orders. I had then, and to a lesser degree still have now, a genuine inferiority complex. In these days, with four trainers' championships under my belt, it may seem odd, but you cannot change your nature.

Baron Blakeney's most exciting run over fences, by far, came at Aintree over the Mildmay course. I can recall it clearly. He galloped with such zest, jumped at speed with a rare accuracy for a novice and galloped a future Gold Cup winner, Forgive 'N' Forget, and a future Grand National winner, West Tip, into submission. The exertion caused a lacklustre performance from both himself and West Tip in the Midlands National, but by then Bob

Wheatley had big plans for generations of his sons and daughters running on British racecourses so Baron Blakeney retired to the enviable if arduous task of mating with fifty or more fillies and mares each stud season.

The tough, talented grey who won on the Flat, over hurdles and over fences at Grade One courses has not yet passed on his better genes to his offspring, but it can be a slow job making a jumping stallion's reputation. Last season, however, Pipe trained Spring To It, bred by the author and wife Mandy, to five wins in six outings – Pipe's first Baron Blakeney offspring to do so well. He is starting to make the grade now, but regardless of what he achieves at stud he remains the horse who put a small West Country trainer on the first rung of the ladder which has since grown like Jack's beanstalk.

Chapter 15

Paul Leach, Our First Stable Jockey

Paul Leach, a tall, stylish rider, had enjoyed seven successful seasons with Kingsbridge trainer David Barons before he slipped into the job with Martin Pipe at the end of the 1981–2 season. Strange as it may seem now, at the time it looked like a retrograde step. Barons had been producing between fifty and seventy winners each season, with Leach partnering anything up to forty of them.

Martin's and Paul's careers initially took very different routes. In 1974–5, when Pipe recorded his first success, Leach drew a blank. Twelve months later the story had changed; Pipe's score was five, and Leach's nineteen. There seemed little doubt then as to which of the two was making the bigger ripple in the West Country.

During the intervening seasons before their paths converged Paul kicked home 119 winners, including Bootlaces, the 20–1 winner of the prestigious Schweppes Gold Trophy at Newbury in February 1980. In the same period Martin managed only forty-five victories.

Pipe
When Paul rode the lunatic Ravens Tower, his first mount for me, he had been lured by the prospect of also partnering the obviously better Baron Blakeney. His rides for the Barons stable were already starting to dry up slightly; it is the same in any walk of life, when the blue-eyed boy starts to lose his hue, he is usually the last to recognize the familiar pattern. The racing press had bandied about a link between us and Paul which did not in fact exist. True, he had just won the Daily Express Triumph Hurdle

on Baron Blakeney for us, but we never dreamed he'd consider joining the stable as Barons was a much bigger fish. I suppose those reports prompted Barons to sever the partnership before Paul gave in his notice. It left the rider out on a limb, though, as we had not offered him a job nor even considered doing so at that time. However, once Paul explained his position we were pleased to take him on as stable jockey. To our little set-up he was a champion.

Paul moved into the main house with myself and Carol for the first year of the partnership. It worked out well at the start. We had great fun together, with Paul on eleven of our twenty winners in the 1981–2 season. But bearing in mind that Carol, myself, our son David, Mum and Dad all worked to one end, the production of winners, Paul's input off the racecourse proved disappointing. He'd already done his share of yard work and tractor driving before he joined us, so I suppose he thought all that was behind him. But here everyone had to earn their corn – and still does.

A bonny little horse called Corporal Clinger became our first major winner together (Barons' Triumph victory was basically a spare ride for Paul). The gelding's first outing, though, went sadly amiss. The horse had been in training with Roger Fisher in Cumbria, running for a partnership between himself and a handsome Greek called Steph Stephano. Corporal Clinger had won two fair handicaps on the Flat before joining Fisher, but on his hurdling debut for the pair at Wetherby received a blow to his fetlock joint and had to be pulled up after only three hurdles. Having bought out Fisher's share, Steph sent the gelding to Pond House to race under the name of Jay Dee Racing Ltd, unaware the horse would not be able to run for some time.

A long rest at grass prescribed by the vet, the late Bill Walter, put the injury right. Steph, a real charmer according to Carol, wanted to get his money back first time out, putting pressure on me to come up with the goods. That grabbed me; I absolutely thrive on that sort of directive. The horse gave us the right vibes at home, indicating he was ready to do the business at Wincanton by the end of November 1983. The eager owner was alerted, the money placed away from the course so not to affect the starting price, Paul Leach was tuned in to the fact that this was not just a day out and I put the finishing touch to the plans.

142

To put people off the scent I purposely left him unclipped; he was a small horse anyway, and this made him look like a pit pony. Remember he had pulled up in his only previous race ten months earlier and looked a complete disgrace the way he was turned out. No one in their right mind would give him a second glance, let alone back him. To complete the set-up I stayed away from Wincanton, Carol doing the honours instead. In those days people thought if a trainer did not go to the races, his horse was not fancied. In this case, though, there was a second and far more valid reason for my absence. This was a local track, and there would be a lot of people attending who knew Dad or me and were sure to ask if Corporal Clinger would win. Being brought up to tell the truth, I could not willingly tell a lie; but the job had been set up for the horse's owner to have a gamble, and it would not be fair to Steph if half the racecourse reaped the benefit. After all, they hadn't paid anything towards his keep over the past year when he'd been injured.

The gamble on Corporal Clinger excited me and Steph smiled at the starting price of 14–1, safe in the knowledge that hiding underneath the unimposing, woolly-haired exterior was a highly charged athlete. The smile was still in place after a mile and a half, when things seemed to be going according to plan, then evaporated when the expected explosion of speed failed to materialize. The horse faded from the second-last hurdle to finish a twelve lengths fourth to Prideaux Boy, trained by Graham Roach. Not just beaten; slaughtered. That was my reaction. Steph naturally let me know his true feelings and I agreed with him. I was useless.

In retrospect the race turned out to be above average for a novice hurdle but, more to the point, the horse was not as fit as I had thought. Rarely has that been the case since. Without attempting to gloss over the sorry affair I took all the blame and Steph accepted my assurance that the lost money should be considered a loan to the bookies. We then planned the retrieving mission.

Two weeks after the Wincanton debacle, Hereford's Grey Bomber Novice Hurdle presented an ideal opening in a race restricted to four-year-olds. Our certainty bolted in at 10–1 under Paul Leach, who produced Corporal Clinger at the final flight before drawing away to beat previous winner Kilsyth by an easy eight lengths. Opting to strike again quickly, we doubled up at Haydock Park nine days later with Chester Barnes entrusted to put Steph's wager on at the course. Another facile victory; but the post-race celebrations were dampened somewhat when bookmaker Len da Costa claimed Chester had put £100 on the winner, not £1,000. Despite the intervention of the Jockey Club's Betting Intelligence Officer, the matter went to Tattersalls, who arbitrate in all such disputes. Da Costa offered to settle before the hearing providing Chester accepted half his claim, which in itself would have been an admission of defeat. Chester declined and got his due from the tribunal.

The following season Corporal Clinger fooled me again, once more needing his first outing to put the finishing touch to his fitness. At that time I did not set enough store by the behaviour patterns of mature horses. Their preferred times of the year and the number of races they can take are two of many factors that need to be established. Reappearing on 12 December, he finished fifth, nine lengths behind Graham Thorner's useful Triple Jump under 10st 11lb. This was a fair mark in my opinion; I thought more of him than that and was delighted the handicapper had not got his measure. The next month, in a lesser contest, he came back to form, scoring in workmanlike fashion by a length at Windsor. A ten-week rest and the gelding won at Cheltenham under the cheekiest of rides from Paul.

Despite wasting hard, Paul put up 3lb overweight on his old pal in the season's final big hurdle, the Swinton Insurance Trophy at Haydock. This, on top of the 11lb overnight rise in weights, in effect meant the gelding ran a stone above the official handicapper's evaluation. He proceeded to laugh at officialdom as well as a high-class field to win by three-quarters of a length from our close friend and neighbour Les Kennard's Statesmanship. Paul and I had certainly consolidated our partnership in style.

In 1985–6 the little liver chestnut turned out four times, every one at Cheltenham. Two good victories and a second saw Corporal Clinger start at 11–1 second favourite in the Champion Hurdle behind the triple winner of the hurdling crown See You Then. His terrible fall in that race injured him so badly it was thought he might never race again; worse still, he might not survive at all. It speaks volumes for the horse's resilience that he

144

returned to Cheltenham nine months later – but only to fall again at the second hurdle.

From the outset Corporal Clinger had showed a bravery in tackling the obstacles that bordered on self destructiveness, and sure enough a neck defeat in Ireland was followed by another tumble at Sandown Park. His final run in the Champion Hurdle placed the over-brave jumper marginally below that class, but he had definitely left his mark.

Peter Scudamore replaced Paul for the last two rides on Corporal Clinger in the 1986–7 season, which proved to be Paul's last as a jockey. The writing had been on the wall for a little while; now it became clearer.

Jonothan Lower had proved more than value for his riding allowance and was obviously in favour. When a young jockey is better than the bulk of the established riders, his right to claim an allowance is worth supporting, but that means taking rides from other people – and Paul was the loser at this stage. Paul and I had had several verbal clashes and his time off through injuries had become more frequent, leaving him feeling less in favour than was comfortable for either of us. Carol tried several times to heal the rift. Paul was not looking for trouble; he had clawed himself up to ride as stable jockey to two good stables and did not relish the thought of sliding down the ladder. We were disappointed, though, that he did not fight for his job. Admittedly Scudamore and Lower were eroding Paul's position with some of the owners, but at the time he did have the advantage of being stable jockey. Perhaps as he had lived with us, and then taken over as head lad when Dennis Dummett went back to Gerald Cottrell for a while, he had got too close to the action. He was happiest simply getting a leg up on the horses in the parade ring and riding them in races; the involvement in getting them fit had lost its attraction.

For whatever reason, Paul's attitude proved sadly lacking. Take the night when ten new purchases, the fruits of six days' labour at Newmarket sales sifting through hundreds of Flat horses, arrived at Pond House. Our exhaustion evaporated in the excitement of taking another look at the fresh ammunition; but Paul, the man who was to ride them, opted to stay in the kitchen with a cup of tea and the day's paper. We felt the workload had become unbalanced.

145

I originally thought Paul should have stayed on as assistant trainer once he had decided to quit race-riding but he wanted to sever the tie. We had probably served each other's purpose. Paul kept a livery yard for a while before setting up locally as a trainer in his own right. Although operating on a smaller scale than us, he is probably more suited to being his own boss and seems happy. He showed he could do the job when just touched off in a driving finish for the Ladbroke Hurdle at Newbury in December 1991 with Galaxy High, and will probably foil our best-laid plans soon.

During the years when Paul reigned at Pond House, the system went through numerous changes, many of which he helped to introduce, others of which were forced upon him. The upgrading of schooling over jumps was instigated by Paul, but the change in race tactics, from holding horses up in the pack to the relentless front-running strategy we've mostly adopted, was something he found hard to accept. Setting a pace to suit ourselves has proved to be one of the stable's strong points, capitalizing on the high level of fitness which is my priority.

This particular change of heart evolved slowly, starting with Carol's evaluation of Baron Blakeney's Sandown run, when the ground he continually and economically gained in the air was frittered away when he was settled back into the field immediately after each jump. Further evidence presented itself when Michael Dickinson sent out twelve winners in one day. I had long been a Dickinson fan, and at breakfast on the morning following 'Dickie's Dozen' I noted that all of the successes had been gained by forcing tactics, either making the running or sitting on the leaders' heels ready to take over at the first signs of weakening. Paul's response, that Dickinson's riders had been able to do it because they'd all been on good horses, drew the counter-argument from me that most often our horses were the best in their races. They may be mainly moderate but if they are running against even worse animals the situation is no different. It took some persuading to get Paul to accept the new tactics, as he had grown up with the popular belief that most horses were better off racing in company. But to me, having come into the game later in life with no preconceived ideas, the change was obvious once we had thought it through.

* * *

Pipe's decision to front-run with the vast majority of his horses has altered the face of British jump racing more than any other single change over the past five seasons. His gift of viewing a given situation without the clutter of received wisdom has served him well, but even so he did not always grasp the truth as it unfolded in front of him. Paul recalls the time at Devon and Exeter when riding a hard-pulling horse which had been gambled on.

'I eventually lost the battle to settle the animal when the struggle between us caused the saddle to be pulled forward over the withers. The horse took over and duly ran himself into the ground, a spent force after halfway. Martin, using a few pertinent and well chosen words, blamed me for going on at a breakneck gallop and strode off without waiting or wanting to hear my explanation. It was a classic case of someone in the grandstand not understanding what his eyes were telling him. The next time out I took the horse to the races, saddled it up myself and partnered it to win. Martin accepted that saddling methods on very hard pullers have to be adjusted accordingly, and that all is not necessarily as seems at first glance.'

Pipe
To my mind Paul was a better steeplechase jockey than over hurdles, but as our successes were predominantly gained over timber until the last four years he never really had the chance to show his full ability. As yet we have not bought stores to put through the system, running first in bumpers, then over hurdles, then going on to become good chasers. When you do this, the rider has the advantage of getting to know his mounts as they grow and really understanding them. However, this may be changing now, as I have recently gathered a handful of young, well bred French and Irish horses around the place with an eye to starting them from scratch.

Another difficulty with Paul was his inability to communicate, either to the owner or to me. When losing, more so than after winning, connections want to hear the rider's considered opinion with a view to righting the situation next time. This is another area where Peter Scudamore excels without ever resorting to the realms of fantasy. We do, like any other partnership, differ on occasions, but we do not air our disagreements in public. We dissect every happening every day, and neither of us is affected by the other's reputation. We talk man to man, often challenging each other's professionalism in an effort to improve results. Neither of us has delusions of grandeur. It works well. Even now I sometimes tell Scu the only reason we were beaten was the jockey, which prompts a few home truths in reply. We can be a fiery pair behind closed doors, but we want the truth, even if it pricks our pride or our conscience.

Pipe felt that Paul bottled things up too much, refusing to discuss or admit responsibility for defeat until months after the event. In any business rapid communication is paramount if it is to prosper. Paul's increasing weight problems also affected him, which again widened the gap between the trainer and his jockey.

Martin accepts, though, that Paul was a top-class jockey to whom he owes a great deal. Similarly, Paul says of his former boss: 'Martin is ahead of the game. At the time I could not see the job escalating to such heights, yet knowing the depths of his inquiring mind, it all looks so obvious now.'

Chapter 16

Riding is the Easy Bit

Two boys attached to Pond House, Jonothan Lower in 1988 and Martin Foster three years later, have become Champion Conditional Jockey. With such a vast quantity of horses in training the chance for youngsters to progress, provided they have ability and drive, is evident. Equally important is the trainer's willingness to promote home-grown talent. Both Lower and Foster joined Pipe straight from school.

Pipe
I prefer to mould young jockeys to my way of thinking before their minds become cluttered by other people's methods. We get numerous staff joining us from a wide variety of stables. Most pick up our approach fairly quickly, although the occasional person finds it harder to adapt to the way I want things done.

It's strange really, but whenever I go into other trainers' stables, either at the sales or to buy horses privately, the lads, more so than girls, tend to run their employers down to me. They all think they can train better than the trainer. I hope mine are more loyal in similar situations. The usual things they say are that the horse has been raced over the wrong distance, needs a different type of track, less or more work, has been forgotten in the third yard, the head man could not feed cheese to white mice and the trainer would have difficulty training ivy up a wall. It could, of course, be a ploy to

149

make potential buyers think they can improve on the horse's handling, but I'm not so sure.

Here we start at 7.30 a.m. which is later than most yards. I feel that as the bulk of our work is done in the winter, it is sensible to work in the daylight. The staff, having each mucked out two stables, taken the inmates' temperatures and tacked up the horse they have been assigned to ride, get the first string out an hour later. With the gallops near at hand they are back in the yard by 9.15, wash off any mud from legs and hooves, sponge out any sweat marks and are tucked into a huge fried breakfast within five minutes of riding back into the stables. I do believe the staff need as much attention as the horses. Rest and food are important to both.

The second string pulls out at 10 o'clock; then the lads and girls who do not have a third horse to ride attend to the swimmers, the solarium, changing groups of horses on and off the automatic walkers, see to the previous day's runners and tidy the place up for a 1 p.m. finish to the morning's work.

The four assistant trainers do all the leg bandaging and administer general medication. A regular team of girls gives hay to all the inmates and others distribute the Ebor nuts and oats prepared by Dennis Dummett according to the horses' individual needs. Everything then shuts up until 2.30 p.m. During the afternoon the horses are groomed. On average each person does three to four animals, varying according to how many staff are away at the races. Also during this second work period, horses that need more exercise – swimming, schooling over jumps or periods on the automatic horse-walker – receive attention. Over the past year we have been riding an increasing number of horses in the afternoon to supplement their morning's work. I do firmly believe that horses benefit from being ridden twice a day rather than getting twice as much work at one stint. Working horses instead of just grooming them after lunch is the big difference from many of the big yards and the one most staff coming from those centres find difficult to accept.

We shut up shop at 5 p.m., which is considerably earlier than most orthodox yards. I don't allow staff in the yard after evening feed time unless they are bringing horses back from the races or are on a specific errand. This practice fuelled rumours at the time of the blood doping accusations: it was all supposed to happen

150

after the staff finished work. The real reason is infinitely less sinister. I believe horses should work in working hours and rest at all other times. Dennis lives in the middle of the main yard and Dad is always poking about mending something or trying to work out how to improve our system or machinery. I also pop down at intervals to monitor the horses which require water-jet treatment to cool inflamed legs or just to soothe them after a hard race. With so many runners from the yard the two stables specifically designed for cooling legs are in regular demand. Between the three of us there is ample cover should anything be amiss with any of the horses.

One lad, who had been head man for David Morley in Newmarket before joining us, refused to accept the way we did things. He repeatedly told me: 'David Morley would never do that.' I must admit it did get on my nerves, and one day I told him if he thought David's methods were better he really ought to go back to Newmarket.

Martin would not dream of saying it, of course, but as he has produced seasonal totals of over 200 for the past four terms, perhaps the Pipe methods have some merit after all.

Pipe and Lower have enjoyed a happy association since the local lad joined the stable from school aged sixteen. Despite enjoying a great deal of success in the show-jumping world, the youngster had always hankered after speed. Show jumping was only a stop gap until he became old enough to be a jockey.

Lower first saw the inside of his future workplace aged seven, when simply going along for the ride to pick up one of the lads with his parents. That glimpse excited him, and after persistent requests he was allowed to join in the action at weekends and during the school holidays. He was entrusted to Carol's grey hack Moony, which proved well within his capabilities and provided a toe in the doorway to his future.

Lower
At that introductory stage I was told there would be a job for me when I reached working age. Neither of us, though, could have known then just how closely we would work together in the future. At the time Paul Leach held the position as stable jockey, with Richard Dennis the established claimer and a dozen other

lads and thirty horses completing the team. The gallops consisted of the rotavated earth strip and the small grass areas. There was no all-weather strip, indoor ride, laboratory or other luxuries. That, extraordinary as it may seem, was only eight years ago.

My first day at work seemed little different from what I'd expected, except for the tiredness it induced. No one could describe the endless afternoons spent picking stones off the gallops as pleasurable, but I viewed the chore as a means to an end. I meant to force my way to the head of the queue for any spare rides that might come up for grabs and had the foresight to understand that menial jobs would not last for ever. From the outset I realized any chances of leapfrogging the other hopefuls would have to come from myself. Having established that most of my rivals were just as conscientious in their daily chores as I was, it became obvious that my biggest advantage lay in the experience I'd gained from show jumping. It proved to be my ticket to ride.

Luckily for me, Martin had only recently been converted to the importance of schooling when Paul Leach joined the stable twelve months earlier.

Pipe
When other boys simply looked like passengers, Jonothan could see a stride pattern for the second obstacle the moment he landed over the first. He had a natural and practised eye. He looked a man in a boy's body, and within a year he had earned his chance to prove he could also do the job on a racecourse.

Lower
That opening is indelibly burned into my memory. My first ride was To-Palikari-Mou, who had pulled up in his two races the previous season. Martin found a conditional jockeys' novices selling hurdle with only four runners at Newton Abbot in August 1984, backed him from 7–1 down to half that price and expected him to give me a good start to my career. I had trouble keeping the gelding anywhere near the other three runners who all simply zipped around the inside rail. My left arm went dead from trying to steer. We ran wide all the way only to rally up the straight to dead-heat for second place.

152

I was absolutely knackered. Both my arms felt like string because the horse had been hanging right-handed on a left-handed course but I was too tired and too ignorant to know what had happened. The boss exploded and I had visions of my glittering career being over before it had started. To no one's surprise I was replaced by Paul Leach when the horse ran at Hereford two days later. It started odds-on, only to finish third of the six runners. Paul was himself jocked off in favour of Richard Dennis for the gelding's third race, the pair finishing a well beaten third. Both the other riders having reported the horse unsteerable, Mr Pipe apologized to me for his hasty judgement on my debut. It restored my faith in human nature as well as some shattered ambitions.

In all I had fifteen rides in my first season, breaking my duck without much effort on Silver Ace at Windsor in March 1985. Making all the running, I never saw nor heard another horse and won by twenty lengths. Such a facile victory destroyed the myth young riders harbour about the emotion and derring-do associated with a winner.

While naturally delighted to have got my name on the score sheet, I mentally noted that the most important factor in my quest to make a name for myself would be getting on the best horse in any race. It also occurred to me that being attached to the blossoming Pond House stable would provide me with a fair chance of doing exactly that. If a stable is having lots of winners the chance of getting on some of them is far greater than in a yard where every half chance has to be capitalized on by using established riders.

The yard topped the fifty-winner mark for the first time that season – by one. Who could have guessed that within a few years we would be sending out a hundred winners before the season was half over? I am still amazed at the growth rate. None of it was ever planned; it just crept up on us.

The next term I really took off, notching up twenty-five winners, the first of which, Morice, scraped home by a length at Devon and Exeter. Being forced to work for victory this time induced the excitement that had been patently lacking after my initial easy win. Twelve months later the winners continued to flow and I became top young rider with a score of thirty-six. That number earned me the Sportsman's Club award for the leading junior rider, together with a cheque for £750, and promoted me to riding on equal terms with the vast number of established jockeys fighting for survival. Since then seasonal totals of eleven, twenty-seven, forty-nine, twenty-nine and twenty have provided the elation of several major winners – and the dejection of sitting injured at home as outside jockeys reaped the rewards of my patient home work and schooling.

Pipe

I cannot speak highly enough of Jonothan, whose work behind the scenes has not been fully compensated by success in public. When Scu retires Jonothan may assume his mantle, but that of course may not be a straightforward decision; certain of the owners might continue to regard him as back-up man instead of front-line rider. Whatever happens, he is an important part of the team here. He understands how I tick.

The all-weather gallop came to life during the first year Jonothan worked at Pond House. I still marvel now at the end product. I must admit, though, that as one of the small army of people who sewed up the sides of the protective membrane encasing the drainage stone Jonothan must have looked on its construction as more of a chore than the most important aid to the stable's future.

Lower

In my first year, when the horses were still regularly transported to gallops high above the stables on the surrounding hills, two of the inmates were best avoided. I tilted the odds in my favour, just as Len Lungo had done ten years before me. Both Silver Maid and Venetian Warrior were lunatics to ride; I thought at the time their regular riders needed medals as well as wages and was quite pleased I'd managed to avoid partnering either of them.

My turn had to come, of course; Paul Leach did the riding lists then and I thought it odd one morning when he continually smiled at me before, during and after first lot. The reason became abundantly clear after breakfast when I saw my name and Venetian Warrior's bracketed together. Paul, as usual, rode Silver Maid, the other nutter. It only delayed the dreaded moment for a day, but I had the last laugh that morning when,

A key element in Martin's phenomenal success is the partnership with champion jockey Peter Scudamore; here a pensive Scudamore is on Bonanza Boy, winner of the Welsh National in 1988. (*George Selwyn*)

Pipe's forays on to the Flat have been increasingly successful; Right Regent (left) wins the Ascot Stakes in 1983, ridden by Steve Cauthen. (*George Selwyn*)

Martin in topper does not appear to be overawed by Royal Ascot; in the winner's enclosure after Atall Atall has won the Windsor Castle Stakes in 1985. (*George Selwyn*)

RIGHT: Having cantered up the hill three times and hacked back twice, the string are totally relaxed as they head for home. (*Gerry Cranham*)

BELOW: Pipe watches the string as they approach the gallops. A half-mile woodchip walkway from the stable will soon be built across his land so that the road can be avoided. (*Gerry Cranham*)

If horses will jump a narrow flight of hurdles without company, they are ready, willing and able to make the running on the racecourse. (*Gerry Cranham*)

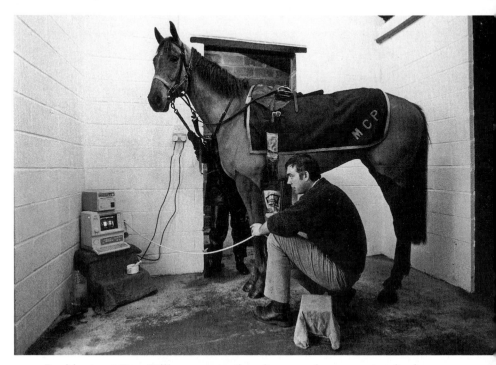

Resident vet Ray Dillaway uses the ultrasound scanner to check Pharoah's Son's flexor tendons prior to galloping. The inner state of the tendons shows up clearly on the screen and is printed out for the files. (*Gerry Cranham*)

RIGHT: Four years after the fifty, the 200 barrier was broken – by which time son David, aged fifteen, dwarfed his parents.

BELOW: The main yard team after breaking the 200-winners-a-season mark for the first time in 1989.

Dave Pipe quizzes Martin on the form while 6ft 4in grandson David does his stint as leg-man for the firm. (*Gerry Cranham*)

Breakfast at Pond House is light but the planning is intense between Martin and Scudamore, with David Pipe observing and learning. (*Gerry Cranham*)

ABOVE: Haydock Park's chairman Bill Whittle presents a handsome bonus to Pipe as top trainer there in 1989.

RIGHT: Because of old injuries, Pipe would struggle to get through the day without his BMX. (*Gerry Cranham*)

ABOVE: Both yards have indoor automatic horse-walkers to accommodate eight horses each. They are in constant use. (*Gerry Cranham*)

BELOW LEFT: Evaluating the opposition prior to a race has proved to be rewarding. All observations are logged for future reference. (*Gerry Cranham*)

BELOW RIGHT: The horse's hind leg in Pipe's study helps owners and staff to understand the complexities of injuries to that limb. Pipe believes that most front leg strains are caused by problems with the hind legs. (*Gerry Cranham*)

On the training gallops at Nicholashayne in 1985. (*George Selwyn*)

The Pond House complex as it was in 1991, with the huge covered ride in the foreground, and the tiny hamlet of Nicholashayne in mid-frame surrounded by lush Somerset acres.

Martin's trademark is the portable phone, which he carries with him wherever he goes – even on the gallops at Nicholashayne. (*Gerry Cranham*)

Omerta (Adrian Maguire) leads over the last to win the Kim Muir at the Cheltenham Festival in 1991. Omerta went on to win the Irish National. (*George Selwyn*)

Chatam (Peter Scudamore) leads Party Politics over the last to win the 1991 Hennessy Gold Cup. Chatam had previously been considered an unreliable jumper. (*George Selwyn*)

Playing to the gallery is a recent innovation. Chatam receives congratulations over Pipe's ubiquitous mobile phone in the winner's enclosure after the Hennessy Gold Cup. (*Gerry Cranham*)

ABOVE: The 1992 Cheltenham Festival was a mixture of triumph and disaster for Pipe. Here, Peter Scudamore on Miinnehoma is taking the last from Bradbury Star in the Sun Alliance Chase. (*George Selwyn*)

BELOW: In a thrilling race, Miinnehoma battles on to beat Bradbury Star by half a length. (*George Selwyn*)

ABOVE: The enigmatic Carvill's Hill, the pride of Ireland, joins Martin's stable and wins the Coral Welsh National at Chepstow in December 1991, but not before making a characteristic blunder at the final fence. (*Gerry Cranham*)

BELOW: Carvill's Hill, with a jubilant Peter Scudamore in the saddle, returns to the winner's enclosure after triumphing in the Coral Welsh National. (*Gerry Cranham*)

Disaster looming in the 1992 Cheltenham Gold Cup . . . Golden Freeze takes Carvill's Hill on from the start, forcing him into a series of jumping errors. (*George Selwyn*)

Another bad jump finishes off Carvill's Hill in the controversial 1992 Gold Cup. (*Gerry Cranham*)

Returning home after early morning exercise at Nicholashayne.
(*George Selwyn*)

despite breaking two hoofpicks in the process, I managed to prise off one of Venetian Warrior's shoes, causing him to be exercised in the lungeing ring instead of making the intended trip to the gallops.

I did it more to wipe the grin off Paul's face than anything else. Funnily enough, after that little trick the nutcases usually came my way.

An obvious danger of using such a short gallop as Pipe's is that horses are far from tired when it comes to pulling up. Over the past eight years this has prompted a few brave hearts to falter as the imposing hedge guarding the work strip from the small field between it and the M5 looms up.

Lower

Only three of us are known to have taken the hedge on, each time with the confirmed runaway Boardman's Style. Rory McNiece's exhibition is the occasion still best remembered. No one knows if he threw himself off or fell off as the horse became airborne. David Richmond's turn came next, but fortunately on this occasion the horse's steering proved more reliable than his brakes. After four laps of the adjoining field the out-of-breath partnership came to a halt intact.

My being carted went unnoticed. Often if I'm due off racing or am riding a runaway, I go up the gallops between the usual lots. One rainy March morning I had taken Boardman's Style up on my own, and got well and truly put in my place. The reins were wet, making them awkward to grip properly. A difficult job became impossible. Trying to fight him from the start saw me weakening dramatically when the brow of the hill streaked past. The advantage the rising ground should have given me disappeared with the horse then totally in charge over the final short, level pulling-up area. Still intent on his battle with me, the gelding was on top of the hedge before he really saw the thing. Too late and too fast to swing around in an arc, he flew the hedge only to stumble on landing, giving me a momentary advantage which I seized. Snatching him round in a tight circle before he regained his equilibrium, I put him back at the hedge. He popped it nicely from the reverse side and was only too pleased to pull up on landing.

By the time the main string cantered up to the top, Board-man's Style had stopped blowing excessively and had become quite responsive. No one else had a clue I'd been made a fool of.

That hair-raising experience taught me the way to end up in charge at the top of the gallop. If in doubt about the outcome of an argument, let the horse run freely from the start, then take a pull just as the hill takes its toll. Once its stride pattern alters you know you're boss.

Pipe
Injuries to Paul Leach helped Jonothan to get and take his early career opportunities, but in recent years the same situation in reverse has robbed him of the chance to capitalize fully on his position as second jockey to Scu. Having said that, Jonothan has won three major races: the Scottish Champion Hurdle on Sayparee, the Welsh equivalent on High Knowl and the Waterford Crystal Supreme Hurdle at the Cheltenham Festival riding Sondrio. The latter dropped in his lap when Scu opted for Paul Green's Irish-trained Elementary for several reasons, prominent among them Sondrio's habit of treating the hurdles with disdain.

A decent colt on the Flat in Ireland with Kevin Prendergast, Sondrio surpassed himself in America when winning four races including the Grade One Hialeah Turf Cup, returning to Ireland to take up stallion duties at the Baroda Stud in 1987. Paying the ultimate price of infertility he was gelded, then sent to me for a hurdling career. He won at Hereford, Haydock and Ascot, despite careless jumping, before that particular flaw proved his undoing at Kempton Park on his pre-Cheltenham outing. Peter Scudamore had ridden the horse in each of his races before Cheltenham but, like the punters, deserted him on the big day.

Lower
Waiting in the wings can be frustrating no matter what line of business you are in, but once the chance came I was ready for it. I knew several days before the race that Scu would choose not to ride ours, so I suggested to Martin we school the gelding both before and after lunch on the day prior to his Cheltenham engagement. After the morning session, when the tussle for control swayed more in the horse's favour, I asked permission to

156

fit a Grakle noseband to the bridle. It had the desired effect by keeping Sondrio's mouth shut, giving me more say in the pace and striding on the approach to a hurdle. After pinging the first hurdle at Cheltenham, I knew instantly his jumping would not stop us from winning.

Pipe
In Britain we do tend to place far too much faith in senior jockeys' judgement, and a glance at their record when faced with a choice shows they are not the best judges of form. As Scu had abandoned Sondrio, the gelding started almost friendless at 25–1. The race stands out as one of the most competitive for the traditional opener at the Festival, and in winning it Sondrio bettered Beech Road's Champion Hurdle time later the same day by a handsome three seconds. He had the likes of Cruising Altitude, Redundant Pal and the fallers Alekhine, Blitzkreig, Granville Hotel and Scu's mount Elementary either well in his wake or on the floor.

Having been asked to partner horses that were attempting to land considerable gambles for the stable since day one, Jonothan does not react adversely to the enormous pressure of large amounts of cash resting on his shoulders. He reasons, correctly, that he can only do his best. It is also no concern of his if people choose to back the horse he's riding. If you try your hardest every time you ride you can do no more.

At no time has Jonothan ever shown me signs of nerves, and funnily enough he looks at his calmest before a big race. I suppose this is due to the discipline and concentration he acquired show jumping as a kid, when he had to pit himself against the fences and the clock, totally alone, time and time again.

Lower
There cannot be any opposites further apart than the loneliness of the show-jumping ring and the scramble of the Grand National. I've experienced both, and my only ride so far in the Grand National, on the grey Star's Delight in 1990, gave me a taste of the ultimate test. Before the contest I felt nothing except anticipation of the challenge; during it, the excitement of avoiding other horses in order to jump every fence with

precision; and after the race, total frustration at having to wait a year or longer to have another crack at it.

We had no fewer than four runners in the National that year, with Scu opting for Bonanza Boy, Jimmy Frost on Torside and Alan Walter riding his own Huntworth. Ever since Strands Of Gold fell at Becher's Brook when still in front on the second circuit going like a winner, Martin has had the bug. Yet, apart from the big race, he does not like Aintree and in fact only went up there on the third and final day in 1991 despite having a host of fancied runners on the first two days.

My memories of the National are still vivid now. We hit the front going to the third fence, that big open ditch. Although Star's Delight is not big, he has a lot of scope, listens to instructions and cleared the first bogey fence with ease. When you and your horse understand each other, confidence is high. To have the first three jumps and the noisy horde behind you is a comforting thought. Being up front, out of potential trouble, the whole thing is relatively enjoyable. I don't expect that sounds very professional but it's the safest way to survive when a horse trusts his jockey and the feeling is mutual.

Having settled down nicely, the sixth, Becher's Brook, looked modest on the take-off side; but surviving the famous drop on landing was one hell of a thrill! Two fences later, at the right-angled Canal Turn, I experienced the most amazing situation, unique to the Grand National. Still up front, towards the outside in relative quiet, as we neared take-off we heard the large crowd start to cheer the field. Not a particular horse or rider; the whole lot. The spectators out in the country, who only see a live horse for the brief few moments they pass by on each of the two laps, must be the most enthusiastic gathering on the course. They were cheering us on simply because we were still on our feet.

My first Grand National attempt started to peter out from that point, quite possibly due to the enormous leap Star's Delight put in on hearing the cheering. It was not immediately obvious that the little grey had burst a blood vessel, but once the energy he had shown over the first mile ebbed and we started to lose place steadily, the National was over for me. It felt just like a car running out of petrol, still moving but without any oomph. After the thirteenth fence it became obvious we would not pick up momentum again so I called it a day. If ever you are in doubt whether to pull up or not, you have already gone past the point of choice. It does no one any good to continue racing when out of contention. There is always another day, provided you do not push a horse over his physical limit.

After a good launch to my career, plenty of follow-up winners, including three major victories, and having established myself among the pecking order, it is frustrating still to be back-up rider instead of literally holding the reins. There have been occasions when I thought I could have been on board one of the stable's decent horses but I have never once asked the boss for a ride and never will.

I used to groom Corporal Clinger at home during evening stables and did think I'd get the call to ride him at Sandown Park in the valuable Mecca Bookmakers Hurdle, which he proceeded to win under Mark Perrett. I was sent to Nottingham instead to ride Afford, who promptly got well beaten at 2–5 favourite.

I suppose to outsiders it looks bad for me when a younger jockey pops up as Adrian Maguire did when he partnered Omerta to win the Irish Grand National, but they wouldn't know that the horse's owner lives in Ireland and had suggested him when the chestnut first ran for us in an amateur riders' race at Cheltenham. I only have to please Martin, and he has never done me wrong. If he has put an outside jockey on one perhaps I thought I should have ridden, he has a valid reason. We trust each other, so neither of us would consider explaining.

I am sure I can recognize all his moods and react accordingly. On a bad day, when things have gone wrong, it's wiser to keep out of the way. Whatever problems I may have, they would not bear comparison with his. We have occasionally fallen out; but it never lasts longer than ten minutes as by then we've moved on to sort out other problems.

As for the job, it is the best. We are all encouraged to pull together for the common good. The riding is the easy part, continually having to lose weight the most arduous, but that would be the same wherever I worked in stables.

With a three-bedroomed house in Wellington and a two-bedroomed flat in Taunton Jonothan has proved there is a wage to be earned under Martin Pipe's direction. More important, this jockey seems to have learned the lesson Dave Pipe has used to amass his fortune: 'Make money work for its owner.'

Chapter 17

Dabbling on the Flat

Sometimes obscured by the relentlessly repeated double centuries of jumping winners, Pipe has an impressive, if somewhat smaller, catch from the deeper waters of Flat racing. Twice he has lifted Royal Ascot prizes, and not just with stamina-laden hurdlers reverting to their roots. The Kampala two-year-old Atall Atall proved one of the speediest juveniles in training in 1985, having been bought almost sight unseen.

Pipe
Fired up by the few winners we'd had on the Flat over the previous three seasons, I decided to expand by buying some two-year-olds at the Doncaster 1985 breeze-up sales in March. I had orders for five juveniles and filled four of them easily enough at prices from £1,500 to £6,000. Tony Millward, from Manchester, did not want any of the horses I'd selected but was still keen to get involved, and when someone is an obvious buyer, he is usually accommodated one way or another.

Willie Stephenson, a founder-director of the Doncaster sales, recognized the signs as the conversation got louder in line with the number of drinks that were consumed. He could see Tony was in the right mood to buy and knew of an animal in Ireland belonging to Mickey Browne, a regular vendor at Doncaster, that could fit the bill. A flattering photograph was produced, Mickey waxed lyrical about the promise the colt had shown in home gallops, and after much old-fashioned haggling the colt was Tony's. When he joined us three days later all I could fault him on was a straight shoulder and front leg. I was more than pleased the trust we had put in Willie and Mickey was vindicated; but I doubt if I would be as rash these days. Being brought up in the bookmaking world where so much business is conducted by word of mouth, you tend to take trust for granted.

As these youngsters had been tuned up to show their paces on Doncaster racecourse prior to being auctioned, they were ready to go on with as soon as they had settled down in their new surroundings. Our purchase by photograph was by far the best of the bunch. By this time we had been using the all-weather gallop for a year and had got to know its worth. The two-year-olds sprinted over three furlongs for a month, showing roughly the same form; but as I had no experience of this type of horse it was difficult to evaluate their worth. I said to Carol, either Atall Atall is a flying machine or the other four juveniles are useless. To find out for certain I pitched the colt against a battle-hardened campaigner a year older and watched in amazement as he proceeded to wipe the floor with the older horse. With the form confirmed, it left only the right venue to be found for Tony Millward to recoup his outlay.

We decided on a maiden at Bath, booked Paul Eddery to do the steering and planned who would put how much on and where. An unraced two-year-old from a jumping stable should not attract too much interest and to throw people off the scent, I also entered him in the seller the same day, hoping it would be assumed that was his mark. That ruse plainly failed to fool anyone, especially when the place came alive with punters from Ireland who knew of the ability the colt had shown on Mickey Browne's gallops while being prepared for the sales.

We still went to town as the horse was a certainty, but had to be content with 5–2 instead of the hoped-for 10–1. In the parade ring Paul Eddery tried to pour cold water on our obvious anticipation with news that the Bill O'Gorman-trained favourite Comcentre had come on considerably for its debut second behind the Henry Cecil Sheikh Mohammed hotpot Mazaad at Newmarket eight days earlier. He went on to put up several similar arguments why we could not win until Carol took matters and, literally, Paul, into her hands to get the message through

162

that no matter what the others could do, ours was something special.

Atall Atall tracked the leaders for three furlongs, moved in behind the favourite two out, joined the issue at the distance and strode away to win by two and a half lengths to unusually loud vocal support for a minor Flat meeting.

A month later we produced him in a much hotter race at Haydock Park over an extra furlong but burned our fingers slightly when he failed to stay the trip and finished third to Reg Hollinshead's Runaway. Paul, to give him his due, thought going back to the minimum trip for the Windsor Castle Stakes at Royal Ascot two weeks later would not see us disgraced.

I'm not comfortable in morning dress but do thoroughly enjoy the whole razzmatazz of the Royal meeting. I'd won the Ascot Stakes three years earlier with Right Regent and was keen to prove I could train sprinters too.

There was a supposedly good thing in our race in the shape of the unraced Irish-trained Bridle Suite and a Tom Jones debutant with a big home reputation called Timberwood. We were a 12–1 chance among the nine runners. Atall Atall took the Windsor Castle by one-and-a-half lengths, having led from two furlongs out to shouts and cheers that are unusual in the owners' and trainers' stand at the Royal meeting. I don't know if I'm wrong, but surely all those regular Flat race owners feel the same thrill as I do when having a winner, yet few ever show their emotions.

The show rolled on to Newmarket for a crack at the six-furlong Group Three July Stakes. The big guns looked on us as a lower-class Royal Ascot winner. The bookmakers took the same view, and also considered us to be running over a furlong too far; so we started at 33–1. According to the market, it was a three-horse race between Guy Harwood's Bakharoff, Cecil's Water Cay and Michael Stoute's Green Desert. The race turned out to be one of the most exciting contests I have been involved in, probably because we were taking on the Flat trainers I respected most on their own patch.

Atall Atall had strengthened considerably in the two months since he'd won his maiden at Bath, convincing me the extra furlong would not prove beyond us. We led right from the moment the stalls burst open, with the more fancied horses bunching on our heels. Two furlongs from home they looked like a pack of vultures waiting for their prey to weaken. Going into the final furlong, the rising ground took its toll on Water Cay with Bakharoff hanging on to Green Desert's tail as he threw down a serious challenge.

In those days, and especially against the top Flat boys, I lacked the courage of my convictions. I fully expected my horse to be inferior when it came to the crunch, yet as the winning post came nearer Atall Atall was still repelling Green Desert, and it was only yards before the line that he was collared by the Stoute horse to go down fighting by a head.

Racing provides incredible elation and desperate despair; the drugs, I suppose, that keep us going. On that day at Newmarket, despite being defeated, our little band of followers was euphoric.

That performance caught the eye of the big league players, with Charles St George the most persistent of the potential buyers. Tony Millward repeatedly went hot then cold on the sale, eventually deciding to keep the colt, who owed him nothing.

After that, Goodwood's Group Two Richmond Stakes saw Green Desert stretch his superiority over Atall Atall to five lengths when they came second and fifth respectively behind Nomination. Lester Piggott then rode our colt to finish third in the Prince of Wales's Stakes at York, and we wound up an unforgettable season when Willie Carson partnered him in the Flying Childers at Doncaster, where sadly he finished lame.

Although he won twice for us the next year, Atall Atall's best run at three was his half-length third to Hallgate and Bridesmaid at Lingfield. Tony then decided to set up a private trainer nearer his home, and so took away the sprinter and the other three horses he had with me. The partnership had been a good one for both of us.

It is worth putting this story into perspective by noting that in 1985 Pipe had only just topped the half-century for the first time, ending the season with fifty-one successes over jumps, none of which were gained over fences. Atall Atall's performances had elevated him on to a very different plane as Pipe's wins on the Flat over the previous two seasons had been gained almost exclusively with hurdlers landing staying races.

He was not to know it at the time, but two of the horses who finished out with the washing when his Baron Blakeney under Lester Piggott fought it out with Willie Carson on Popsi's Joy for the 1982 Ascot Handicap were destined to join the Nicholashayne team and benefit from the change of air.

Pipe

The Baron responded to Lester's driving but was simply not good enough to peg back Popsi's Joy on the first day of the Royal meeting. Even so, he had not disgraced us and gave Bob Wheatley the fun he had hoped for. Nine lengths behind us Guy Reed's home-bred Flying Officer never got a blow in, while David Elsworth's Right Regent could only beat one of the thirteen runners home.

Both horses were to join me, though in different circumstances. Devon publican Sidney Hindle sent Right Regent to me. David Elsworth had won two of his previous three starts with the colt, including the Great Metropolitan Handicap at Epsom, and must have been surprised and annoyed to lose him. Flying Officer, on the other hand, came up for sale at the November Doncaster sales as a part of Guy Reed's annual clear-out of older horses to make way for his yearling intake: this is always a good occasion to buy. I secured the gelding for 6,800 guineas, which seemed cheap for such a good walker who had won once over a mile and a half and twice at two miles that season. The new owners were a syndicate headed by Brian Westcott and Alan Sheldrake, key figures in the South West Racing Club, who have not only supported me since then but have ensured their club's growth despite the recession.

I had been convinced after Baron Blakeney's win in the Triumph Hurdle that staying Flat horses were the type to buy for jumping because all the speed in the world is no use if the animal peters out before being able to deliver its challenge. What's more, they could be snapped up for a fraction of the cost of the speedier Flat cast-offs.

Flying Officer did the syndicate proud, winning four of his six Flat races in 1983, though running inexplicably badly in the other two. His victories came at Bath, Lingfield, Warwick and Wolverhampton, with the first of them almost causing me to lose Right Regent only months after he came to me.

Extraordinary as it sounds, that year the ground at Bath's early May meeting rode heavy, putting a premium on stamina in the Box Handicap run over two miles one furlong and what proved to be a decisive twenty-seven yards. Right Regent, with the benefit of a good third at Newbury twenty-two days before, was my fancy to win. Flying Officer had shown less ability at home, which was reflected in his starting price of 25–1, and was really only running to give his enthusiastic band of owners a day out and me a chance to find out more about the horse.

As the contest unfolded Right Regent, under Brian Taylor, went to the front six furlongs from the finish and quickly put the issue beyond doubt. Or so it seemed. When I turned to Sidney Hindle and his partner Bert as their horse passed the two-furlong pole to congratulate them on their inevitable win, Bert ventured the opinion that the horse with the black and white colours would be second. Retraining my binoculars on the race I saw that it was Flying Officer who was running on, but when passing the tiring pursuers he swerved violently left-handed towards the running rail. Up front Brian Taylor sneaked a glance over his shoulder and having confirmed he could not be caught, dropped his hands to give Right Regent as easy a race as possible. Then, just seconds before we saw it, he felt his mount interpret his relaxation as a signal to stop. Little Ray Still on Flying Officer, working away purely to keep his mount going in the taxing ground, suddenly found that the bird who had flown had suddenly slowed to walking pace, allowing him to force the outsider up in the dying stride and snatch the verdict by a neck as Brian Taylor's frantic efforts to restart Right Regent came to nothing.

You can imagine the widely different reactions in the unsaddling enclosure: an ecstatic bunch of winning owners on one hand, a furious partnership only yards away, and me in the middle not sure whether to laugh or cry. I naturally congratulated and commiserated with the respective parties, but then had to face the punters, who already thought I'd put one over on them, and Right Regent's owners, who were convincing themselves I had by the minute.

Two weeks later Flying Officer, again doubled up with Ray Still, put Baron Blakeney in his shadow. Right Regent also obliged at Wolverhampton and Kempton, ridden by Steve Cauthen on both occasions. Sidney could not make it to the latter; it was an evening meeting and as he kept an hotel near Newton Abbot, he felt he should be attending to business. An unusually big silver cup went with the prize, and this, Bert decided, should be filled with champagne – several times. As dusk descended Carol and I left the party with the cup perched proudly on the roof of Bert's Range Rover as the centrepiece of the continuing celebration. When it finally broke up the emotionally charged part-owner left Kempton Park unaware his trophy was still adorning the roof. When it finally dawned on him that the cup was not in the car, he retraced the fifteen miles he had driven only to find no sign of the missing cup. Fortunately, on reporting the loss to the Sunbury police station it transpired that an honest member of the public had handed the by then much-dented trophy in. To the day he died Sidney Hindle didn't know how close he came to not having the silver to display in his hotel.

When Royal Ascot came around the following month I was three-handed in the Ascot Handicap with poor old Baron Blakeney, who had finished well clear of the other two twelve months before, the outsider of the trio. Carson's mount Prince of Princes attracted the heavy money, displacing Right Regent as favourite with Flying Officer fifth best in the market and the Baron offered at 25–1.

Cauthen on Right Regent tracked Baron Blakeney into the straight in third and fourth place respectively, with the favourite two behind and looking dangerous. Steve kicked for home two out as Baron backpedalled and that move proved decisive as the late challenge from Carson failed by a rapidly diminishing neck. My first Royal Ascot victory prompted a surge of uncontrollable joy during which I grabbed the horrified woman next to me in the grandstand to hug and kiss her. She and her husband were total strangers; I only hope they were foreign visitors and not regular racegoers who have ever since been saying what a horrible man I am.

That season had given me some heady moments and some quite strong pointers as well. To win at Royal Ascot and land a gamble or two gave me the confidence to trust in my judgement.

167

Believe me, once a trainer knows for sure his methods and yardsticks are sound, the guessing goes out of the job. Then only luck can interfere with his plans.

Pipe was only too aware that the major Flat trainers had a nucleus of long established owner–breeders to supply annual drafts of yearlings from proven bloodlines. On top of that, they attracted big spenders to vie for the best blood on offer each year at the sales on both sides of the Atlantic. He had neither group to help him break through the barrier that separates the band of jumping trainers who mount an occasional successful raid on the Flat from those who make the complete transition. However, a year before his encouraging wins with the trio of winning stayers, the emerging breeder and buyer Peter Savill had given Pipe some hopes in that direction when sending Filario to deepest Somerset.

Pipe
The early to mid-eighties was the period when things came together for me. I had increased my understanding of training from nil to a fair degree of competence, expanded the facilities, seen the jumping winners swell from fourteen in 1980–1 to fifty-one in 1984–5 and had produced two vastly different Royal Ascot winners.

Serious participation on the Flat had started with Baron Blakeney but was fuelled when Peter Savill sent me Filario. He represented a totally different type of owner from those who had supported my earlier career. He and Bob Wheatley were men who could breed or bid for serious Flat race horses.

Filario had been tailed off on his only start as a juvenile for Alan Jarvis but patently trained on at three. Peter Savill liked to monitor his horses' progress more than any owner I've had before or since. He entered his horses and decided where to run them, which he said gave him as much pleasure as the end result. Although not fully wound up, Filario ran at Salisbury on 23 June 1982, finishing in the middle of an eighteen-runner maiden. He came on for the run and ten days later, having worked well at home, was dropped to selling class at Bath to land an off-course touch for us both at the unbelievable odds of 6–1. The coup looked even better when nobody bid for him.

Three weeks later, upped to handicap class at Warwick, we

played the winnings at 9–1 and drew again. It was a perfect example of a strategy that has stood my gambles in good stead ever since. Run fit and below your class to land the first bet; then, when you move up in class next time out, the stigma of having won a moderate race rules you out of serious consideration in the eyes of form students and bookmakers. Of course, when the ploy has been exposed the value disappears, but the horse should still be ahead of the handicapper and if it's good enough will add further to his score.

We were only able to run once more that term and in fact had to give best to Jarvis, who beat us with Sniffy, ridden by his son Tim. All the same, we had taken the value when winning twice and still finished well in front, despite the losses incurred on the last attempt. Alan did not lower himself to crow at foiling our treble, but he would have been inhuman not to have been secretly chuffed with the result. No one likes losing a horse or owner and when it happens the trainer lives in dread of the horse making him look silly.

Filario did us another good turn on his only start of 1983 when, once again ignored by the public and bookies, he went off at 12–1 to win a modest Wolverhampton handicap. His legs, though, gave us a great deal of concern and but for the swimming pool he would not have reappeared in 1984. We ran him in a seller again to reaffirm in people's minds that he was moderate, but knew he could not win under 9st 10lb. Another outing over too long a trip put suspicious punters off the scent before we reverted to his ideal trip of ten furlongs at Warwick, where he carried only 8st 1lb and started at the rewarding odds of 10–1.

I dwell on Filario for no other reason than that he is the perfect example of a gambling horse. Once we had evaluated his true worth, which was slightly above selling class, it only remained to find the opening to go to town. The horse had obliged four times and been beaten just once when we had backed him. He owed us nothing; quite the reverse, in fact. Peter Savill left the fold after that – an amicable parting on both sides. He loved Yorkshire and has since developed his large string in the north. For my part, I did not entirely relish his level of involvement, but for both of us the partnership proved successful.

Having proved to myself I could do the job equally well on the Flat, I had to make a decision on my future. Which way should I go? After a lot of thought the attractions of the Flat – handling a fresh bunch each year and not agonizing over so many training injuries – were counterbalanced by the realization that I would have difficulty in attracting the right sort of owner. My jumping team was rapidly increasing in size and because of the policy of having a big early-season string, my stables were full all year round. Added to that, many of the jumpers bought out of Flat stables retained enough speed to run under both codes. So the decision became easy: I would concentrate on the winter game.

Since arriving at that decision, Pipe has continued to keep his hand in on the Flat, with a commendable ratio of winners to runners. In 1991 this sideline brought him seventeen winners, including Tamarpour's victory in the Northumberland Plate – the 'Pitmen's Derby' – netting £20,000 for his friends Alison and Frank Farrant.

Chapter 18

Vets

Almost without exception, the people Dave and Martin Pipe initially sought out for help when moving into the horse business were contacts from the greyhound world. Their original veterinary adviser, Sam Loughridge, is no exception; although basically a horse vet, he also attended Exeter greyhound meetings where he and Dave Pipe struck up a friendship, eventually extending to a business relationship. Besides working with Thoroughbreds, he also bred and owned the brilliant steeplechaser Diamond Edge, whom he produced to win a point-to-point at Buckfastleigh before sending him to the late Fulke Walwyn, who trained him so well to win two Whitbread Gold Cups and the 1981 Hennessy Cognac Gold Cup.

Pipe
He's the best castrater in the job, so quick and efficient horses don't know they are done until the anaesthetic wears off. He'd geld you in two seconds if you turned your back on him! It's an education to watch Sam at work. He gets a horse into the corner of a stable, manoeuvres him into the best position with his legs set apart, leans into his side with his shoulder, then snip, snip and on with the clamps to stop the bleeding. It's all over within seconds. He is totally fearless, too. Sometimes horses are ticklish or obstinate and try to put up a fight, but after a few grunts and a shove, Sam invariably wins the battle.

People who don't have much to do with horses probably think it isn't necessary to geld the vast majority of jumpers, but I can assure them it is. Few entire horses would enjoy the discomfort of brushing through fences; once gelded, the nastiest of characters becomes a much more amenable animal to deal with.

Sam is also a superb judge of a horse's character from the few minutes he spends with them prior to and during his operations. He'll always come out of a stable and deliver his opinion, 'Gutless/tough/useless/a real horse', and most times he'll be right. When we sent him in to geld Chatam, he thought it was a sin to rob the horse of any chance of being a future stallion, said it was too nice a horse to castrate. He may have been right; yet I am sure the horse would not have been as good a racehorse if we'd left him entire. He was far too clever. It is also extremely difficult to make a jumping stallion, as we found out with Baron Blakeney. I'm still convinced that if we'd continued to race him instead of packing him off to stud we would have won the Cheltenham Gold Cup by now.

Sam still attends to the gelding here. He's a smashing chap, and we've always got on well, even though we use numerous other vets for various jobs. I firmly believe in hiring an expert for every problem – gelding, respiratory system, blood content, leg strains and all the other regular headaches. Sam makes his point now and again when leaving us to stew for a couple of weeks when we want him, as if to say, 'You're not the only stable on my books.'

Les Kennard put us on to the late Bill Walter from Badminton, who saw us through the formative years until his death in 1990. Bill was one of those rare, larger-than-life chaps who not only know their job inside out but are fun to work with. I'll never forget the time I was dithering about whether or not to try Baron Blakeney over fences, as he was still an entire and not very big. We'd just finished a fair morning's work and were in the kitchen having a cup of tea. Bill jumped on my words, saying there was only one certain way to find out: try him over the schooling fences, and no better time than the present. What's more, he gulped his scalding hot tea down, prodded me into action and rode the little horse over fences himself without any company. And until that moment I had no idea Bill Walter the vet could even ride! Baron Blakeney responded to the evident horsemanship of his strange jockey, pinging the fences several times. Bill then returned the grey to me, saying, 'He'll do the job all right.

You could run him tomorrow if you had an entry.' What a man! Of course, it later transpired he excelled over natural terrain around the Beaufort hunting country in Gloucestershire. Stupid of me, really, to have thought that because Bill was a vet he could not be good at anything else. The episode taught me a valuable lesson: never pre-judge a person, speak as you find.

It was Bill, too, who decided our blossoming yard needed more in-depth help and suggested that the proximity of Bristol University, with its veterinary wing under Geoff Lane, could provide the ideal opening.

It was in 1980 when we noticeably started to move forwards. I wanted to understand what makes one horse better than another. That is still something of a mystery, but what did become plain was the fact that if our moderate horses had everything right – health, fitness and jumping – they would beat horses of a similar class who might only have two of those three attributes correct. Better still, if ours were spot on and we found a contest against inferior horses, we were even more of a certainty. Now that did appeal, and it was probably that which convinced Dad it was worth investing in better facilities.

I'd always been keen on eliminating dust from horses' environment and feed to keep their breathing right, so when Geoff Lane expressed his belief in the principle we had a strong mutual interest from the start. The first innovation he introduced me to was examining horse's throats through an endoscope. It took all the guesswork out of respiratory infections and stopped us doing lasting damage to horses by racing them when, unbeknown to us, they were ill. Obviously we could not expect to scope all our horses every day, but the twice-daily temperature readings alerted us to those horses that need their throats and lungs checking.

Geoff is inexhaustible in his quest to extend the range of methods we can command to foresee trouble. The pressure pads that forewarn us of strains before they are visually obvious are just one example of developments that have interested me. Even more fascinating is his research into scanning tendons and investigations of which muscles are used for what purpose. I am convinced that in the not-too-distant future there will be discoveries in these areas that will turn long-held beliefs upside down.

Realizing my interest in how things work, rather than just what they do, Geoff conspired with Carol to obtain an unusual Christmas present for me after I'd attended a course at Worcester on horse husbandry. They bought me a complete horse's hind leg in bone form, and were trying to put the thing together when I made an unscheduled visit home. The back door was locked at 10 a.m., which is enough to rouse any husband's interest. When I pressed the bell there seemed to be a great deal of scampering about with no signs of anyone wanting to let me in. I flew around to the kitchen window, only to catch the pair of them crawling around on the floor and a garbled shout to go away. Still inseparable, Carol and Geoff shuffled out of the kitchen to the windowless passageway leading to the rest of the house, leaving me more mystified than ever.

Lame excuses were offered, flushed faces added to the impression of guilt and both parties refused to tell me what they were up to. Even in those days there was enough happening here to divert my interest – we were scoping a bunch of horses, which did grab my attention – and it was not until Christmas Day that the completely reassembled hind leg was produced to explain all.

The bleached bones now stand next to my desk to help ease owners' anguish or explain the extent of the problem when their horses have injured a hind leg. It also comes in handy when physiotherapist Mary Bromiley comes down to lecture the staff on what to do and where to do it after their charges have fallen or made serious mistakes when racing. As with everything in life, common sense is the most reliable course to take, and too often we ignore the obvious. Mary tells the grooms to relate to their own experiences. If we fall over, the first thing we do is to rub the point of contact with one or both hands to ease the pain. What we are in fact doing is encouraging the flow of blood to the injured limb and massaging the stiffness away. We now do this to all our horses after a fall, or even after making a bad mistake at a fence. All the staff soon get to know how and where to massage for the best results. Every little bit of help we can give the horses must amount to something when it is all added together. Short-head verdicts count as much as an easy victory so if every little detail is covered the short heads should go our way more often than not.

Attending the Worcestershire College of Agriculture equine

studies course certainly opened my eyes. Besides the usual topics like the digestive process, the blood system, respiration and disease organisms, lectures on joints, muscles, leg and hoof abnormalities proved fascinating. We dissected legs, hearts and lungs under supervision, giving me access to a completely new field that I had hitherto taken for granted. On my way home it struck me that if I did not know what was under the skin, how the hell could I prevent or cure injuries? The course spurred me on to continue those investigations on my own at home, which I did on a table in the garage, much to the revulsion of my mother and Carol. It was easy enough to get hold of limbs and organs from the abattoir and, surprisingly, in no time at all the thirst for knowledge overrode the initial unpleasantness of post mortems.

Michael Dickinson had been the only licensed trainer to attend the course before I did, although no end of my younger colleagues have followed suit since. I've said before that apart from maths my schoolwork left a lot to be desired due to my total lack of interest in everything else. After leaving school the bookmaking business grabbed me in no uncertain terms; learning about the inner workings of a horse did the same thing. If something interests me I can totally immerse myself in it, whatever it is. If it doesn't, I won't even try.

From 1975 up to 1980 people were entitled to say I was a complete idiot, a joke, and I did not object because it was true; but over the past twelve seasons we have made so many changes to the way horses are trained here that it does now hurt me to be the subject of trashy rumours or totally inaccurate stories in the papers. I try to get on with everybody, but do get annoyed with those people who say things behind my back. Pub talk comes cheap but can do a lot of damage as it spreads. If any trainer or owner has a grievance and is honest enough to confront me, at least I get the chance to defend myself against the accusation or explain the reason for this misunderstanding.

Having evolved our present system, I am convinced that long steady cantering makes horses slow. Ours never come off the bridle at home, although they do quicken up over short distances. If I see a lad pushing the head off one or using a whip up the gallops, he's not long with the stable. There will naturally be times when a horse needs correction, needs a smack, but that's all. I had the occasional smack as a kid when I wilfully opposed my parents, but only when it was absolutely necessary.

Every season I get the conditional jockeys together and tell them they are like prefects at school. It is their duty to let me know if someone is mistreating one of the horses. Far from being a sneak, it is simply taking proper responsibility. If I know what is going on, I can sort it out quietly. Who knows, the horse they see being abused may be their ride in public the next week. It's in all our interests to work to the same end: happy horses and lots of winners.

Sometimes apparently harsh methods are actually the kindest option. We have a row of stables with the doors and window-ledges wired to a low electric current to stop horses that crib-bite, which inevitably leads to windsucking and eventually impairs their breathing. Horses are sensible enough only to grab the electrified edges once; it does not hurt them a great deal but it does give them a shock. The method has a draw-back though; when we turn off the current to take a horse out of one stable, the rest in that row know immediately and grab the nearest available toothhold to start windsucking. Dad's working on that problem now.

The desire to know more about this side of the job took Pipe to Newmarket in 1977 for a series of lectures at the Animal Health Trust. It was the first time scientists and trainers had been brought together in this country. Barry Allen, a professional biologist who had moved from research in humans to join the AHT at racing's headquarters nine years earlier, stimulated Pipe's interest most of all the lecturers and during the lunch-break it was no coincidence to find Martin and Carol seated next to him.

Pipe
I took notes of everything he said on the subject of the virus and how to recognize it in the formative stages. We took all the precautions suggested then, yet it was not until 1982, when we were decimated by some bug or other, that I went back to Barry for help. The blood samples we sent to him revealed that the prevalent strain was actually on its second or third round among many of the affected horses. It came home to me that I had foolishly wasted the five years since first realizing the sense Barry had talked at Newmarket. The immunity period is so short in

horses that by the time the animals infected first had recovered, they were catching it again from newly stricken horses. Barry saw we had quite a problem on our hands and agreed to come down here to sort it out.

Allen
The most encouraging thing about Martin was his willingness to eradicate the problem. Sadly, some people prefer to pretend it does not exist. Horses can excrete a virus for up to twelve days, making immediate isolation paramount. The bugs are transmitted from horse to horse directly and also via humans. That means the moment you find an animal with a temperature it must be removed and the horses either side of it tested, as well as any other horses the infected horse's groom cares for or has ridden.

During my first stay with Martin we decided exactly what equipment he needed to prevent a recurrence of a virus and agreed on the importance and cost-effectiveness of an on-site testing capability. There followed a series of financial discussions with Mr Pipe senior, who claims to be able to obtain anything at the cheapest price. Eventually we agreed to differ. Buying these specialist machines required someone who knew the life-expectancy of second-hand equipment, but on the whole I would agree that Dave Pipe could squeeze the last five pence out of any deal.

The machinery came from human research units, only needing different calibrations to set it up for equine application. In lay terms, if a human blood-testing machine records on a scale of 1/100, for horses the scale needs to be 1/20, which means the margin for error is far greater and it is consequently more important that testers know what they are doing. I've spent twenty-four years now solely researching the effects of blood-related problems in horses, and yet I've learnt more in the past two years than in the previous twenty-two.

Given the go-ahead, the lab was up and running in no time. I spent all my free days down at the yard; it was an exciting and rewarding period, and what is more it provided the first winning streak I'd ever encountered as a punter!

It also fell to me to select a technician. From an original list of 185 applicants, which included one hopeful betting shop manager, a group of ten fitted the bill; Katie Redgate turned out to be

177

the most suitable, and she stayed through the formative years, then handed over to Sue Challacombe who only occasionally has recourse to calling me in.

Martin became worried in late January 1992 that several of his younger horses were wrong. The eight samples he sent showed five horses to be affected but, not satisfied he had identified the problem soon enough, he went to the bother of sending me samples of all 166 horses in his two main yards. The results of these tests cleared all but the suspected quintet. Martin fully realizes the importance of prompt action and also is fortunate enough to have the facility on-site to test daily if he suspects the spread of a virus.

Sadly, the virus is as endemic to Britain as malaria is to Africa. You have to realize that research into such things as vitamins was being carried out as long ago as 1900, which means our blood research and its viral evidence has a lot of catching up to do. Trainers are walking through a minefield without realizing it.

Regular testing now also reveals stress in a horse and, when explored further, can tell us if the pain causing the stress is the result of infection; if not, there is a hidden injury. Respiratory viruses have developed to the stage now where even scoping into a horse's lungs does not always tell the true story. If scoping fails to reveal anything amiss, a tracheal wash will flush out mucus and this tells us a whole lot more about the particular problem. Basically, the horse's system produces mucus after a virus to protect the lung's lining, but it is this muck, nature's protection, that blocks the airways and stops the horse performing to its true ability. After years of research and experience, I can now look at a horse in the parade ring before a race and know it is not right.

The trouble is, though, that horses in stress or in the later stages of a viral infection can and do win races despite their condition. This has led to several trainers challenging the worth of testing at all. The question they should really be asking themselves is, what damage are they doing to the horse's future health by racing it while stressed?

Dust in anything is a source of respiratory problem and I am convinced that bedding horses on straw is one of the main culprits. Even the advent of paper bedding has not eradicated that scourge: in 1991 Dick Hern's horses showed undeniable signs of paper dust in their lungs. With this in mind, Louis Jones has installed a process of dust extraction within his paper-chopping machinery in Lambourn.

As a result of the recent advances in blood testing for viral infection and stress, there are a lot of semi-qualified people around trying to break into the field; but there is no doubt in my mind that badly read results are worse than no results at all.

It is one of Pipe's great strengths that he is able to recognize true experts, and he is quick to enlist them to his cause. He values their opinions accordingly, and this has contributed largely to putting him ahead of the game, especially in veterinary matters.

Chapter 19

Eliminating the Risks

Martin Pipe is the first to admit that his early trial-and-error methods of training produced their fair share of errors. However, over the last six seasons he has developed a process of eliminating errors to arrive at a set of methods that is now firmly established. To do so he has questioned received beliefs, explored the benefits of new technology and recruited experts in every field. The results in recent years speak for themselves.

Of course, to a degree his success is a numbers game, with his two yards together able to house 166 horses. Yet the spiralling success story hinges on more than numerical fire-power: his high percentage of winners to runners is still hard to better, and that from a staple population of very ordinary horses – though the pattern has changed of late as the stable's record of getting the best out of whatever horse he is sent has attracted the big players and their quality steeplechasers.

Pipe
I try to relate horses to humans, especially when they have injuries or problems, and it is that group who require most attention. People say no one can handle this many horses properly, but I deny that totally. I am able to give my horses more individual attention now than when Dennis Dummett and I had only six horses to look after. In those days we were flat out simply to get the work done; there was never any time to step back and observe them. With the system that has evolved now,

my eyes and ears are constantly taking in changes in behavioural patterns or appearance. That is the crux of training: changes are the horses' way of telling us something is amiss. They can talk all right if only we have the time and inclination to listen.

Quite often I don't look at the list of horses working as I watch the gallops. The mind needs to be emptied of preconceived ideas if it is to spot discrepancies. Some horses are natural oddities, and then I would be worried if they departed from their idiosyncrasies. I start every day afresh and let my eyes and ears work for me. I cycle around the yard listening and watching. The sounds from stables are many: a cough, a hoof scraping the floor, windsucking, groaning, a horse rolling or kicking the stable door. There are always sounds hitting me when the yard is at rest. If whatever I hear is normal for that horse, fine. If not, I check it out. Even such apparently small details as the amount of water a horse has drunk overnight or the state of its droppings tell a story. Dennis will already have checked all the horses when doing the breakfast feeds before the main body of staff arrive. We compare notes in case a horse we intend to gallop or race needs further investigation. If in doubt, we never take a chance.

By the time first lot pull out of their stables the staff will have taken their horses' temperatures, checked their mangers for any leftover food and generally looked for any deviations from normal. I trust the lads and girls to report anything to me, even if it is only a gut feeling that all is not right. We watch the string walk around the yard and then the covered ride as the horses warm up and stretch their muscles. I like to see most of them acting fresh, but if a usually docile horse is bucking and kicking you can bet there is something hurting his back. The same sympton can mean totally opposite conditions in different horses.

Our gallops are only half a mile from the stables and that journey is the only time our horses ever see a road; soon a new wood-chip lane across the paddocks will do away even with that. To make one last check for abnormalities before they gallop I slowly pass the string in the old Range Rover Dad gave us for our wedding present in 1971. This is to take a view from the girth downwards to look for signs of stiffness. We have a man on his feet to close the gate from the road into the gallops in case a horse gets loose; they are like homing pigeons and are no respecters of traffic.

Every rider knows what work his or her horse is to do from a list pinned up daily in the tackroom. Steady, half- and three-quarter speed are the only instructions they get, although they vary according to the fitness of their mount. My horses canter every day on the all-weather wood-chip strip in groups of three. They never trot, either on the road or on turf; it is a gait I consider alien and damaging. It puts too much pressure on the joints and causes concussion in the cannon bone. I've also been following studies in Sweden where they have established a third tendon deep down that is never used at the trot, and implanted microchips into all moving parts to establish what exercise is most beneficial. By all accounts I have been doing the right thing without knowing why.

Having cantered up the strip, the horses circle until the last group has completed work, then they about-turn and lob quietly back downhill to the start, where once again they wheel around on the spot to do their second piece of work. That process is repeated for three uphill canters and two downhill.

Horses soon learn to accept that there is no need to surge into action the moment they turn around at the top. Visitors constantly remark at how settled the horses are while waiting their turns. Another fact worth noting is the uncanny habit of routine they develop when actually working. First time up, the horses take a normal hold of the bridle; then they hack back off the bit. Second time up, they pull harder, only to drop the bridle again to canter downhill before really pulling for their heads when doing their last piece of work. They work hardest when wanted and relax when cantering back to the start. Even old Melendez, who had to be forced to canter in either direction on the first four trips, always happily obliged on the final time then contentedly walked back to where I stand to observe them. Now how could he know the fifth canter is the last – unless horses can count?

Watching my string do the same thing every day has convinced me that horses are happier in a daily routine. Most people advocate a change of scenery to keep horses' minds fresh, but that is a line of thought I do not accept. I think they expend too much mental energy if they are taken to strange places. Many trainers take their horses to racecourses to gallop after the last event, but although they do no more work than at home, they lose a lot of weight and that can only be as a result of the box ride and change of venue using up nervous energy.

Obviously I cannot try one horse against another over my short four-furlong gallop, and as they are never stressed off the bridle they are keen to work every day. The close proximity of the gallops to the stables means they are only out for forty minutes at a time, although the stuffier ones will swim afterwards and in some cases canter again after lunch.

The way I tell when a horse is ready to run – and I don't run them until they are able to win – is purely by listening to its breathing and monitoring its recovery rate. The fitter a horse is, the quicker he stops blowing and his heart rate returns to normal. I have a particular place by the strip where I stand to listen to their breathing when working and often I close my eyes to sharpen my hearing. When I hear unusual or laboured respiration I quickly open my eyes to check out the identity of the horse in question and note it on a pad. Here, *everything* is noted in writing. I will not accept the lame excuse that something had been spotted but forgotten, even from myself.

On the walk home I always ask every rider their opinion of their mounts; they tell me 'fine/lazy/keen/excitable/ready to win/ not sure'. Only I ever say a horse is useless, but that's just to goad them. The staff defend their horses fiercely and if ever one of them agreed on that score, a horse would indeed be very moderate. And I still get a buzz from winning with bad horses. Providing an owner gives me a free hand to run in its class, I'll win with it. Every dog has its day.

To start horses off from grass we walk for a minimum of six weeks, then go straight to cantering. At that stage they may also swim, depending on the amount of fat they are carrying. I'll take as long as is necessary to get a horse fit, although the norm is three months. Once fully fit, horses can take races close together but running fat horses to attain fitness is wrong in my mind. It does more harm than good, putting strain on tendons and muscles when the horse is tiring. People accuse me of being too hard on my horses, but the reverse is true. Mine are never put under stress at home; they are built up gradually, and if they are showing signs of weakness or immaturity, we lay them off. Careful monitoring of everything a horse eats and daily short-term cantering produces lean, hard equine athletes ready for the fray. You don't see fat human runners, do you?

Like all good horse handlers, I pay attention to a horse's state of mind. Although I do not agree with the change-of-scenery idea, we make a point of giving the animals love and affection in and out of the stable, ensuring they feel safe with their surroundings; and we try to make exercise enjoyable, so that they can't wait to get at it in the mornings. By using the pool and the automatic exercisers, schooling youngsters over small jumps or even taking horses up the gallops again, we manage to get most inmates out of their stables twice a day, breaking their confinement up as much as is possible.

The gallop I use cannot tell me which is the best horse out of a pair, but so many times the horses that come up the easiest are not the fastest on the course. We've had some slow home workers who turn out to be good racehorses: Pharoah's Laen, for one, Terry Johnsey's chaser who won eight out of his first fifteen starts for us before a freak racing accident saw a piece of birch slice up into his tendon, almost severing all the working parts in the lower leg. Quite a lot of our regular winners would come into the slower bracket, but simply because they are fully fit they keep galloping right to the finish, and it is that, more than sheer speed, that wins races. Scu says ours is the only stable to produce slow horses for him to win on, everyone else tells him how fast their horses are. Few live up to the billing. On the subject of slow horses, I bought Sporting Mariner from Doncaster sales for no other reason than that *Timeform* stated he was slow, and he proceeded to win seven of his twenty-two starts. If they all won a third of their races the game would pay for itself.

A good example of misleading gallops came at Devon and Exeter in the late seventies when Lorna Vincent was in her heyday. She rode work here and was in no doubt when choosing to partner Cherchez La Femme instead of my own Weston Bay. Kay Rees got the ride on Lorna's rejected mount and was told to toddle around and enjoy the outing as she couldn't win on any known home form. Lorna's horse went backwards as if shot and Kay swept through on the wide outside to win easily with tears of joy streaming down her face.

There is no big secret to training winners. Proper feeding and exercise is common sense. Horses tell you when they are ready to run if only you listen to them and don't guess. If any of us spots something amiss we locate it then hand the problem over to the vets to sort out before attempting to bring the horse to the boil. Just like us, horses accumulate aches and pains through life which need treating accordingly. Swimming, relaxing under heatlamps, physiotherapy and proper grooming all do the trick. Grooming is important, and I don't mean tickling with a soft brush. My staff use old fashioned strapping on horses during the half hour each one gets every evening. Strapping is a form of massage which soothes bruised muscles and helps to develop others. Many racehorses don't get groomed because their lads don't have the time, now that economics have forced many trainers to increase the lads' charges from two each to as many as five; but I consider that false economy.

Most horses come in from a summer's grass far too fat. Excess blubber has to be worked off, which in turn puts undue strain on joints. It also takes far longer to take a lot of the weight off, which adds considerably to the training costs. Much better to control grazing sensibly to avoid the horses getting obese in the first place.

As so many horses join us with injuries to their backs, I devised a simple method of confirming my eyesight, or, in a lot of cases, finding what the human eye misses. The moment a new charge arrives we photograph its quarters from behind, using a camera on a tripod placed level with the top of the horse's tail. The print is developed within seconds and as soon as it is dry I place an equal-sized piece of tracing paper over the photo and trace the outline. I then fold the paper in half, and the outline shows any discrepancies in the quarters.

Trying to train horses when all their parts are not able to function wastes my time and the owner's money. Here we work with the horses like a fitness centre does with humans, honing the parts that are faulty or damaged. The vets have helped me develop an eye for locating problems and latterly Mary Bromiley, the human and equine physiotherapist, has added new dimensions to the art of returning horses to soundness.

My own experience of recuperating from car crashes and falls has been applied to the horses' problems, too. After my ankle was smashed in a car accident it healed solid, and I can still vividly remember Carol forcing me against the wall to regenerate even the slightest movement. After a month of grappling against each other there was half an inch of flexion. It was uncomfortable, but it got me going again. With that in mind, I have come to believe that many horse injuries benefit from controlled exercise much more than from rest. There are many human ideas we can use with horses, but we must understand and respect their animal senses and sensitivities. I liken them to children, who seem far happier if they know the routine and rules in the home. Kids like stories read to them in the safety of their bedrooms, and likewise horses feel comfortable with particular grooms and stabled in the same place each season.

Our stable bedding these days is shredded paper or wood shavings. We used to use straw because we grew our own; basically, it was cheap. These days we don't: it is too dusty, too much is contaminated with pesticides, and worst of all the horses eat it. If they fill themselves up with rubbish they are not going to eat a balanced diet.

I want to know exactly what goes into every horse's stomach: feeding is just as important as the right work. Dennis does all the feeding, except on Sunday mornings when I take over to give him a break. He is a master feeder and knows to the oat what each horse will take without going off its feed. He's drummed it into me that the moment one oat or nut is left over a horse will quickly lose its appetite, and before long there is a problem. We feed Ebor nuts from Newcastle, oats off our own farm and Visorbin as a vitamin supplement. Visorbin is quicker than anything to perk horses up. No end of feed merchants have tried to get me to change to another brand by offering reduced prices and in some cases free supplies, but to no avail.

We also grow all our own hay, samples of which we send away to be tested before use. This is another area where I deviate from standard practice: I employ a team of girls to give all the horses their ration so they know exactly what to give each horse according to its size and workload. The night before a race I like a horse to have no more than a bird's nest. Hay is fed on the floor; I've seen too many accidents caused by haynets and racks. After all, horses forage off the ground by nature.

I make a point of listening to everyone, then sitting back and forming an opinion of my own. Coming into racing from a bookmaking background, I am not blinkered by old beliefs handed down within horsy families. For example, I conducted my own research into the effects of the mandatory injection against equine flu. Guidelines vary on how long a rest period should be given after the virus has been injected; some trainers canter the horses again as soon as two days later. I blood-tested two horses every day after their flu jabs to determine the infected period; one recovered in fourteen days, the other took eighteen. Imagine the discomfort and possible damage caused by working horses before they are clear.

Feed additives have also been tested via the blood picture, while our own scope, used by resident vet Ray Dillaway, alerts us to respiratory problems before they become evident rather than afterwards.

Tendons can be scanned on site to affirm strains, although both Dennis and myself, plus a large number of the staff, pride ourselves on being able to feel trouble before it becomes visible. Strangely, though, I'm only able to get the correct messages through my left hand.

The only innovation that failed to enthuse me was a pressure mat linked to a computer to alert us to a horse favouring one leg over another, indicating the onset of lameness. I tried it for two years and thought it interesting rather than essential. Yet despite my lukewarm reaction to that idea, I am convinced that science and facts have to be better than guesswork. I'll try anything I think might eliminate a risk. Even so, I make time to watch, listen and feel every horse every day I am at home, and if I am not Dennis does it for me. In the end it is down to my judgement, and if anything fails to add up, an intended runner stays at home.

Horses kept at livery before joining me are monitored by means of a daily form describing the horse's work, feed, comments on behaviour, vet's remarks and twice-daily temperatures. These forms are faxed or posted to the office every Friday for my inspection on Sunday.

No matter how much care is taken of their health or how much training is done, horses will still struggle if jumping badly or running against better-class rivals. It took me too long to put the jumping aspect right here but pitting horses against their inferiors has been the biggest single factor in getting winners. I suppose that stemmed from my bookmaking days when we evaluated form to decide whether to hedge or keep a bet. It may sound boring and even prompt a few sniggers when I tell you I take the form book to bed and on the few holidays we have. Carol suffers this indulgence very tolerantly, considering that quite often she has just dropped off to sleep when my excitement at finding the ideal race for a particular horse elicits a shout of joy which wakes her up.

When we tried to go through the card at Devon and Exeter last August the real excitement for me was months before when marrying the horses to the right races. On the day when Sweet'N'Twenty went lame prior to racing I knew we would fall flat in the final contest so the day itself felt like an anti-climax. That sounds silly, really, when we ended up with five winners; but the fun was in the plotting.

Another long-range victory planned with the form book on the pillow was Trifolene's win at the Galway Festival on 30 July 1991. Dublin-based accountant David L'Estrange wanted to win there to achieve a long-held ambition. The mare was among the batch owned by Pipe–Scudamore Racing plc being sold at the company's dispersal sale in early June. I had already seen the race that had been made for her and told David she would take the third race on the second day at the Festival. And she did. David had a large punt on his new purchase and achieved his ambition. Sadly, though, Trifolene strained a tendon in winning, which is sometimes the price of victory over fences at that time of year.

Chapter 20

Scu's Part of the Big Time

Peter Scudamore, who had originally thought of the Pipe stable as no more than a small West Country yard, took note of its steady progress in the early eighties and when stable jockey Paul Leach was injured in February 1985, was keen to take a slice of the action. Thus began the association that has since become the most numerically successful in the history of National Hunt racing.

At the time Scu initiated this partnership he was way ahead of his rivals, with the single glaring exception of John Francome, who constantly held top spot, not only as far as winners were concerned, but also as the darling of press and public. No matter how expertly Scu performed to win a race, John got the headlines. Scu constantly seemed to be trailing in Francome's wake, and even for such a modest person the situation had become depressing.

Scudamore
I saw Martin Pipe's stable as the ideal addition to my armoury that I needed in order to match Francome's strength. John had early- and late-season runners from John Jenkins's powerful stable to complement his mainstay of quality mid-term winners from Fred Winter's Lambourn operation. At the time of my first tentative approach to Martin, he was still going strong and at thirty-two looked to have several good years to go on kicking dirt in my face. The secret of his durability was his outstanding horsemanship, which saw him dramatically alter the usual ratio of falls to rides in his favour.

My initial approach to Martin was far from accidental. I wanted the job with him to maintain a steady supply of winners throughout the year, but at that stage I was quite prepared to pick up the spares or ride when Paul Leach was injured or could not do the weight. Jump jockeys do have morals regarding other people's regular rides; even when a stable's main rider is out of action, there may be others in the wings who have earned the right to take over in such circumstances. I did not want to tread on anyone's toes although I would have been slow not to make myself available.

Our first venture resulted in the type of victory people have come to take for granted from us. Riding the diminutive Hieronymous at Haydock Park, my orders from Martin were simple: 'Make all the running and you'll win.' That proved to be a huge understatement as the 5–1 shot went thirty lengths clear of some useful opponents, kicked several hurdles out of the ground without altering his stride and proceeded to make some highly-thought-of juvenile horses look decidedly moderate. We scored by a facile fifteen lengths easing down. I have never been so fast on soft ground yet still able to maintain the pace to the end in a staying race. On dismounting I told Martin that was the fittest horse I'd ever ridden, which seemed to throw him somewhat. He was bemused at the thought that all horses were not fit to run a race out to its conclusion.

Ironically, John Francome rode Horn Of Plenty into second spot that day; had he not surprisingly retired later that season I am convinced he would have tasted similar frustration too often for his liking. Martin's depth in strength was the weapon I had lacked to challenge Franc.

Ten days after Haydock Park, the Cheltenham Festival saw Paul Leach back in the saddle without much joy, riding four unplaced mounts for his stable. I rode in thirteen races without success, while John Francome had nine mounts including a faller in the Arkle Chase, The Reject, who started his doubting as to the wisdom of tempting fate too often. With his foot caught in the stirrup when his horse got up, John dangled dangerously upside down while onlookers froze to the spot. John had the presence of mind to grab one rein just as The Reject was deciding to pursue the other horses, forcing him instead to pirouette around his hapless but then safe rider. A month later the same horse fell in the Welsh Champion Chase, again hanging John out to dry. That prompted him to think 'Someone up there is trying to tell me something,' and taking note he instantly retired, despite having a lucrative contract to ride in the World Jump Jockeys' Championship at Cheltenham two days later.

The season following Francome's premature abdication, Simon Sherwood won the sought-after job to partner the Jenkins horses, leaving me in much the same state as before. I did not immediately jump into the vacated job with Fred Winter, instead opting to remain as stable jockey to David Nicholson although that liaison had not hitherto proved numerically strong enough to make me outright champion jockey. John and I did share the title with a final score of 120 winners in 1982, in quite exceptional circumstances. There is no doubt I would have ended up outright champion that year but for breaking my leg when twenty winners clear of my arch-rival a month before the season finished. Equally certain, though, is that I would not have eventually shared that title had Francome continued riding after drawing level with me.

It still amazes me now to recall the widely differing interpretations the press put on John's actions. He made the gesture unselfishly, purely out of a sense of honour, knowing in his heart I would have taken the title that I so desperately wanted had I stayed in one piece. Totally missing the point, some sections of the press intimated that John had done it to gain public favour! Nothing could be further from the truth.

It is a popular misconception that all jump jockeys are poorly educated. In fact, several of my colleagues have taken degrees prior to turning professional, and many others managed good A-level passes. My own schooling produced two A-level passes in Medieval History and British Constitution at Belmont Abbey, but I did not need to be a genius to see the formula needed if I was to assume Francome's mantle. Martin's job was the answer, provided it came by a natural process of retirement not an engineered sacking.

The 1985–6 season saw me increasingly getting off David Nicholson's horses to ride Pipe-trained good things, which naturally grated on my main employer. I have never taken a retainer from trainers, preferring to assure them verbally of my loyalty, with the proviso that I could choose other stables' horses if a race was patently one-sided. To me that seemed a logical path.

Martin has never offered a retainer, for two main reasons. It would add considerably to owners' bills; and if a horse holds an obvious winning chance, leading jockeys or their agents scramble to secure the ride. He knows full well that most of the top riders would leap at the chance to fill my boots and in the times when I've been injured he has been courted by them all. Ironically, this job is the first I would consider being bound to by contract yet it is the only one I've had where I haven't been offered one!

That season proved to be the last for Paul Leach, who rode twenty-five of Martin's total of seventy-nine successes. Although he could sense it slipping away through more weight and less enthusiasm than the trainer demanded of his jockey, Paul actually started the following campaign, only to give up the ghost after a couple of rides.

The 1986–7 season saw me start off with a live chance of breaking records, with the pick of Martin's quantity stable supplementing Fred Winter's quality string. The theory failed to become reality immediately; the first seven runners I rode for Martin's stable all found others too good. I sensed the situation was under review; Mr Pipe senior started to mutter about me being an unlucky jockey, what he says has a large bearing on what happens. You need results in this job; bad luck does not wash.

Yet from that sluggish beginning the job evolved to the present level. Martin and I are like-minded; we are never satisfied with just winning, especially if we think a victory has been in part the result of good fortune. Then as now, Martin constantly asks me to bring a matter to his attention immediately if I see anything I think is wrong or can be improved on the training side. Conversely, if Martin is less than happy with an aspect of my riding he tells me.

My initial suggestions centred on the schooling facilities which, although upgraded by Paul Leach, nevertheless fell short of Fred Winter's and David Nicholson's standards. Martin had only two small steeplechase fences when I joined forces with him. His policy still leaned towards the principle that horses were more likely to injure themselves schooling than galloping.

This theory fitted in with his basic pattern of eliminating every risk; only in this instance the decision worked against his goal. Once I'd pointed out that the removal of the home risk by doing as little schooling as possible actually increased the chance of injury when racing, Martin set about building whatever schooling facility I requested. He is a man of definite opinions, yet is perfectly willing to reverse them if convinced by logic and reason. It is situations like this one that illustrate his strength of character: having been argued into realizing that his long-held belief was in fact wrong, he did an about-turn.

Now we have a row of five uphill fences running hard against a hedge, thus eliminating distractions from one side at least. They are in constant use, putting the finishing touch to the increasing number of steeplechasers in the Pond House string. With as many as three contenders in most major steeplechases these days it is hard to imagine that only eight seasons ago the stable had 50 hurdle winners before sending out its first victor over fences.

Before a novice horse attempts the biggest jumps it has repeated sessions indoors over tiny obstacles, leading to more daunting logs and tree-trunks, also shielded from distractions, within the confines of the enormous covered canter. Portable hurdles and fences are used on the wood-chip gallop, saving the turf from being ravaged in wet times and also providing an alternative for the horses who get too excited on days when work is switched from the strip to the schooling ground.

The new-found emphasis on teaching horses to jump accurately and with confidence enabled us to expand another hallmark of the stable: dictating the pace of a race. Ours do not need to be pampered on the course by getting a lead from others, whether it's their first time or their tenth. Most happily cut out the running without question. The benefits are threefold. First, ground gained at the start while others are dithering has to be made up at some stage by the pursuers, using up valuable energy while ours are only cruising. Second, from the front we can dictate the pace to take advantage of stamina over any trip. How many times do you hear the excuse 'they went too slow, it turned into a four-furlong sprint instead of a two-miler'? We have eliminated that factor. Third, a true gallop capitalizes on our undeniable fitness edge. Martin only runs his horses when satisfied they are ready, while in every jumping contest a large percentage of runners are patently in need of the outing. When we go on from the rise of the tapes, those rivals who are a bit short of peak fitness will be found out, whereas in a slowly run event untuned horses can and do win. It is a fallacy that Martin's runners go like scalded cats then sprint again when tackled. My aim is to race at a high but level cruising speed, which in practice puts challengers under pressure just to get to our tail. Usually it is the challenger who weakens, not we who quicken.

To illustrate that point, Tom Clapton, a novice hurdler on whom I won at Newton Abbot, finished dog-tired even though racing on good ground. Martin thought I had gone far too fast over the first mile, bursting instead of nursing my mount. I was adamant I had not, agreeing to settle the matter back at Pond House by sectional timing of the race from the SIS televised recording. I was exonerated when the stop watch conclusively proved a constant pace between the hurdles until the horse tied up going to the final flight. Martin capitulated, but, still far from content with the performance, tested the winner for any medical sign that would explain the weakening in the final furlong: a blood test revealed the muscle enzyme's level to be widely amiss. Few other trainers would have conducted such in-depth inquiries into a ten-length winner's well being.

Our regular review of each other's roles can only be of benefit to the end result, and it is probably because Martin came into the game as an outsider that his often obvious battle plans are not offensive to me. 'Don't go near the top weight at the start, he may shy at the tapes/Bradley's mount jumps right handed/ Elsworth's horse doesn't stay the trip/the second favourite looks bad in the paddock and is drifting in the betting, he's no danger/ Keep away from Dunwoody, his horse hates jumping open ditches/' – these are more the kind of comments a young rider would expect. It could sound patronizing; from Martin it is genuine help.

Dave Pipe has often told me he thought I was useless when I first rode for the stable, just like the majority of riders who are only happy when sitting in mid-division to pounce after the last jump. Now I have perfected the front-running tactics the trainer's father considers me to be a proper jockey!

My Cup Of Tea was a rarity: he never responded to schooling, remained unpredictable at the jumps and when fresh was

196

positively frightening. Faced with the type of ride that makes laxatives redundant and left to my own judgement, I popped the gelding out in front at Newton Abbot to make him think about the job in hand instead of spending his vital energy into the equine/human struggle, which, whoever won, would be detrimental in the long run. That sort of decision would, of course, normally be the jockey's. However, if the trainer knew more about the horse than the man asked to execute the plan, he would be definite with the orders. Martin knew this to be a tricky ride and as it was my neck on the line, he was happy to let me decide the best tactics.

Celcius came into the opposite category. Told to hold the ungenerous gelding up for one short, sharp run in a four-horse race, I decided the funereal pace set was far too slow and decided to disregard the orders, attempting to make all the running after the first flight of hurdles. We got well and truly stuffed as the little sod downed tools when challenged. Martin was so furious I thought he would bust a gut, but I made my decision at the time thinking it to be correct and was unrepentant. Neither of us raised our voices but to those who know us it was perfectly obvious we both felt aggrieved. In time events proved Martin correct, and I accepted I was wrong.

In the case of Walnut Way at Wincanton Martin's own lack of riding experience caused the biggest rift between us. The horse hung left-handed from the start on a course that has sharp right-handed bends. The ground, slippery from rain on a hard surface, required caution at the jumps and I did the sensible thing by keeping hold of Walnut Way's head. Nobody gains from a fall, especially not the horse who, even if not injured, could lose his nerve. The gently, gently approach saw us come back beaten but, significantly, in one piece. Martin saw it differently. He was convinced I'd lost my bottle, which really did hurt me. That is the one insult which will penetrate a rider's inner core. There is a time for throwing caution to the wind, just as there is for using the experience of previous similar situations. Kamikaze pilots look good when a daring ride comes off, but history shows that calculated precision – cool nerve rather than blind bravery – must be the long-term favourite. In this instance Martin had reacted to the story he saw without inquiring further into the reason why I acted with caution. Although the incident hurt my pride, once we had talked it through, the unsavoury episode faded away, as both of us only wanted to work for better results. Personal feelings do not enter the equation.

Martin is often full of self-doubt. He is much happier dealing with horses than people, works better under pressure, is quite superstitious and if left to fend for himself would not survive. Newbury's parade ring before the 1988 Hennessy Cognac Gold Cup is a typical example of the self-doubt he is prey to. Beau Ranger had won the valuable Edward Hanmer Chase at Haydock Park only three days earlier on his seasonal reappearance, yet in the limbo period before the bell to mount up rang, Martin continually doubted Strands Of Gold's fitness on this, his first run of the season. After listening to the mutterings for a while I asked the simple question: 'Is this one as forward as Beau Ranger?' When told yes, I insisted he stop his mithering, Strands would win. And he did.

As to his handling of humans, the year long anti-press period reveals the way Martin thought. In his own mind he was still a small-time trainer when to everyone else he had arrived. Initially he could run horses as he pleased, do virtually what he wanted without anyone noticing or, for that matter, caring. Then suddenly the press were demanding to know why, when or where horses were running, which to Martin seemed an invasion of his hitherto unthreatened privacy. He was brusque, even rude, to some and totally ignored others, resulting in some pretty adverse comments by the snubbed reporters. We all suffer from endless misquotes and watch helplessly as one line develops into a whole story. The *Cook Report* changed all that for Martin, when the majority of the journalists supported him. Now he sees we need the media more than they need us.

With the horses he calls the tunes and they invariably dance to them. There would also be a fair amount of secrecy emanating from his father's example. At that time Mr Pipe senior had told us all not to speak to the press; then the following day's *Sporting Life* displayed a large photograph of him discussing the transactions at Ascot sales. When the situation was raised and his words queried over breakfast, Mr Pipe had the cheek to deny the photo was of him. What changes? If you are the person who signs the cheques, you are right even if you are wrong.

Yet in his professional dealings with people, Martin is formidably efficient. Apart from the occasional times he shuts himself in the office to cut himself off from the world, Martin is able to deal with a dozen queries at the same time, make decisions and carry on several conversations while scanning papers on his desk.

The majority of trainers are superstitious and Martin more than most. His aversion to green is obsessive and on too many occasions to recount he has ignored friends and owners sporting green clothes. Worse still, he's caused several pile-ups on escalators when attempting to avoid contact with the dreaded colour. Another superstition of Martin's is standing in the same place in various parade rings where he has experienced previous successes. I know exactly where to find him when I go into the most crowded paddock, then every now and again he's missing when we've experienced some bad luck and the formerly lucky spot loses its magic. Of course, nothing alters the results; but if adhering to firm beliefs sets someone's mind at rest, it's got to be helpful.

As for my assertion that Martin is helpless except for training racehorses, when you are as successful as he is it makes little difference. Carol understands Martin better than anyone except perhaps his mother – and having said that, there must be quite a few traits he's developed since Betty Pipe handed over custody of her only son to Carol twenty years ago. Carol does every mortal thing for Martin in the home, as well as ordering his meals when they dine out. She is the most marvellous lady, absolutely secure in herself, never doubting a decision, runs the office and keeps everyone together. With his father monitoring everything mechanical or practical (he was catching mice when I went to the yard recently), Carol overseeing the accounting and Chester generally mopping up owners, press and the telephone tipping service, Martin is free to concentrate solely on training the horses, a luxury not enjoyed to the same degree by many of his colleagues with much smaller strings.

A prime example of Martin's in-depth view of any given situation came at Southwell during the full-scale trials of the artificial racing surface. Having sent horses for three of the mock races, not content to take things at face value my orders covered all eventualities. In successive trials they ranged from 'make' the running' to 'stay in the middle of the pack' and finally 'drop out last then make progress up the inner before switching to the outside'. As a result I returned to Nicholashayne well armed with the probable outcome in any future circumstances encountered on the Fibresand surface.

Not content with sounding out one of the new surfaces, Martin dispatched another batch of horses to Lingfield Park to assess and compare the Equitrack. One of the Lingfield batch provided me with a rare chance to play at being Lester Piggott. Riding Regal Ambition, I dropped in last on the rail, still eyeing the leading group as they fought for the prime positions on the run to the final bend. Letting out a bit of rein I felt a surge of power from my partner, providing me, normally a front-running rider, with an opportunity to test my own ability to time a late winning run and take victory by a short head. In indulging myself I deprived poor Ray Goldstein of success. Such unusual tactics from me were not lost on the press, who swarmed over anyone and everyone even remotely connected with the stable to extricate the flying machine's name. (In those trials horses' declared names were not necessarily their real ones.) With our team adhering to orders of secrecy, no one on the course discovered the horse's true identity; the most persistent were fed a false name to get them off our backs.

When Regal Ambition next appeared under his rightful name, he was in fact beaten a head at Worcester, but by no less a star than Remittance Man. The defeat alerted me to the fact that stamina was the gelding's forte, a valuable lesson and one which soon paid dividends. The evaluation proved correct next time out when we made all to beat the Jenny Pitman pair Strong Gold and Black Moccasin by fifteen lengths and the same. The next time out saw me force the pace once again to beat Mrs Pitman's talking horse Danny Harrold by a facile twenty-five lengths at Leicester. Jenny bleated about hers being wrong afterwards, but the truth was that ours was very good, which he proved when taking the Sun Alliance Hurdle at the Cheltenham Festival by an easy twelve lengths.

When Regal Ambition broke down on both front tendons in the $750,000 Dueling Grounds Hurdle in Kentucky under Jonothan Lower, having been sold for a reputed $300,000. I was upset. He had so much ability; it was a tragic ending to such a promising career. Prior to that we'd lost Out Of The Gloom at home, another horse who looked seriously good. Obviously I was distraught by both happenings, but Martin was even more so. People think it's just a winner factory down here; they are very wrong. Horses do count, and we hate to lose them or see them suffer.

Of the stable stars, Sabin Du Loir is the best hurdler I've ridden – never mind fences. Bonanza Boy is quite amazing, he toddles along doing nothing then goes into a turbo-charged scuttle. Carvill's Hill is an enormous powerhouse, a real thrill and I am just so sorry that the racing public did not see the best of him. To ride him at home or on the course is beyond description, he was in another league. Chatam is a potentially brilliant time bomb, as is Rolling Ball, and Terao could be anything.

Reflecting on my position in January 1992, halfway through my first full season as Martin's stable jockey, it occurred to me that I'd previously really been a journeyman rider enjoying plenty of middle-of-the-road winners: I could see Martin was heading for an onslaught on the major steeplechase prizes some years ago and fervently hoped I'd still be in the saddle when it happened. Thanks to the Hay diet, which has removed the drudgery of harder wasting habits, instead of pondering retirement I now feel five years younger. Add to that the more comfortable stirrup length I now use, six holes shorter, and the signs that the best is yet to come from the Pipe stable, I shall ride until I no longer enjoy the sport.

Chapter 21

Today's Opinion

Everyone in the Pipe team is given the chance to express an opinion on whatever horse-related subject falls within his or her scope. Martin calls it Today's Opinion and will digest it before storing or discarding the thinking. He is always flexible enough to change even his long-held views if convinced they are wrong.

Pipe
Situations change and we are prepared to go with the flow here, although on certain subjects, such as use of the whip, I would need strong evidence to change my beliefs. Horses are not dissimilar to us. There are occasions when they need to be corrected or encouraged by using the whip; but too often it is used in the wrong situation. Quite often we have more than one runner in a race, which naturally creates rivalry between our younger jockeys who are all trying to establish themselves. I repeatedly explain that if any of them is in with a chance of winning they can give their mount a couple of smacks to help get the result. But I will not tolerate them getting into battles with each other purely to finish ahead of a stable companion regardless of where in the race they are likely to finish. A keen youngster thinks it will impress me to finish closest to the winner but that is my last concern.

I'm looking for jockeys who use their brains. Most damage is inflicted when horses tire, towards the end of a race, so that is when most care should be taken. Weston Bay was killed as a result of two jockeys going hell for leather at the last fence trying to beat each other. What is the point? Finishing sixth or seventh makes little difference. It makes my blood boil to see beaten horses hit when they are going backwards. Lots of riders, and that includes established jockeys, hit a horse for too long and too late. More action should be taken against these offenders rather than those battling it out for a win, provided of course, the horses being encouraged by the stick are responding to the driving.

Perhaps the answer is to restrict the rider's arm movement to no more than shoulder height; at least then the blow would not land with the severity that changes the use of the whip from encouragement to bullying. Quite a few horses are branded as ungenuine, but if they have had a thrashing every time they got to the front it is hardly surprising that they associate leading with pain.

The whip issue leads me on to the thorny subject of local stewards. I was once told by a steward to instruct my jockey not to hit a particular horse because it had shown a tendency to be marked from the slightest whip contact; can you imagine the outcry from punters if the horse lost in a photo-finish having been ridden out with hands and heels only in accordance with that instruction?

I think the stewards have got things about right. They do a good job overall, and when they do get it wrong it is not for any sinister reason but simply a case of their honest opinion. They do a difficult job well and they are impartial. They are human, after all, and all humans make errors.

My riders fill in reports every time they school or ride in a race. I call it Today's Opinion, because it is amazing how opinions change over a period of time. Good jockeys know what trip will suit a horse, whether it prefers going left- or right-handed and what ground it acts on, and will determine how it is best ridden. Some, of course, feel they have to appear clever and invent things when there is nothing new to contribute.

It is asking a lot of men who only sit on a horse at the races to evaluate it after a minute's contact on the flat or five minutes over jumps. Most of them know their jobs as riders, but it never ceases to amaze me how little the majority of jockeys actually know about horses once they are out of the saddle. My riding ability was definitely lacking but because I'm dealing with the horses every day I have an insight to their make-up and ability. That in turn gives me the right to comment on how they should be ridden or what chance of victory they have. When the media interviews a jockey about a horse's chances they are asking the wrong person because in most cases he won't know what his mount has been doing in the lead-up to the race. The horse could have been in its stable for a week, could have been coughing or have gone off its food. The jockey will probably not be privy to that information. Also, they will not have been through the opposition as thoroughly as a professional form student. Every man to his job: I like to get feedback from my jockeys, handicapper, betting spies and home staff. Today's Opinion is vital.

Of all the excuses given for beaten horses, I really can't understand why trainers tell owners their horse blew up. Surely that in itself is no more than an admission of incompetence on their part? Is it not the trainer's job to ensure a horse is fit and can jump? Just as it surprised me when Scu said his first ever ride for me was the fittest horse he'd ridden all season, it baffled me when Martin Foster let it slip the other day that some horses he partners for outside trainers positively blow up when cantering down to the start.

Intelligent riders pick up things as they observe others going about their business. These days Jonothan Lower and Martin Foster stand with the owners in the paddock and correctly evaluate their rivals. 'That can't win, it's not fit. The top weight's got too worked up, it doesn't jump when it gets in a state. The danger is number three, it ran well last time when needing the outing.' I'm proud to listen to them; they realize what is required to win races. I'd go as far as to say those two would be streets ahead of most of the top twenty riders in the jockeys' table as regards understanding horses in more than just race-riding terms.

The week after Scu rode his first winner for us Jonothan Lower won on My Dominion and Bob And Peter. Both were little bigger than kids' ponies but they were fit to run for their lives and we backed them accordingly. Scu admitted he had given them no earthly chance on looks or form. Opinions are what keeps the money going around in racing. Scu is brilliant with our new jockeys, he encourages them and often gets them in the house here to instruct them, using video evidence to prove his point. He will also guide them through the intricacies of a course the first time one of the boys is in action at a fresh track. He'll get a video out of a previous race to demonstrate the way to handle bends, note where horses hang towards the racecourse stables, point out tricky obstacles and advise them how the terrain affects the way we decide to ride different courses.

Both Scu and I tell the boys the whip is to be used to encourage, not to punish. The only time one of our riders carries a whip at home is when he or she is on a horse that is naughty, and they are thankfully few and far between. The odd one who is shy of traffic can be encouraged to pass vehicles by the pressure of the rider's leg or a tap down the shoulder with the stick. If they are dithering, prompt action from the saddle makes their mind up before they whip round, which is far more likely to inflict injury than a slap with the whip.

Being a large stable we need the horses to win, but not at the expense of being beaten up to do it. I think Scu has got it about right. He drives them from his pelvis with his bottom half going backwards as his trunk and arms stretch forwards in time with the horse's stride. He uses the whip to complement that body movement rather than as the main function, encouraging the horse, not intimidating it.

The same kind of thinking is behind my obsession with Trebor mints. Every member of staff has unlimited access to them. We encourage horses to take them as a sign of friendship, a bond between man and horse. I am sure it is the same for animals as it is with humans: you get far more cooperation from them if they like and trust you. Most new inmates treat us with suspicion and many will not take a mint at first; but once they realize it is a token of goodwill, or a reward, they lower their defences. When Jonothan Lower looked after Corporal Clinger he taught the gelding to lift a hoof when he wanted a mint, just like a dog will beg for a biscuit. It is a mirror of my young days when Granny Nation used to give me sixpence for doing well at maths.

There is a school of thought that mints encourage horses to start windsucking as they salivate and lick their lips to savour the taste. I do not subscribe to the view and can honestly say none of mine have ever done it as a result of eating mints. We get through over a hundred tubes of Trebors every day, and it is money well spent.

When it comes to evaluating a horse's ability or prospects Pipe is refreshingly open to owners and has been from the time he was unknown. Stories abound of trainers keeping animals in work just to get another weekly fee or doubling the amount of straw bedding to hide tendon strain when the unsuspecting owner visits his pride and joy. Pipe learned early on that honesty pays.

Pipe
Until Baron Blakeney won the Triumph Hurdle no one rang up out of the blue to ask us to train for them. Then a few days after Cheltenham Carol came running up to the top of the drive where I was trimming the hedge to say a man wanted to find out more about the set-up. I ran down to the house expectantly, only to be told that Steven Harvey had half a dozen other trainers to sift through before deciding where to send his horse. He had bought an animal called Lucky Eagle from Michael Dickinson and wanted to know what I thought of it. A quick glance through the form book told me he had paid too much money for it and placing it to win after Michael had used up its novice engagements would prove difficult. I explained that I would not have bought the horse for him if given the brief to find a champion, which he clearly thought it was. On paper the horse's form looked good, but its potential had been exposed. Having set myself up to be shot at by drowning Mr Harvey's hopes, I told him if he sent it to me I'd do my best to find a small race for him to back it to win in order to salvage some of his inflated purchase price.

Carol went mad at me for pouring cold water on the man's hopes and bet me that would be the last we ever heard of him. In my own mind I had not been rude, just told him the truth as I saw it; and to cut a long story short he sent Lucky Eagle to us as he appreciated my honesty.

The horse had won two novice chases and a handicap the previous season from only five starts at Southwell, Wolverhampton and Uttoxeter for the best trainer in the country. In my book it was a hard act to follow, and indeed it was not until his fifth outing for us that Lucky Eagle added to his score, and then only after the intervention of the Uttoxeter stewards.

The horse died the next year but that contact led directly to Steven's uncle Steph the Greek sending us Corporal Clinger.

Pipe, however, can still get it wrong. Any reference to a hard-pulling grey called Spanish God stops him in his tracks.

Pipe

The trouble as I saw it was our inability to work out where we were going wrong. In his first race in August 1979 he ran away with Ron Atkins after the first hurdle, jumped violently left-handed at the next and beat a hasty retreat after the third. Following that display we put all sorts of gadgets in his mouth to give the rider some control but he got beaten in eight more incredibly bad selling hurdles until scrambling home at Devon and Exeter in November. When the bidding reached 650 guineas I was delighted to let him go. In my opinion the horse was useless.

When Spanish God reappeared on the same course two months later to win another seller by eight lengths I felt sick. Mark Stevens, his new trainer, went to 1,800 guineas to retain the grey and then proceeded to win several open races with him the following season. I wanted to commit suicide every time it ran. Dad kept reminding me what a complete idiot I was and he was right. No trainer likes selling a horse he thinks will win for someone else and my opinion had been way off-line. We were not setting the world alight anyway, so a blow like that was enough to make me doubt whether I could train at all. There are still times now when I feel insecure.

The management pattern is the same now as it was when Pipe first realized the value of having key personnel to manage different areas of the business. Carol's department includes hiring and firing staff.

Pipe

She's a far better judge of character than I am: I can be taken in by any old sob story. There was one who slipped through the net, though. In May 1989, when the stable first broke the two hundred winner mark for a season, the *Daily Star* decided to put in its own mole to discover the secret of our success.

When their girl Kerry Allott applied for a job as groom/rider she told us she had no previous experience in racing stables but had ridden all her life. Some of our best girls have joined us from a similar background and quickly picked up our ways. Unusually, Carol did not bother to check back with Kerry's immediately previous employers. She took an instant liking to the girl and felt sorry for her. When her article appeared a week after she left us, Carol and I were sad that she had used us and we both agreed that had we been approached openly by the paper, we would almost certainly have let her join us anyway. The headlines proclaiming the *Star* girl had the 'inside story and secrets of the punters' pal' were misleading to say the least. A few quotes from Scu, Carol and myself lifted from numerous previous articles, plus a lad moaning: 'All we go for here are winners, nothing else matters. If we don't get one there's a lot of disappointment' proved rather shallow. That quote, though, did sum the job up well in a way; we are in the business of producing winners and do get depressed when they don't oblige. I wonder how content that disgruntled lad would be working in all weathers *without* winners to make it worth while.

Forming correct opinions of people is paramount when buying horses with form. Some people I am delighted to buy from, because I know that their inmates will not have been overworked, or because their methods are so different to mine that a change of routine will bring out the best in the horse. Conversely, there are trainers I steer well clear of, for various reasons. For instance, I had attended several lectures on the horse given by the vet Brian Eagles, who impressed me with his in-depth knowledge of the endless list of things that go wrong with the Thoroughbred. In my opinion he had mastered the game. When I later discovered he was private vet to Guy Harwood, I decided that if Harwood was selling, I wasn't buying. If there was any mileage left in his horses, Eagles would be working on them to win more races for his employer, not allowing others to reap the benefit of his time and expense.

Chapter 22

Gathering Momentum

It had taken ten years for Martin Pipe to improve his seasonal total of winners from a single one in 1974–5 to one past the fifty mark in 1984–5; and yet only two more years saw him break the century barrier. Even then, though, the still relatively low takings in prize money emphasized that though the horses were winning a lot of races, they were not winning the big ones. The 106 victories in 1986–7 brought prize money averaging out at £1,500 each – barely enough to cover two months' training fees and running costs at the time.

That situation soon changed, largely as a result of the increasing number of steeplechasers coming into the yard, most of them sent to Pond House by owners looking to rekindle their horses' enthusiasm. Beau Ranger started the trend.

Pipe
I knew Beau Ranger's owners, Arthur White and his nephew Peter, from meetings at a local charitable organization, the Stand Club, which was based at the County Hotel in Taunton. We often got round to talking about their horse, who had won seven of his nine starts in 1984–5 for another Somerset trainer, John Thorne, among them the valuable Kennedy Construction Gold Cup at Cheltenham's December meeting and a good handicap at Aintree, striking up a marvellous partnership with claiming rider John Hurst in the process.

The next season Beau Ranger paid the price of his success when he was hit hard by the handicapper. He returned to

211

something like his best when second to the subsequent Grand National winner West Tip at Cheltenham, but only managed one win, beating Wayward Lad at Aintree.

The entire racing community was deeply saddened when John Thorne died six weeks after that win, but we were pleased to hear that his daughter Jackie was to take over the training. Unfortunately for her, Beau Ranger never fired the next season: from five starts he managed only one third, having fallen on his reappearance, and was pulled up on both his last two outings, including the King George VI Chase at Kempton Park. Arthur and Peter felt that time was running out for Beau Ranger and, having given Jackie a season holding the reins, decided to move stables.

When I was approached to take Beau Ranger, I talked the situation over with Carol and we decided that if we did not take charge of him someone else would. As Jackie was fairly local the situation was far from ideal, but we had never chased after the owners nor asked them to send the horse to us. My conscience is clear on that score. While I felt it would have been embarrassing or even seemed patronizing to have asked Jackie about the horse after he had been transferred, I did write to her to express my sadness at how things had turned out. I was disappointed for her, and did not really need him myself at that time. It looked as if his best was behind him.

When we checked him over on arrival at Pond House, it became apparent that Beau Ranger's problems emanated from a bad back, possibly incurred when he fell first time out the previous season. Mary Bromiley worked on him, then advised plenty of good old-fashioned strapping to massage, stimulate and strengthen certain muscles. One of my best girls, Mary Horswell, took on the job and used to pummel his back with a wisp – a rope of hay plaited into a solid lump twice the size of a hand. It sounded like a training session in a boxing gymnasium. I like horses to get at least half an hour's grooming each every day. We may have a high-tech set-up here but I don't like the modern trend of fewer staff doing more horses; to me, that old-fashioned grooming is an integral part of training.

Beau Ranger was a stocky individual who benefited greatly from swimming, which visibly muscled him up. His home work impressed me and I was aware the handicapper had given me more than a sporting chance to get him back winning again. His first run from our stable saw him attempting to give 25lb to Dudie at Sandown and only failing by half a length. Dudie's rider Dale McKeown was fined £100 for excessive use of the whip, but Scu ensured Beau Ranger came home having enjoyed his outing. We were there to win, but not at the risk of undoing everything we were trying to build up – and in any case, he loved life so much, he'd give his best without being bullied into it.

Scu felt obliged to partner Fred Winter's Malya Mal in the following month's Mackeson Gold Cup at Cheltenham, so I engaged Mark Perrett to ride Beau Ranger off a generous 10st 2lb. Looked well, jumped well, made all and won by fifteen lengths, says the form book. In the Cheltenham Gold Cup Beau Ranger showed us that stamina was not his forte, yet still finished a creditable third, sixteen lengths behind Charter Party. We finished off a thoroughly satisfactory campaign with a win in the South Wales Showers Mira Chase, worth £17,000. In beating Chief Ironside, Scu, who had realized how able Beau Ranger was, rode a vigorous finish using hands and heels but did not go for the whip.

In all, £57,000 had been added to his career winnings that season, but the handicapper had restored him to the top end of the ratings and I thought matters would prove more difficult the next term.

Horses continually surprise me, not always pleasantly, but after his first two outings of the 1988–9 term Beau Ranger was rated as good as any chaser in Britain with the exception of Desert Orchid. He trotted up at Haydock Park on his reappearance then, carrying 12st, went under by one-and-a-half lengths to Pegwell Bay, a year after winning the A. F. Budge Chase over the same course and distance with twenty-six pounds less on his back.

That autumn there were some niggling problems associated with general wear and tear that caused Beau Ranger's bold jumping to deteriorate. He did win again, at Worcester, but lacked sparkle at Aintree and the Cheltenham December meeting, though he put up a pleasing performance in the Queen Mother Champion Chase at Cheltenham over two miles, finishing third behind Barnbrook Again and Waterloo Boy, some eight lengths adrift. When you consider he had not been tried over the minimum trip for four years, the run was no disgrace.

There was no real championship for the two-and-a-half-milers then; the choice was between the Queen Mother and the Gold Cup, a gap of a mile and a quarter.

In his third season with us Beau Ranger, now twelve years old, strained a tendon on his first run and was not seen out again for a year. We discussed retirement then, but as he loved his lifestyle, had the best of everything from food to total devotion from Mary, we decided to let him race another term.

In his third run of 1990–1 season Beau Ranger fell fatally three fences from home at Kempton Park, having dropped out of contention. It was the worst day of my life. Everyone was gutted and even now I still expect to see his white-blazed head looking out over his old stable door. He was a proper gent, too, which naturally created a stronger bond than an irritable or nasty horse would have. We all felt Beau Ranger was almost human; his death struck a very deep chord. I really do miss him.

Once owners saw for themselves that Pipe could bring the best out of a quality chaser just as well as he could produce Flat race culls to win over hurdles, the snowball gathered momentum. No sooner had Beau Ranger rediscovered his form than the list mushroomed, with the team quickly growing to include Strands Of Gold, Rusch de Farges, Sabin Du Loir and Bonanza Boy.

The last-named joined Pipe from another local trainer, Philip Hobbs, a transfer which resulted in the cessation of diplomatic relations and the birth of another anti-Pipe rumour: that he was stealing owners by offering to train their horses for nothing.

Pipe
I categorically deny that accusation and I am still very upset that Philip went into print blaming me for his loss. I have never poached other trainers' owners. Quite apart from the ethics of it, I would risk committing economic suicide. The business is still Dad's and he is not in the habit of subsidizing other people's hobbies.

As it happens I could have taken charge of Bonanza Boy six months before I did. George Malde asked me to have the horse as he could see the fire had gone out of Bonanza's general outlook. He would not take part at all unless hard ridden. George hated to watch him run when he was patently unhappy. On that occasion I suggested he stayed put to the end of the season in case things picked up when the spring arrived. Philip had, after all, not only bought the gelding cheaply but had also produced him to win five of his seven starts in 1986–7.

Bonanza Boy's emergence was one of those tales that encourages sportsmen to buy less than fashionable types. He is by Sir Lark, second in the Ebor Handicap, out of a Vulgan mare who showed no ability on the racecourse, and whose only previous offspring to reach the track from five foals was a poor selling hurdler. Even so, the female line had its high spots as Bonanza Boy's dam was a sister to Midsprite and Airsprite, both regular Grade One course winners. Hobbs bought Bonanza Boy from his father-in-law Bertie Hill, who had hunted him – then named Crow Point – with the Dulverton West Hounds. There is surely no better way of educating a young horse for steeplechasing than to take it hunting, but the costs in terms of time and labour can be prohibitive.

At the end of his first season, in which the gelding took both the Challow Hurdle at Newbury and the Persian War Hurdle at Chepstow, Philip told the press that his horse would not be seen at his best until he was faced with three miles plus and fences. How right he was. The little bay won his first three novice chases, including the Peter Cox at Ascot, but then lost his confidence over fences and returned to hurdles to finish third at the Cheltenham Festival behind Galmoy in the Stayers' Hurdle.

Before that trip to Cheltenham, Pipe remembers watching Bonanza Boy sulking at Taunton.

Pipe
I can distinctly remember saying to Carol that he would be lucky to ever win again. Starting odds-on in a Mickey Mouse race, he absolutely hated it, didn't jump and had Graham McCourt hard at him all the way simply to keep in the contest. To be honest, I suppose, when I was approached to have him the prospect of rejuvenating such a fed-up horse did not look like the plum job it turned out to be.

Despite some improvement when he was run over hurdles

again, George Malde repeated his request that I take the horse. It was obvious that the relationship with Philip had broken down and, as with Beau Ranger, if I turned him down this time someone else would have taken the horse.

To this day Philip and I avoid each other at the races. I would have much preferred him to have faced me with his accusations than complaining to the press. Somewhere wires became crossed, and I doubt now if they will ever be straightened out. Despite my annoyance at being wrongfully accused of luring the horse away, I hope I am not so small-minded as to let the issue cloud my judgement or general behaviour. There are occasions when Philip phones me to find out if one of my horses is running in a race he is hoping to win. There are no pleasantries, just a question and an answer.

When Bonanza Boy joined us after his summer break high on Exmoor with George and his wife, Angie, we took things gently to restore his confidence. My first move was to give him to Donna Cornforth to look after, as her record of establishing a bond with her charges is remarkable. I can't stress enough the importance of good staff. A groom can make or break a horse's general outlook on life. Donna is unique here as only non-riding groom on the payroll. We call everyone by a nickname – it's part of the friendly environment, there's no forelock-touching – and Donna started off as Dopey Donna; but with her record of changing jaded has-beens into keen winners, she soon became Darling Donna.

Besides Donna making a fuss of Bonanza Boy in the stable we consciously let him do his own thing at exercise, within reason. Once again swimming played a big part in his work, and that is the key: he was working without realizing it. As our gallop is so short he was never stressed. Being a stocky sort, though, he needed a lot of exercise, and so he often went out three times a day to get the required amount of work to clear his wind. After a while I could see him change his mind and decide to get involved instead of simply tagging along. As his jumping had let him down we also set about persuading him that that could be fun by popping him over small and varied obstacles.

Before long it became obvious that his approach to life had turned the corner. He started to prick his ears when faced with a jump and to quicken instinctively of his own accord. The velvet glove technique prevailed where the iron fist could not.

By the time the ground had eased enough to consider running him for the first time from our stable, it was getting close to the entry stage for the Coral Welsh National. I didn't want to show my hand to the handicapper, so we decided to keep him ticking over at home in order to capitalize on the lenient weight he had after his loss of form the previous season. Then we let him loose at Newton Abbot five days after the Welsh National weights were announced and as the horse had showed up well with other good winners on the gallops I told George and Angie their Christmas present was as good as won. It may sound cocky to be so sure of victory, but sometimes conditions do fall exactly right. This was one of those times.

Bonanza Boy absolutely hacked up, after which he had an equally easy success in the Welsh National. Our plan had been executed, leaving us with the rest of the season to indulge ourselves in running for fun. A win in the valuable Racing Post Chase brought a lump to my throat as Bonanza Boy showed the guts to haul himself back into contention, having struggled to keep tabs on even the back markers for much of the trip.

He was a remote fourth in the Gold Cup and no match for the faster horses in the Whitbread, but in between those two races he surprised most professional observers when jumping round Aintree to finish eighth in the Grand National.

Scu had every confidence in the little horse's ability to jump those huge fences and he was proved correct. It gave us all a great deal of satisfaction to have fired his flame sufficiently to do what he did, remembering that only twelve months before he had patently hated every stride in a tinpot chase at Taunton.

That season saw the stable send out 208 winners, an achievement previously thought all but impossible. It was only two seasons ago that Martin had cracked the hundred mark for the first time; his rise to double that figure finally drew respect from many of the sceptics who had been slow to accept him as a big-league player.

Another significant change was the sharp increase in winning chasers, from nil five years earlier to seventy, fully one third of his total. Quality had risen, too, to match any stable in the land; Strands Of Gold took the Hennessy first time out, one of forty-one horses from the stable to win on their seasonal bow that term. He was yet another sent in the hopes of salvaging lost enthusiasm.

Pipe
He'd joined me towards the end of the previous campaign from
Jimmy Fitzgerald, who took the removal badly and is still very
offhand towards me now. The horse had bad hocks and his
jumping had gone to pot. We fell in love with him the moment he
stepped off the transporter; he's a Christian in every way, in or
out of his stable.

Again it was only a question of playing around with him,
building his muscles up to equal proportions on both hind
quarters and popping plenty of tiny obstacles to let him realize
nothing unseen would grab him. I firmly believe horses should
not be schooled over jumps until they are sufficiently muscled up
to allow them to engage maximum thrust. Most damage to the
fore-legs emanates from faults at the rear end.

On his first run for us Strands finished fifth at the Festival in the
Ritz Club Chase, a contest that at the time held two future
additions to our set-up. The race was won by Aquilifer, trained
by David Murray Smith, while the third home, Von Trappe, was
ridden by Eddie Buckley. Both the winning horse and the third-
placed jockey were destined to join me later and were to become
valuable contributors.

None the worse for his Festival outing, Strands lined up
for the Grand National with Scu on board as a 20–1 shot.
When the runners passed the stands with another circuit to
go Strands lay happily in tenth place and was jumping those
big fences for fun. This race does get to me but I refuse to
allow myself to get carried away, and it was not until he hit
the front going to Becher's the second time that I thought we
could win it. Twenty seconds later Strands and Scu were out
of the contest: yet another casualty of the famous drop on
landing. I do get quite wound up generally but there is nothing
like the National to lift you to the heights only to send you instantly
back to earth.

A final run that season to finish third behind Desert Orchid and
Kildimo in the Whitbread prompted mouthwatering thoughts of
the next season's Hennessy and in due course he obliged, helping
us not only to top the double century for the first time but also to
endorse my standing as a producer of big steeplechase winners.

218

The latter meant a great deal as we had never really been taken seriously before.

Besides Strands, Beau Ranger and Bonanza Boy, others who helped make this a truly memorable season were Sondrio and Sayfar's Lad, both Festival scorers. Travel Mystery took the Imperial Cup, Out Of The Gloom, Pertemps Network and Sabin Du Loir added other major contests and Anti Matter became the horse to win the two hundredth first prize that term.

Two wins from three starts also pinpointed the French import Voyage Sans Retour as a future star, but he was to prove a reversal of the trend we'd become used to, for in his second season with us the colt took the former Oteley Hurdle at Sandown, won previously by such champions as Bird's Nest, Sea Pigeon and See You Then. A good fifth to Morley Street in the Champion Hurdle was followed by a second in the Welsh equivalent, but his final appearance that season saw him finish a disappointing last in the Scottish event. The horse was then destined to go to Ireland for a summer's grass, which we took to mean we were losing him.

Soon after he arrived at his holiday destination with Georgie Wells, the owner, Peter Leeper, telephoned to say Jonjo O'Neill would be having him to train the next season as Wells had reported the colt to be jarred up and suffering from diabetes on arrival. Our records and vet's examination prior to him leaving Pond House showed the colt to be in excellent condition for a horse at the end of a campaign in the highest company. All telephone calls to our accuser failed to obtain either a retraction or permission to visit him to confirm the slur on our handling of the horse.

We intended to jump straight on a plane and arrive unannounced at Mr Wells's yard, complete with our own vet, to put his claims to the test. Naturally such confrontations are both embarrassing and expensive, but it is only too easy to toss about accusations which then escalate like wildfire if they are not quashed firmly. As it turned out, we were unable to go, but the vet Ned Gowing did check the horse and vindicated our reputation: the horse was fine. But although we'd proved our case, once an owner has decided to move a horse there is little point in trying to change his mind. We'd lost a good horse and that hurts the pride. I hope, though, that we accepted the reversal better than some of the trainers who'd lost horses to us, and in this case it evened matters out a bit as another owner, Eric Scarth, had sent us Granville Again from Jonjo's stable. For the horse, though, the move had an unhappy sequel: after winning his first two chases for his new yard, Voyage Sans Retour had to be destroyed after falling next time out.

It is that irreversible loss that makes training jumpers hard. We went through a terrible fortnight when three horses had to be put down, including Buster Joe who died of colic only a week after George Bisgrove had bought him for £30,000. When that happened I was very low. Death leaves an empty, helpless feeling about the place, affecting everyone. I thought at the time perhaps the sport demanded too high a price; but at least by eliminating as many of the risks as possible we can reduce the threats to our horses to an absolute minimum.

Chapter 23

Brian Kilpatrick: A New Breed of Owner

Pipe had good reason to notice Sabin Du Loir years before his owner thought of sending his horses to Pond House. He had backed the compact bay gelding to win the Sun Alliance Hurdle at the 1983 Cheltenham Festival when trained by Michael Dickinson, a man whose methods Pipe had monitored faithfully over the years as he sought to establish his own career. In the course of that study Pipe had made money backing his rival's horses, but readily admits that he was amazed when Dickinson chose to run his French import against older horses at Cheltenham instead of taking on his own age group in the Triumph Hurdle.

Pipe
Sabin won Michael's chosen race all right, beating no less a horse than Dawn Run in the process. He finished that season unbeaten from five starts and as I kept bumping into Michael at equine seminars and demonstrations, I asked him to elaborate on the French connection. He told me the French horses were tough, acted on soft ground and as there was practically no second-hand market in that country, horses that had won decent Flat races could be bought reasonably.

Sabin's front legs needed firing, necessitating over two years off the track, and when he returned to action he went into training at Lambourn with David Murray Smith. The gelding's legs obviously continued to cause concern as he only managed to get on to the course five times in the next two seasons, but a second to See You Then in 1986 and a twenty-length victory the following year proved that the horse had not lost his ability.

I was approached by Mr Kilpatrick at Ascot in June 1987 with a view to his vetting me as to my suitability to handle his horses the next season. My emergence into the big time was not the issue; he wanted to see for himself how I operated at home and also to satisfy himself that my jockey was not reliant on the whip. Brian Kilpatrick is a tall, quiet and very private person, a thorough gentleman, and I was excited to think that he might join us as an owner, as unlike the majority of our clients he was retired from business and had the time, money and patience to buy young potential chasers and wait for them to mature. The inspection went well, but I had a slight reservation in my mind that Scu's will to win might prove fiercer than was acceptable to my potential new owner.

We were racing at Chepstow the afternoon Mr Kilpatrick went to evaluate my jockey. Scu was riding a grey of Bob Wheatley's called Up Cooke who had fallen with him on her chasing debut at Worcester, unseated him at Devon, had a confidence restorer over hurdles and was now to be back to fences. With fifteen runners in a competitive chase we agreed that Scu should look after himself and the mare, not throw caution to the wind. I was embarrassed to watch the race as it looked a typical instance of non-trying with Scu joining the leaders on the run to the second last but sitting as still as a mouse. The last two jumps at Chepstow are both downhill and, aware of the danger of over-jumping only to crumple on landing, Scu sat tight until he was safely over the final obstacle. Then he simply let out half an inch of rein to win stylishly without ever looking likely to go for his whip. I could have kissed him. Scu delivered his most artistic ride when it mattered so much to me.

When Sabin arrived, the customary inspection revealed the most horrible pair of front legs imaginable, but they were as hard as iron and cold as ice. In and out of his stable Sabin proved every bit as much of a gentleman as his owner. He used to get a bit lit up at first when asked to wait his turn at either end of the all-weather gallop, but we took to letting him go first and he soon adapted. I gave him to Martin Foster's sister Dawn to look after and to ride and the pair struck up an immediate bond.

In his first season with us Sabin won a hurdle over two and a half miles at Ascot in November and finished third on the same course a month later over an extra three-quarters of a mile, giving lumps of weight away to Bluff Cove and Miss Nero. The legs had shown no signs of heat or swelling but I had been careful to minimize further wear and tear by swimming him a lot and, as with the rest of the string never trotting or putting him under pressure on the gallops. However, on his third outing for us in heavy ground at Cheltenham in January, I thought the worst when Paul Croucher, deputizing for Scu, pulled him up having led to the second last hurdle. There was no apparent reason, but the horse was not himself for some time.

We spent three months getting him back to racing fitness and the combination of his optimum trip of two and a half miles and good to soft ground at Aintree gave me all the encouragement I needed to fancy him. In the event Sabin had no answer to a horse four years younger, the Champion Hurdle third Celtic Chief, but he did put several Cheltenham rivals well into his shadow. That ended Sabin's initial campaign from our stable; having established his preferences, we sent him back to grass in Buckinghamshire sound, leaving me with mouthwatering thoughts of what we might do over fences the next term.

The most difficult job proved to be persuading Mr Kilpatrick that Sabin would jump fences. He reasoned sensibly that the horse had been running over hurdles for so long now that he might find it difficult to adapt his style. His horse was on the small side for a chaser and was almost ten years of age. He would never forgive himself – or me – if Sabin got hurt. In response, I pointed out that until we tried Sabin over the bigger obstacles we had no way of knowing if he could adapt. Smaller horses had won recent Gold Cups and although he was older than the norm for the transition to fences, he had fewer miles on the clock than many horses half his age.

Under duress, Mr Kilpatrick agreed to have a home trial but insisted he attend to see the outcome for himself. I must admit we did pop Sabin over one fence the day before his owner came down for the decision day and I knew at once that this was where his future lay. The full-scale schooling session went well and Mr Kilpatrick gave us the go-ahead, although he still felt marginally unhappy. He is a very sensitive and caring individual; he will not allow his horses to be hit and has grave reservations about running any of them in the Grand National.

An easy victory over hurdles at Ascot put Sabin spot on for his chasing debut at Newton Abbot on Boxing Day, only six days short of his tenth birthday. Jumping like the proverbial stag, the little horse had to exert himself no more than if he were schooling at home, much to the relief of all concerned.

Since then Sabin Du Loir has done us proud. He just seems to enjoy every day of his life. Since taking to steeplechasing Sabin has beaten and been beaten by the very best at all distances from two miles to three and a quarter but is best at two and a half miles on decent ground and, like Beau Ranger, would have benefited from a two-and-a-half-mile level weights championship. I am sure he will win more decent races despite his advancing years. As with humans, so with horses: some are old before their time while others retain their youth. Sabin Du Loir is definitely one of the latter.

Another horse of Brian Kilpatrick's, and another former cripple, Aquilifer, joined Pipe from the stable of David Murray Smith, who, along with the late Paul Croucher, had produced the big chestnut to win six chases in the 1987–8 term, including the Ritz Club Trophy at the Cheltenham Festival. The following season Aquilifer totally lost his form, pulling up in the last of his five runs for Murray Smith, and duly followed Sabin Du Loir to Somerset.

Pipe
I enjoy a challenge and Aquilifer was exactly that. He was eleven when joining us, had been off the course for eighteen months and was as lame as a cat every morning from a broken knee sustained in his last race.

In many ways the old horse was just like me and I trained him on similar methods to those I employ to get myself through each day. Halfway through a normal afternoon I am a cripple from all my old car crash and racing injuries. By riding the bike around the yard and keeping my weight off the legs, I am able to keep going, but if I spend a long day at the races where I am forced to run about, I have a job to walk by tea time.

Aquilifer is a big, heavy-topped horse, which makes him his own worst enemy. Because of his size and shape he needs a lot of work to get him to racing fitness and keep him there, yet his old battle-scarred legs will not stand it. The answer is swimming: Aquilifer swims five days a week both in the morning and after lunch. Quite often he'll get a dip three times a day to get the required amount of work into him without any strain on his legs. On the two days he does see the gallops, he is never asked to quicken faster than he wants to; we let him dictate what is comfortable. I know I keep banging on about listening to the horses but it really is the key: by constantly observing them you find their attitudes tell you what they can't say out loud.

Coincidentally, I recently noticed something about Aquilifer when he canters that had never struck me before. That made me look for similarities in other horses and sure enough a large proportion have the same trait. I can't enlarge on it at this stage as it is too early to determine its importance – and anyway to remain ahead in this game a man must keep his discoveries to himself for a while . . .

Aquilifer had had a solitary outing at four in a National Hunt flat race, for education, but proved too weak to resume competition until two years later. The fact that he went straight to fences aged six without a run over hurdles indicated that he was bereft of speed. He is the typical Grand National candidate, the exact opposite of the horses I had worked with to establish myself. Ironically, his owner refuses to let me enter the bold-jumping chaser in the Aintree marathon and I respect his wishes.

I gave Aquilifer to Sarah Hancock to care for. She's done enough good horses to recognize one when given time to get to know a newcomer. Sarah thought he felt like a horse half his eleven years and I suppose with his late start to racing and almost two years off through the broken knee, he'd only had three full terms prior to joining us.

His first run from here was an encouraging second to Twin Oaks at Haydock, another eleven-year-old to have made a remarkable comeback from injury that season. Afterwards he was eased down when taking a long-distance chase at Warwick and, so poignantly, the Newbury race named after his former regular jockey Paul Croucher, who was killed in a road accident. In between those victories Aquilifer ran a blinder when pipped by Bonanza Boy for second in the Greenall's Gold Cup, again in Twin Oaks' hoofprints. His third win from five starts that season was presented to him by Norton's Coin's attempt to demolish the penultimate fence and disinclination to jump the last in Aintree's Martell Cup. Having said that, though, the third horse home, Stay On Tracks, was fully twenty-five lengths adrift, which stamped the form as distinctly useful.

As with Beau Ranger before him, and Omerta at the same time, I am aware that much of Aquilifer's initial success on coming to me was attributable to the dive they had taken down the handicap before joining our stable. Of course, their changed physical and mental condition was down to the staff here, but winning a sequence of races proves a double-edged sword as the handicapper kicks them back up the weights.

Although Aquilifer did not win for us last season until Punchestown in April, he also ran some fine races in defeat; and there is no better loser than Mr Kilpatrick, who acts no differently whether winning or not. A second and a third to Carvill's Hill in Chepstow's Rehearsal Chase and Coral Welsh National, plus a second to King's Fountain at Wincanton, netted almost £14,000, proving that it can be perfectly sensible to run chasers at the age of twelve or more provided they still enjoy the sport.

Mr Kilpatrick is a modest, unassuming man who despite owning horses of the calibre of Aquilifer, Sabin Du Loir and the giant Terao would not be known to the vast majority of racegoers. He buys his youngstock from or through Jeremy Maxwell in Northern Ireland, which has in turn opened up a sound and valuable avenue for me. Maxwell's record goes back to the Michael Dickinson days and he has maintained his high standard through to the present time. Terao could be the best young horse I've got; he's certainly the biggest and heaviest. After surprising us all when winning his bumper he has gone on to look more than useful over hurdles and given an injury-free run will make up into an exciting chaser. Bred by Jeremy out of an unraced daughter of that top-class racemare Grangewood Girl, Terao could be anything.

Jeremy also bred Pectorus by his stallion Denel, a French St Leger winner. Mr Kilpatrick bought this one, like Terao, unbroken and having won his bumper with Jeremy, Pectorus was put away to mature. He is another one we are looking forward to training and again is a completely different sort of horse from the bulk of ours. I must say it is nice to have some owners who will buy the seedcorn and have the necessary patience to watch the youngsters grow into their strength. I still enjoy my tough ex-Flat horses, but this diversification gives me a whole host of options.

With a view to the future, now that I have found I can handle the pure-bred jumper, I have bought a load of yearlings and will add to them annually to ensure the supply continues to flow. By nature I am a restless person, and originally my owners were not able to live on future hopes, which forced me to tap the Flat race stables for established horses. Perhaps the ratio of newcomers will now alter in favour of Mr Kilpatrick's type of horse. Now that I am getting older, the attractions of a slower development process do sometimes appeal. There are days when I look to the future and cannot see beyond training; then there are others when the immense pressure of keeping all the balls in the air seems too hard a job.

Chapter 24

Spreading the Net

The idea of multiple ownership had been growing in Martin and Chester's minds for a while before they hit on a formula that grew into the current Pipe–Scudamore Racing Club, itself an outgrowth of Martin and Scu's company, Pipe–Scudamore Racing plc. The present syndicated string of between twelve and twenty horses, depending on the state of the kitty and the soundness of the animals, evolved from a handful of the stable's existing patrons.

Pipe
The original idea was to spread the load so that more people could share in the winners. Although most of our horses manage to provide a return for their owners, the occasional person with a single horse could end up going through the season with very little to show for their money. Racing is meant to be fun and that is what I try to promote, but undoubtedly there is far more fun derived from winning than from owning a beast that never shows any form or, worse still, having an unsound one that hardly sees the racecourse.

I canvassed the people I thought would get on if brought together and had no difficulty in extracting a one-off payment of £7,000 from each of eight existing owners. A single advertisement attracted the remaining four we needed to form the twelve-strong syndicate. The £84,000 we thus collected was to buy, train, race and insure five horses each season, with Chester managing both horses and owners. They produced a hatful of winners with the likes of Sea Island, Adamstown, Royal Wonder and Don't Ring Me. One season the group cheered home sixteen winners and, more to the point, backed them as well.

One side-effect of bringing people together is the lasting friendships that blossom. Frank and Alison Farrant and John Fairbrother met through joining the syndicate and have since become very good chums. In fact, since those early days both the Farrants and John have established good strings of horses.

Adamstown took a £10,000 Flat race, which attracted the bloodstock agents' interest, and off he went to race in Dubai, but the members turned down the real profit they could have taken on Sea Island. Nicky Henderson's brother-in-law George Sloan came here to try the mare to see if she was suitable for racing in the States. I can recall the trial gallop vividly. Chester and myself were standing beside the all-weather strip when George whizzed by and I'd only just mentioned what a good partnership Sea Island and George made when Chester spotted the mare cantering back towards us with no sign of George.

Despite that incident she impressed him enough to bid £60,000 but after much deep and sometimes heated discussion the members decided not to sell. Ironically, when the syndicate split up a year later Sea Island only made £32,000 at public auction and that was mainly because two of them, Roger Warren and Charlie Eden, both wanted her. Sod's Law, she got a leg after her first run for Roger, but has come back to be better than ever now.

Frank and Alison Farrant really immersed themselves in racing after those initial shared winners. In the seven years they have been with us their blue and red colours have come in first fifty-seven times out of 164 starts, and this from only twelve horses. Alison bought Liadett as a surprise birthday present for Frank and they have never looked back since. Tamapour even took the £20,000 Pitmen's Derby last Flat season for them. He started to have his own ideas about exerting himself after that victory so I had him gelded and now he's Mr Nice Guy again.

The Farrants derive so much obvious enjoyment from their sport that it really is a pleasure to train for them. Some folk do whinge when things go wrong and quite often they are the ones who should know better. The Farrants are not of horsy stock, yet they still seem amazed every time they have a winner. In defeat they are generous, taking the inevitable disappointments well without ever thinking of looking for a scapegoat.

John Fairbrother loves a bet and seems to do well at it. He phones me daily for advice, but knows how tight my time schedule is and never keeps me on the line for long. John runs the extremely successful Fairlord Confectionery Ltd business in London which has proved a godsend for me: I am a confirmed chocaholic and the horses here consume literally thousands of Trebor mints every week.

The group attracted people from widely differing walks of life, including Lady Craddock from Sussex. She and her son Richard bred and raced some good Flat horses with Guy Harwood, so she must think it is a very different job down here; but she definitely seems to enjoy her frequent visits. She usually brings a couple of friends with her to see the horses, stops off for lunch in the country and makes a day of the trip. If only more owners planned their days out around racedays or watching gallops they would get so much more out of a sport which is, after all, expensive enough to participate in.

Another founder member, Roger Warren from Cheltenham, has also branched out on his own since. Besides buying out his fellow syndicate members when Sea Island went under the hammer, he owns three others with me. Roger, too, likes to bet daily and is good enough at it to make the game pay. He keeps meticulous records of every transaction which he in turn produces for the Inland Revenue to substantiate his earnings – which is a very sensible policy, because so many people have used the bookmakers as a vehicle for laundering money over the years that the tax inspectors are highly suspicious of anyone who purports to make gambling pay.

Most of the big bookmakers have closed Roger's accounts, but there are no end of new outlets willing to oblige anyone wanting to gamble. Bookmaking is similar to training in that respect; for every one that drops out another two are trying to start.

Pond House was the obvious name for our first syndicate. It had had a three-year life from 1988 to 1991, by which time the bulk of the owners had complemented their involvement with horses of their own. We then decided to go one further, to allow the people who could not afford to stake £7,000 a chance to join in. Chester and I had seen the success of BTRB, Full Circle and

Gymcrak Thoroughbreds, which had attracted thousands of working men, housewives and former owners into multiple ownership, and decided it was an avenue worth exploring. It may sound corny to say I didn't need more owners, but that's the way it stood. The idea behind mass involvement was to enable lots of people to have the chance to experience the thrills of racing for a relatively small outlay.

On reflection, forming a public company was the wrong move. The amount of work and prohibitive costs involved in making the business legal means that the set-up is top-heavy, with the administration requiring serious funds that could otherwise be used to buy more horses. After the two-year life of the original company and the subsequent twelve months of its successor, which ended in July 1992, we decided that the idea was sound but that there must be less demanding ways of putting it into practice. The start-up costs of the company alone amounted to £62,000 of the initial intake of £700,000 gathered from the 2,800 shareholders. Administrative costs and the annual audit added to the drain on resources and then the cost of winding up the companies at the end of their fixed duration took another £5,000 out of the kitty.

When we first advertised our invitation to join the stable I was very much aware the cream had been skimmed off the market by the companies that had preceded us. We were consequently totally unprepared for the deluge that followed. The phones screeched at us from seven in the morning to ten at night, logging over four hundred calls a day. As a result of this barrage we sent out over twenty thousand brochures to inquirers. If we'd had the nous to have used an 0898 premium phone number, we could have accrued a big bank balance before we started.

Carol, Chester and myself were already far too busy to deal with the volume of inquiries, which led us to enrol former professional golfer Barry Simpson to administer the company. Barry had the added recommendation of running the prestigious Straffan House estate in County Kildare, which included a twenty-mare breeding operation. His wife Susie also trained under permit in Ireland, where among her other runners she won a bumper with the mare Dalkey Sound, who has since gone on to take a string of chases for Mary Reveley.

Barry's arrival took the strain off the rest of us. He and Carol ran the office and Chester set up the chat and tipping lines on the premium rate service leaving me to get on with the training. Neither Carol nor myself took a wage out of the company, Chester got his income from the phone service and Scu took an annual retainer for his involvement.

We managed to be up and running by June 1989 and during the inaugural year of the company's two-year life the shareholders cheered home twenty-four winners from only sixty-one runners, a winners-to-runners ratio of thirty-two per cent. Not having to wind the company up for another year, we were able to sell off a few of the lesser lights, retain the bulk and buy some replacements.

Among the new stock we bought was the tiny mare Hopscotch, acquired for 11,500 guineas in the Queen's annual dispersal draft. As with My Dominion, it was the athleticism she exuded that drew me to her, overriding her lack of inches. I loved her the moment I saw her, and I also thought she possessed a high residual value as a broodmare being out of a half-sister to the Queen's St Leger winner Dunfermline and by Dominion, whom I rated so highly.

The first day Scu sat on her up the gallops he agreed the mare had class and by the time she had collected eleven first prizes over hurdles in 1990–1 she rated among the top five juveniles. Of her defeats, two came when travelling badly for no apparent reason; she was swallowed up in the Triumph Hurdle at Cheltenham and found the Aintree track too sharp. But she went out on a winning note, recording her sixth success over Cheltenham's demanding course.

Hopscotch's eleven wins helped boost the company's tally that season to forty victories, netting £133,000 in prize money. By the terms of the company's articles of association the business then had to be wound up, with the stock sold at public auction. Hopscotch realized £30,000 to race for Jonothan Sheppard in America. When Scu went to Buckingham Palace to receive his MBE from the Queen, the former owner expressed her amazement at the improvement a flight of hurdles had wrought in the mare.

Another disadvantage of a public company became obvious when, despite pulling out all the stops, it still took six months to wind up the financial affairs and to be able to declare a dividend of £40. Naturally there was some dissension at the AGM, but when you consider the shareholders had been associated with sixty-four winners in the two-year period, it worked out as quite inexpensive fun. The prospectus pointed out perfectly clearly that the investment would be unlikely to show a profit; and in any leisure activity there is a cost. Like the housing market, the bloodstock bubble had burst and, having bought at the top only to sell at the bottom, the dispersal disappointed, apart from Hopscotch.

The shareholders, who came from all backgrounds, included a number who had no previous experience of the sport. One lady who sat quietly throughout the AGM periodically looked agitated, as if she wanted to say something, but without ever actually doing so. When I approached her after the meeting to find out in private what she obviously did not want to say in public, I was rendered speechless by her query: 'It just seems odd to me that you have invested money in racehorses. Everyone knows they are a high-risk commodity!' I was too dumbfounded to explain that racing is our business; it seemed simpler to take the rebuke. Conversely, at Devon and Exeter a couple who had bought each other a share for fun without any prior knowledge of jumping got their money's worth on their maiden voyage. The wife looked thrilled to meet Scu before racing in the parade ring, was privy to the orders I gave the champion jockey and watched with fascination as he carried them out to perfection. I let her lead the winner into the enclosure, pose for the photographers and accept the trophy. Immersed as she was in the whole proceedings, just that one day must have been good return on the share price of £200. A lot of owners spend fortunes on buying, training and racing a horse without ever having as good a day out as that.

Scu rode in a novice chase for the company half an hour later, only to be unseated at the second fence, and I had to smile when the same lady turned to her husband and said: 'Martin will be cross, he didn't tell the jockey to fall off.'

There were about fifty shareholders who turned up every time we ran a company horse which, of course, gave them tremendous value. Others came when possible, some were in it for the betting only and a section simply wanted an interest to get them out of the house. For various reasons, not least the recession, the second company attracted only twelve hundred shareholders at a reduced cost of £200 per share. Initially one thousand people signed up; we took stock of the situation and eventually decided to try advertising on SIS, the daily satellite service that goes into the betting shops. For an outlay of £5,000 we attracted £20,000 worth of business, but we took the view that we had swept up most of the spare money and have not repeated the attempt yet.

This last company has enjoyed thirty winners, a strike rate of over forty per cent, so I do feel that in terms of fun and the thrill of winning the returns are good. Those in it for the betting have not found prices generous but with winners so plentiful they are in profit none the less. Chester does a daily phone message for shareholders only on which, besides giving tips and telling listeners future plans, he gets myself and Scu to record in-house chats. He claims to have made a profit every season and to watch him at the races you'd think he has fortunes on for himself. He goes bananas when one of mine is coming through to win, although a lot of his verbal outward encouragement is team spirit. He's a dedicated enthusiast.

At the races we tend to watch most of our horses on the closed-circuit television in the bar. The coverage is so much better these days and you can read a race far more accurately than when being jostled in the stands. I have to laugh when Chester's £20 bet escalates with the telling to become £200, but then most racegoers habitually exaggerate the winning bets, conveniently forgetting about the rest.

The sheer weight of work involved in administering a public company has led me to revive the Pond House syndicate for a dozen owners again, this time at £8,000 a share. That was up and running from August 1992. The very first to send his cheque was Sir William Garthwaite, a member of the Jockey Club who took up the offer from a promotional article in the Pipe–Scudamore magazine.

Having run its course, Pipe–Scudamore Racing plc was wound up at the end of the 1991–2 season, with the Pipe–Scudamore Racing Club filling the void. I have decided to pitch membership at £100 to involve the former company shareholders. The halving of the cost reflects both the current financial situation and the idea behind the whole thing which was to help a wider range of people to get a toehold in the operation. The benefits of the club as I see it are the flexibility afforded to us by freedom from the red tape associated with the legalities of a company, the opportunity to continue for as long as we wish and the reduced running costs. Other than that it is business as usual.

Quite a few of the group-owned horses were bought in France as a result of both contacts and hours of hard graft. We have the French runners faxed over daily, twenty-four hours before they run. In France a horse has to be declared a runner two days prior to its racecourse engagement, and this gives us time to go through the claiming races with a toothcomb. Barry Simpson spends as much as two or three hours on the form of a single race. If he is interested in one or more runners he phones our contacts in France for their opinions and if these sound encouraging we fly over for the sports and usually come away with a bargain. The joy of picking up these horses is that they have seldom been faced with ground faster than good, minimizing the likelihood of jarring or stressed cannon bones. I have seriously considered running horses in France or even setting up a second stable over there to run in conjunction with the home base, but as French laws stand at the moment, it would be difficult.

The people who support our stable encompass the whole spectrum, with the syndicates and club just as important to me as the major players. The main difference obviously lies in the buying power and goals of the likes of Paul Green. Paul came to me from David Nicholson and Reg Hollinshead, and in only a few seasons has sent some exciting prospects here – none more exciting than Carvill's Hill.

Chapter 25

Shattered Beliefs

When Paul Green and his two partners, Gordon Gray and Liam Marks, decided to transfer Ireland's enigmatic chasing prospect Carvill's Hill from Jim Dreaper to Martin Pipe the move had every chance of causing a rift in Anglo-Irish relations, for the Irish hold Dreaper in high esteem and considered the horse a national property. Still, the Pond House magician had worked his miracles with every other fading star to join the stable from Beau Ranger to Omerta, and it was assumed he would do the same with this huge, troubled horse.

Pipe
Paul had told me when he bought Dermot McMorrow's two-thirds share in the horse that it would stay with Jim Dreaper for a year at least and, should he get the horse right, would remain there. In case he did come to me I started to take notice of him and was interested to hear the reports, albeit second-hand, of visits to Ireland by the equine muscle expert Maggie Turner, who monitored the gelding from his holiday at grass to full training. The horse, it seemed, was wrong in his neck and also relapsed too easily into muscle spasm in his quarters. By December it was thought his problems had been ironed out and he was ready to carry Paul's colours for the first time from Jim's yard. He jumped around pleasingly to win the Durkan Brothers International Chase at Punchestown by an easy twelve lengths from Larchmont at level weights. The contest looked to be an ideal pipe-opener for the season. Sadly, next time out in the

Thyestes Chase at Gowran Park Carvill's Hill became unsighted at the first fence, falling heavily and sustaining pelvic injuries that kept him off the course for the remainder of the season.

He came to me in June 1991, straight from the paddocks, and although I was thrilled to have him, I was only too aware that a horse is basically only as good as his latest run. In this case that was six months previously. I must admit to being nervous that I would fail to put him right. He was a vastly different prospect from the others we'd rejuvenated. This was not a case of locating a problem, solving it, then nipping in down at the bottom of the handicap. This was a championship horse who would be on show every time he set foot outside the stable. He was public property.

I never let myself believe he could come to me until I saw him walk out of the transporter. He hesitated at the top of the box ramp to survey the new surroundings, held his head high and looked down on us with the air of someone who knows he is of a different class. The pride and tingling excitement I felt watching him standing there surveying the world ebbed with the very first step he took. He was evidently lame behind.

We let him settle down for a few days then packed him off to Bristol University for Geoff Lane to examine him in depth. They took him apart, metaphorically speaking, with the help of sophisticated scanning machines that probe deeper than is normally required. Every bone in his body was examined for old fractures before we tested functioning organs like heart and lungs. In both those areas, at least, he had a clean bill of health.

From the evidence of my own eyes, backed up by the photographic and subsequent tracing tests, it was immediately apparent that the horse's near-hind quarter had wasted as a result of damage within the pelvic area almost certainly consequent on his latest fall. Geoff Lane confirmed this as the trouble spot, but otherwise pronounced him a fine and healthy specimen. The pelvic girdle and associated bones form a complicated area and damage there causes pain and malfunction; that in turn leads to muscle wastage as the horse tries to avoid using the parts that hurt.

Sarah Hancock was still holidaying when Carvill's Hill returned from Bristol so Debbie Stokes, another of my leading girls, took on the job of caring for the patient. His reaction amazed me. He would not take to her and simply chased her out of the stable. I then asked Mary Horswell to fill in until Sarah returned, but not to become too attached as it was only a temporary measure. We get very little aggravation among the staff except when I ask someone to attend to another person's horse. Then all Hell is let loose, especially among the girls, who guard their charges jealously.

Carvill's remained aggressive for some while – quite understandably, when you consider he was in permanent pain from his dropped pelvis. We also noticed he rolled more than most horses which was a sure sign he was trying to relieve the discomfort. Again, if I related how he must have felt to the times when I was recovering from various breakages (self-inflicted in my case) it was easy to sympathize.

Carvill's Hill is in fact an aggressive horse by nature, but we agreed to try to soft soap him using Sarah's charms and as many Trebor mints as he would take from her. He steadfastly refused to eat a single mint at first but Sarah was equally determined he would do so. She crushed them, licked them and ate loads herself in front of his nose. Eventually, curiosity got the better of him. It may sound insignificant, but his acceptance of the titbits formed the basis of trust between human and horse. Once Sarah had won him over he then came to me for the offerings, but never with the same degree of trust he showed her.

Once we had pinpointed the trouble and started on changing his attitude, Mary Bromiley came down to get to work on the injury, but before she could do this Barry Park had to perform a tricky injection deep into the sacroiliac joint to ease the evident pain the horse was suffering. Both Barry and Mary correctly described Carvill's as 600 kilos of pent-up anger brought on by pain or discomfort. I certainly did not envy Barry the job of inserting an eight-inch needle into the horse's back. Only a mild sedative could be used, otherwise Carvill's would have relaxed too much, prompting him to rest one leg and so throw the injection area out of line. Conversely, if he were to object violently it is unthinkable what damage he might do to his back. Fortunately, the trust he placed in Sarah and the mild sedative combined to keep the patient still long enough for Barry to complete his job. He said it was like pushing the needle through cardboard as old muscle tears and fibrous tissue had formed to protect the injuries. It was all too much for me. The moment I was happy they had Carvill's in the frame of mind to accept the needle, I did a runner until they came out smiling.

The process of recovery follows a logical sequence of steps. Now we had established the seat of the trouble, got Carvill's confidence and relieved the pain, it was time for the remedial exercise. Mary advocated controlled activity, refuting the old adage that rest cures all things. She argued that now the pain had abated we could get the horse to use the wasted muscles, just as a human athlete would use weights to work on specific areas in a modern fitness programme.

A four-ounce-heavier work shoe fitted on his near hind foot meant that Carvill's was forced to use the wasted quarter with more effort than the off side, thus eventually equalizing the two hind quarters. Ed Buckley, who had joined me from Ireland as an assistant when his race-riding days finished the previous year, had the tedious job of driving the horse in long reins over logs and in circles. On Mary's advice we went back to the basic principles of classical dressage, which, directed from the ground with the aid of long reins, altered the horse's carriage, muscling him up over the back and neck. Although I do not normally trot my horses, Carvill's problems required use of that gait and as building his body back to its pre-injury state came highest on my list of priorities, I was content to watch Ed running behind the big horse as he executed his planned routine at the trot for two and a half months.

During the time Carvill's was being driven, Ed also rode him with the string and from the outset it was evident he had an excitable nature. To begin with I let him exercise in company with a few reliable companions and took the precaution of leading the group in the Range Rover on the half-mile walk to the gallop in case he met any traffic. I was blowed if I was taking any chances now, having gone to the lengths we had to put his pelvic area back into working order. I was definitely over-protective towards him.

At first Carvill's wanted to tear up the all-weather strip, but soon displayed his brains when realizing that our canter, walk, canter routine held no surprises for him. With a few weeks of regular visits to the strip he learned to relax between canters and to wait his turn, taking comfort from the old hands who'd long accepted our methods.

What did immediately strike us all was the ease with which he covered the ground, even at a steady pace. I'd never trained such an imposing horse. Even when still only half-fit his stride, at the canter, made other good horses look very ordinary. In fact before he ran from our yard for the first time he had never galloped fast at home but still made the others struggle without being extended himself. He really was in a different class from any other horse I have had through my hands.

What pleased me most was the fact the big horse remained sound from day to day. Keeping him sound worried me a lot as Mary Bromiley had warned me he could undo our work by rolling in his stable or by kicking the stable wall if upset or too fresh. Although it sounds crazy, for the first time in my training career I welcomed the daily batch of usual problems as it stopped me from dwelling too long on Carvill's Hill.

The importance of his first schooling session could not be overestimated. Admittedly Ed Buckley had already driven him over poles and small logs as part of his recuperative routine, and the horse showed willing. However, the real test had to be over regulation fences to see if the healed sinew, tissue and muscles could stand the additional strain of jumping. Paul Green, in whose colours he was to run, insisted on seeing for himself what his horse would do. Apparently in Ireland Carvill's Hill got so revved up it was safer to school him on racecourses instead of the home grounds which he knew too well. As with Mr Kilpatrick and Sabin Du Loir, we could not resist having a pop over a fence the day before. This was no time to be playing blind brag. The importance of the occasion even tempted Carol out of the office and, much to the relief of us all, he jumped with scope and precision, even if somewhat keen. The next day, in front of his owner, Scu sent the big horse up over the line of three fences several times, satisfying us that at schooling pace he could leap with the best of them.

When we went to Chepstow for his reappearance in the Rehearsal Chase I can honestly say he was not fully wound up, and for one of mine that is a rarity. He had been with us for five months which in a dry autumn is not a long time to get a massive chaser to racing fitness. Remember Carvill's had never worked over further than four furlongs and had not touched grass other than when he schooled over fences. His breathing told me the race would bring him to peak but also that he was fit enough to do himself no harm. Three miles on good to soft going with Celtic Shot and Cool Ground already boasting winning form that season, Katabatic trying the trip for the first time, plus Aquilifer and Bonanza Boy from our stable, provided a fair test.

Taken on by Aquilifer after the third fence, Carvill's Hill made two jumping errors in the first mile, more from ring-rust than anything else, but was never off the bridle. For a moment between the fourth-last and third-last fences I thought Carvill's was weakening, then he did scare me properly when over-jumping and very nearly failing to get his front feet out in time to keep him upright. After that the show was over as he ran on stoutly to win by ten lengths from Aquilifer.

We were all relieved and excited. Even Paul Green's permanent suntan had lost its strength during proceedings. Scu reported that the first two mistakes never felt likely to dash our hopes and the blunder at the third-last was nothing more than a typical Chepstow error as horses gallop on the downhill run to the finish. All that remained was to check how long the horse blew, recovery time being the indisputable evidence of a horse's fitness. Carvill's blew heavily for ten minutes, then took a further twenty-two to return to normal respiration. (Aquilifer had stopped blowing altogether after only eight minutes.) This confirmed we had a live Gold Cup contender provided he pulled out of his stable sound the next morning, which happily he did.

The horse had attracted mass media coverage since first putting a foot on a racecourse and this performance further fuelled the interest. You cannot imagine how much more difficult it is to train a horse that is considered public property. Every time it goes out of its stable a story is concocted and we spend a ridiculous amount of time either reporting on his well-being or denying scurrilous rumours.

The next two outings are history. He won the Coral Welsh National unchallenged by twenty lengths, doubling his super-iority over Aquilifer, who only forfeited second place to Party Politics by a short head in the last strides, though it made a difference of £4,500 in prize money to Mr Kilpatrick. We had dodged the King George at Kempton Park, not through fear of defeat but more to get another comfortable win under the horse's belt on a left-handed course, which he marginally prefers. After all, the Gold Cup was our objective and it seemed prudent to me to go to Cheltenham with as much jumping practice as possible.

In the Welsh National, his second run, the big horse jumped beautifully until a clumsy clamber over the final fence, but notwithstanding that momentary loss of concentration his obvious superiority drew accolades from most observers. As we left the course that evening the feeling of satisfaction was rewarding. We weren't cocky; just pleased that the arduous and costly treatment had worked.

A return to Ireland for the Hennessy Cognac Gold Cup at Leopardstown, a level weights contest, saw Carvill's outpoint the best his home country had to offer at that time. Except for a single, though far more serious-looking error, at the third he thrilled the huge crowd. Again Scu felt the mistake was less worrying than it probably looked. He, at least, was not worried about the Cheltenham fences or the opposition. Although Scu blamed himself for over-relaxing Carvill's, which, he said, directly led to his lapse, from where I stood it looked more like Scu asking and the horse not answering quite as his jockey had anticipated.

I do love racing in Ireland. The public are knowledgeable and caring and, unlike in Britain, the racecourses genuinely welcome visitors with open arms. When our party turned up it was not a case of the owners being entitled to just two badges; rather, it was 'How many do you want and would you all like lunch?' More heartwarming than anything else, though, was the fact that not a single person, and that included Carvill's Hill's former trainer Jim Dreaper, showed any animosity to me or to Paul Green. When you consider we had removed the horse from one of Ireland's most popular trainers, you might have expected quite the opposite.

After Leopardstown I was convinced that this powerhouse of a horse possessed more ability than any other I had the privilege of training. On the run-up to the Festival the air around the stables was electric as we prepared our raiding party of twenty-seven from an original entry of one hundred and twelve. Besides Carvill's Hill, Granville Again and Miinnehoma were major players for the Champion Hurdle and Sun Alliance Chase respectively, and with a barrage of requests from the press and television stations it became obvious there would be no peace unless we let everyone in at the same time.

Over forty newspapers sent reporters and eight television crews turned up for the Cheltenham preview. I had decided to parade the main three, with slight reservations that Carvill's would soon get annoyed at the invasion of his privacy. In fact he played so much to the gallery people must have thought I had been overplaying his intolerance of strangers. A great deal was made of the big horse, less of Granville Again, and poor little Miinnehoma was almost totally ignored. Small and scrawny besides Carvill's Hill, Freddie Starr's horse was overshadowed in every way. I am positive the assembled hacks thought I was trying to put them away when I named Miinnehoma as my banker of the meeting.

We had planned for the visitors to photograph and film the leading trio, then repair to the house for sustenance and questions. This did not work out quite as expected, as everyone wanted to get their own exclusive. Ed Buckley and Sarah Hancock became very popular, the lab was invaded and even Dad was cornered and pressed for his tip. He chose Barry Window in the opener and to this day he will not say whether he was taking the mickey.

Having surprised us by almost going to sleep during the photo-call, Carvill's Hill displayed his true nature once back in his stable. Those members of the press who wanted a shot of him in his box were treated to a show of bared teeth and flattened ears. Like most animals, the big horse tolerated public attention until it encroached on his domain.

Several people remarked on being logged in when they arrived, but memories are short; following my public wash and rinse by the *Cook Report*, I was half expecting them to send a crew down to update their footage. All my life I have been open and trusting and find it alien to have to behave otherwise.

When the Cheltenham horses did their final gallop I could not have been happier with Carvill's Hill, who bounded up the strip as if he had wings on his feet. He would not have blown a cobweb apart his wind was so good and I can honestly say I have never been more satisfied that a horse was ready to do his best.

Seven runners on the first day gave us only a bad omen: when Granville Again fell heavily at the second last in the Champion Hurdle. Paco's Boy, a good second in the amateurs' chase, was our only placed horse. Of the twelve runners on the Wednesday, most were out for social reasons, but the owners let me go where I want with the horses during the bulk of the season and a run for fun keeps everyone happy. Pragada found his first bit of form since joining me from Josh Gifford to finish second to the first Irish winner My View in the Coral Hurdle Final. Sea Island also filled the runner-up spot in the Mildmay of Flete and Run For Free produced his best to finish third to Miinnehoma in the Sun Alliance.

As I entered the winner's enclosure a jet-lagged Freddie Starr phoned me from his home to savour the moment as much as possible. Many people see the use of mobile phones in public as a gimmick, but having lost owners in the past through being inaccessible I am only too aware of their value. When Freddie contacted me in the winner's spot while watching the television, he felt more a part of the action.

The fancied horses had performed well enough over the first two days to give me every confidence that Carvill's Hill would go to post for the Gold Cup in ideal shape to lift the big one for us. The five Triumph Hurdle runners from the stable ran pretty much as expected, with Snowy Lane finishing nearest in tenth place. Aquilifer ran his normal game race in the Ritz Club Chase – and then it was time to saddle up Carvill's Hill.

I have never lacked confidence when I fancy a horse and having saddled the gelding I admit to looking at him and thinking there was nothing else I could have done to give him a better chance of victory. Of course we were nervous; Paul Green rates the Festival so highly and the Gold Cup is the top prize. Of all his winners, only two have been at Cheltenham and neither of those at the Festival. Considering how used Paul is to coming out on top in massive business deals, he was being very philosophical that day, reasoning that if our names were on the cup we'd win it and if not, too bad. This was D-Day without a doubt.

Scu's armful of records had been important at the time, but he ached for this one. For me it was the moment I'd worked for since taking up the job eighteen years ago. Scu and I had considered every conceivable twist to the plot, especially in light of a telephoned warning days earlier from a Lambourn source that we were being targeted to be forced out of the race approaching a fence. We were content to sit in behind the leaders if the pace proved suicidal or go about our own business if left alone. The diabolical mistake at the first had me worried; the way he ballooned the second confirmed my worst fears. I knew then we had lost it. Carvill's had hurt himself. Taking into account the other, albeit less serious, jumping errors en route, just still to be in contention off the last bend speaks volumes for the horse's bravery. When he dropped out of the race after the final jump and walked over the finishing line I was totally speechless, drained of emotion and hurting for the large number of people who would share my sorrow for the horse himself. I rushed down to the course and was relieved to see Scu still in the saddle. I remember thinking, 'Today we got it wrong but he's sound so at least there'll be another chance to prove how good the big chap is.' Carvill's looked slightly distressed when unsaddled; then as he cooled down in the vet's testing stable the first signs of lameness emerged. We always wrap forelegs up in a cooling agent immediately after a race as a precaution, but I did not kid myself the damage would be gone by the next morning. Sure enough, the main flexor tendon had broken down, he had severe cuts on the outside of his fetlock joints and when Mary Bromiley put her hand between his front legs he showed great distress.

The cuts were probably caused by his own hind feet as he tried to save himself on landing at the first. The strained tendon could have happened at the same time, or more likely as he desperately struggled to maintain a gallop despite the injury to his chest, which would undoubtedly have impaired his breathing. Whatever the case, he was very brave to continue galloping for as long as he did. Many people will remain convinced he was exposed as a wimp or that that is as good as he is. I hope that in time I can show the detractors Carvill's Hill's true worth. He possesses so much ability that it grieves me to go into his stable at night thinking what might have been; but he at least does not know any different because we all still make just as much fuss of him.

Reflecting on the team tactics used to defeat us, I have only one observation to make: how much fuss would Jenny Pitman have caused had the roles been reversed?

In the twelve months between Festivals, from March 1991 to March 1992, we had endured the *Cook Report*'s attempted public assassination of our whole operation and then seen our dreams collapse at Cheltenham amidst controversy. Tired, deflated and lame, it did occur to me that the price of holding the show together might perhaps be too high. Then two days later the stable sent out four winners in one afternoon, dissipating the tiredness and putting a spring back into my step. This is a game of continually changing faces, but the team captain needs to be as fit as his charges if he is to see it out right up to the line.

Epilogue

Behind the Next Door

Pipe

There are still so many mountains to climb. I dearly want to win a Cheltenham Gold Cup and a Grand National, and to go through the card one day – which is probably the easiest of the three to set about achieving, as there is always a host of opportunities in the first few months of every season. The two major chasing titles need the right horse and you only have one crack at each race each year.

Having created this place by accident more than design, I could never turn my back on it, but I can certainly imagine myself taking a sideways step in another ten years' time to help our son David when he's ready to take the reins. He's already had a taste of the public responsibilities that accompany success when starting his riding career this year. On his debut in a point-to-point, television crews and the press followed his every move and he knows that being the centre of attraction means your slightest flaw is highlighted.

When I embarked on the training and riding scene no one took a blind bit of notice if I made an idiot of myself. For over a dozen years I was able to do my own thing without being questioned, blamed or praised. By the time the leap into the spotlight came a few years ago, I'd had a fair grounding.

I'll know when the time is right to hand over to David. It'll mean far fewer worries for me and I couldn't care less whether my name appears in the papers. I don't think I've ever been a show-off or anything like that. Quite honestly, I hate the limelight but the very size of our stable makes anonymity impossible now, and that is why David will need a lot more exposure before he's in a position to cope. He's quickly eclipsed my riding escapades already and I'd love him to wipe my training landmarks from the record books by sending out four hundred winners in a season. The only limits are set by the hours in the day and the frailties of the body.

Carvill's Hill is recuperating, and I nurse hopes that his low mileage will mean another chance to show everyone just how good I know him to be. In the meantime the equally huge Terao has only to continue his present level of improvement to become the first champion from the stable to have evolved from an unbroken store horse. He'll keep my own unsound legs moving for the foreseeable future.

At the moment I'm ploughing my way through the renowned Federico Tesio's *Breeding the Racehorse*. This is definitely heavy stuff compared to some of my previous reading, but even after the first third of the book I'm questioning more of my long-held beliefs. Who knows what doors will open next? One thing is for sure, I'll always want to take a look at what's behind them.